The Logic of
Democratic Exclusion

The Logic of Democratic Exclusion

African Americans in the United States and Palestinian Citizens in Israel

Rebecca B. Kook

LEXINGTON BOOKS
Lanham • Boulder • New York • Oxford

9012671

LEXINGTON BOOKS

Published in the United States of America
by Lexington Books
A Member of the Rowman & Littlefield Publishing Group
4720 Boston Way, Lanham, Maryland 20706
www.rowmanlittlefield.com

PO Box 317, Oxford, OX2 9RU, UK

British Library Cataloguing in Publication Information Available

Library of Congress Cataloging-in-Publication Data

Kook, Rebecca B., 1959–
  The logic democratic exclusion : African Americans in the United States and
Palestinian citizens in Israel / Rebecca B. Kook.
    p. cm.
  Includes bibliographical reference and index.
  ISBN 0-7391-0441-1 (alk. paper)—ISBN 0-7391-0442-X (pbk. : alk. paper)
  1. African Americans—Civil rights. 2. Marginality, Social—United States. 3. National
characteristics, American. 4. United States—Race relations—Political aspects. 5. United
States—Politics and government—1989-. 6. Palestinian Arabs—Civil rights—Israel.
7. Marginality, Social—Israel. 8. National characteristics, Israeli. 9. Israel—Ethnic
relations—Political aspects. 10. Israel—Politics and government—1993-. I. Title.

E185.615.K59 2002
323.1'1927405694—dc21   2002013069

Printed in the United States of America

♾ᵀᴹ The paper used in this publication meets the minimum requirements of American
National Standard for Information Sciences—Permanence of Paper for Printed Library
Materials, ANSI/NISO Z39.48-1992.

Contents

Preface and Acknowledgments

Each piece of research is the product of a personal story and of a historical context. Yet, political scientists, as self-proclaimed scientists, are expected to provide objective and value-neutral analyses of political processes and behavior. This quest for objectivity usually implies that subjective stories, narratives, and contexts are deemed irrelevant, or worse—unscientific. Nonetheless, the questions we ask, the theories we produce and the interpretations we proffer are all part of our own historical experience. They stem from our attempts to understand our own personal realities.

My concern with the particular juncture of democracy and national identity then, is the product of a life lived within and between these two frameworks and ideas, which gradually evolved into a strong awareness of the constraints, as well as the opportunities they offer. I was born in the United States, to an American mother and Israeli father. My father, Hillel Kook, was a man who, like others of his generation, class, and historical context, took upon himself the responsibility of shaping history. During his engagement with history, he learned two lessons that in retrospect strongly influenced my own political and intellectual consciousness. First, in the early 1940s, when he lobbied the American Congress to pass a rescue resolution to save the Jews of Europe, he found himself at odds not merely with a recalcitrant administration, but with a hostile Jewish American establishment. Afraid he would bring anti-Semitism to America by speaking out, they fought for his extradition from the United States. At this time he learned regardless that Jews thought themselves bound by a common heritage and history, they were in fact separated by politics and national interests. Lesson number one: shared cultural identities do not necessarily dictate shared political interests, and similarly, shared political interests can bridge cultural differences.

Returning to Palestine after the war, my father learned another lesson. The secular Zionist leadership of the new state, in its desire to control the forces of religious opposition, refused, in a move of somewhat dialectical political reasoning, to separate between the religious and national definitions of nationhood. This resulted in a religious-national hybrid that was culturally defined and politically exclusive. The entire apparatus of the new state was then used to stifle any aspirations for a secular, liberal, and inclusive *Israeli* or *Hebrew* nation (nationally, and not religiously, defined). Redefining the "identity" of the sovereign nation, from a Jewish to an Israeli identity, became, for my father, a quest and an obsession. In the aftermath of World War II— and at the peak of the popularity of notions such as "national character"— particular political experiences led my father to awaken to the constructed nature of national identities, and to recognize the ability of political institutions to promote such changes. Lesson number two: politics, and the state, matter.

These "lessons" hovered over my childhood. My father's attempts at political change moved us back and forth, between New York and Tel Aviv, every few years. Hence, on many levels, "identity" featured very prominently in my life, yet the constant backdrop of my fathers particular experiences reinforced the feelings that while identity was clearly *important*, it was never given, nor taken for granted. Identities were there to be questioned and challenged. Yet, almost everywhere I turned, identities were imposed and defined, presented as intractable and natural—whether in the euphoric, and charged ideological atmosphere of the post-1967 Israel, with its deterministic idea of a nationalist *Jewish* identity, or in the 1970s American discourse of identity-politics, where ethnic, gender, and racial identities were promoted as essential elements of ones very individuality. Finally, in graduate school in the late 1980s, the modernist ideas of imagined communities and constructed identities seemed to provide a partial resolution. Identities were at once deep and meaningful, yet both constructed and fluid. I had discovered an academic discourse that contextualized the ideas I imbibed from my own family's history by defining and articulating them in an elegant and convincing theoretical and historical framework. Reading Gellner and Anderson, and reflecting upon the different ways in which identity and politics played themselves out in both of my "homes," my fathers "lessons" found a general, theoretical context.

Shuttled between two homes—both of which were equally adopted, and equally authentic—the idea that we imagine our community, and construct our collective identity, resonated very strongly. Yet, from my particular status, of belonging yet not belonging, I could see that within each community there are those who imagine, and those who, to paraphrase Partha Chatterjee, *imagine others' imaginings*. Within the margins of identities— the space that I occupied—imaginations and constructions were not homogeneous. As different as my two homes were, their boundaries and margins were surprisingly similar. These spaces were inhabited by minorities who were at once included yet severely excluded—citizens of the state, yet not entirely members, their identity distinct and excluded from the homogenized and constructed identity of the core. African Americans in the United States and Palestinian citizens in Israel inhabit this common place—this twilight zone of citizenship. They are accorded certain rights, yet denied others—accepted, yet rejected. From the margins looking in, Israel and the United States were thus revealed as exclusionary democracies, managing to propagate exclusionary policies towards their own citizens, while maintaining a facade of democratic legitimacy.

To me, the robustness of a democratic regime is most clearly exhibited by the status of its minorities. This then raises serious and central questions concerning the nature of these two democracies. Indeed both societies remain plagued by the complexities of racial and ethnic divisions that have come to set the context of economic, social, and political inequality. Issues of membership, and the nature of majorities and minorities, lie at the core of both societies' socioeconomic agendas. Reminded of my fathers lessons, I wondered what precisely was the role of the state, or of politics, in both constituting, and then reconstructing these differences.

This book is the outcome of an investigation which began with my fathers lessons, and resulted in my own efforts at investigating their validity, as well as thinking through my own particular status and space. Convinced of the potency of the state and its ability to form and promote collective national identities, yet needing to understand the logic behind it, this book has emerged in response to two very basic puzzles. The first relates to the ability and motives of the democratic state to manipulate boundaries of identity: why are democracies concerned with identities, and how do they promote them? The second puzzle concerns the nature of these boundaries: why do democracies maintain exclusionary identities, and how is this exclusion reconciled with democratic values? Similarly, why do acts of inclusion occur, and when and where are they most likely to happen? Reaching beyond simple notions of "culture" and essentialist arguments, I aim to unravel the logic of democratic identity-politics. Thus, while considering the extreme potency of cultural identities—be they racial, ethnic, or national—this book sets out to examine the ways in which these identities contribute to the politics of order and stability. All avenues led me back to where my journey began: politics, the state, and political interests.

Many people and institutions helped me throughout the process of researching and writing this project. Thanks go to Columbia University, to the Institute for Mediterranean Affairs, and to Ben Gurion University for providing me with the facilities and fellowships to conduct this research. Special thanks to Lisa Anderson, Alex Motyl, and Charles Hamilton, who witnessed—and nurtured—the origins of these ideas. To Joel Migdal for his continuous support and help. To Serena Leigh and Martin Hayward from Lexington Press, for their support and enthusiasm. Also—to Gad Barzilai, Doron Ben Atar, Charles Hauss, Susan Kennedy, Ben Mor, Ilan Pappe, Joel Peters, Batia Roded, Meirav Riklin-Shapira, Rogers Smith, Oren Yiftachel— all offered invaluable comments and suggestions at different stages and on different parts of the manuscript. Thank you to Tania Forte for helping me through the critical final stages.

I completed the final stages of writing at Ben Gurion University, where I now teach in the department of Politics and Government. Special thanks to all members of this special department—David Newman, Renee Poznanski, Joel Peters, Neve Gordon, Dani Filc, Ahmad Sa'di, Fred Lazin, Udi Lebel, Nurit Klein, and Anat Segal—for providing such a supportive and stimulating work environment.

Final and ultimate thanks to my family. To Gideon—who's belief in this project (and in me) often surpassed my own, and to Batia, Talia, and Hillel— for their love and constancy. They are my own, invaluable, community of solidarity. Special thanks also to Nili Kook, Nili Garinkol, and Astra Temko for their love and support through all these long years.

Finally, this book is dedicated to the memory of my father—Hillel Kook— visionary and statesman, whose cries fell on deaf ears, whose ideas were before their time and whose life should have made a monumental difference. *Yehi Zichro Baruch.*

Part One

Democracies and the Politics of Collective National Identity

According to mainstream democratic theory, the legitimacy of democratic regimes is rooted in the consent of the governed. No further rationalization and legitimation is needed beyond a majority at the polls. This legitimacy is grounded in the belief that every vote is counted, and that every vote is counted equally. Hence, consent and equality are the building blocks of the democratic structure. Our knowledge and understanding of democratic politics at the beginning of the twenty-first century instructs us, however, that what is construed as consent is often thinly veiled apathy and alienation, and that equality at the polls is rarely translated into social, economic, or even political equality. Democratic governments, as often as nondemocratic ones, rely on other mechanisms to engender legitimacy, and distribute rights and benefits unequally through different mechanisms of inclusion and exclusion.

Why, and how, do democratic regimes distribute rights unequally? Why are certain groups discriminated against, and others not? Moreover, why, once exclusion is maintained successfully, are these very same groups often included? In the introduction to this book I first examine the different theories and discussions of nationalism to see if they provide adequate explanations for the particular relationship between nationalism and democracy and then explain why democratic regimes rely on national exclusion. In the second chapter, I focus on the different mechanisms of coercion and cooperation employed by democratic regimes in their efforts to maintain stability. Specifically, I focus on one such mechanism—collective national identity—and examine the way in which promotion of a collective national identity facilitates the provision of public goods and minimizes free riding.

Chapter One

Introduction

On March 5, 2000, there was cause for celebration amongst human rights activists in Israel. Early that morning, the Israeli Supreme Court ruled that the Kaadan's, an Israeli-Palestinian couple,[1] be allowed to purchase a house in Katzir, a small picturesque settlement in the north of Israel. In the fall of 1994 the couple responded to a newspaper ad and applied to the Katzir settlement to purchase one of the lots. Wanting to escape the overcrowding and poverty of Baqa el-Garbiya, a nearby Arab town, they sought the relative prosperity of one of Israel's expanding suburban developments. Despite the fact that they fit the professional and economic profile required by the acceptance committee of the settlement—middle class professionals—their application was denied. Without mincing words, the committee notified the couple that "while they seemed like very nice people" their application had to be rejected because they were "Arab" and not Jewish. This, it was explained, was prohibited by the terms of the charter of the Jewish National Fund (JNF) adopted by the Israel Land Agency.[2]

The couple promptly turned to the Supreme Court and filed suit against the settlement on charges of discrimination. For five years, the Israeli Supreme Court hemmed and hawed, reluctant to intervene in an issue of such critical political and ideological importance. Finally, on March 5, 2000, in a seminal ruling, the Court declared that equality was to be considered a supreme value. Equality, explained Supreme Court Chief Justice Aharon Barak, was to serve as the guide and measure of all state policies, and as such, the acceptance committee of Katzir was prohibited from utilizing the relevant clauses in the JNF charter as a basis for their decision. From now on, the Israel Land Administration could no longer administer Israeli state land according to the renowned JNF clause which explicitly stated that land in the state of Israel was purchased and guarded exclusively for the Jewish people. Israeli citizens, continued Barak, included Jews and non-Jews alike, and all must have an equal right to purchase and settle on the land. Liberal, bourgeois property rights trumped conservative ideology.

Although faint, the celebration in Jerusalem was an echo of a larger celebration forty-five years earlier in Washington, D.C. The cause for celebration then was the signing of the voting rights bill that ensured African Americans in southern states the right to vote. For one hundred years, since the end of Reconstruction, African Americans in the South were prevented from exercising the most fundamental democratic right of all: the right to vote and to stand for election. Despite significant improvements in the civil rights status of African Americans gained since World War II, by the mid-1960s close to 90 percent of Southern Blacks were still prevented from voting, and no Blacks had successfully competed for an elected office. Southern politicians were extremely creative in devising mechanisms that prevented Southern Blacks from registering, ranging from literacy tests to poll taxes, and culminating in the infamous grandfather clause. All constitutionally sanctioned, democratically legitimate, mechanisms of disenfranchisement. The passing of the voting rights bill changed all that, and for the first time in the history of the United States, African Americans were able to exercise this basic democratic right unhindered by democratic mechanisms of exclusion. One hundred years after gaining citizenship, African Americans enjoyed the fruits of equality. Liberal, democratic notions of equality trumped racism.

Two celebrations in two very different societies, separated not merely by time, but by geography, culture, and history. Nonetheless, an underlying similarity links the two. Reading about these celebrations, as well as the stories of the minorities who participated in them, a very particular democratic reality is revealed. Often, apparently, fundamentally democratic societies discriminate not merely against resident or illegal aliens or migrant workers—*nonbelongers*—but against citizens of the polity, potential recipients of equal rights, legal and legitimate vessels of entitlement. These stories therefore attest to a veiled aspect of democratic reality—the existence of differential categories of citizenship.

The existence of different categories of citizenship which accord differential rights is a much more common democratic practice than is commonly acknowledged. In most former colonial states, such as Britain and France for example, different citizenship and residency categories were devised and implemented, allowing the state to distinguish between former colonial and commonwealth "subjects" and "authentic" citizens. In Great Britain these distinctions survived up until the legislative reforms of 1981 and 1984.[3] In other democracies, whose colonies were internal rather than external—

Australia, New Zealand, and the United States, countries or territories inhabited previously by indigenous populations—the practice of maintaining differential categories of citizenship (particularly regarding issues of property rights) went by unquestioned for years. The impact of colonialism on the policies of citizenship is not merely a thing of the past. Unequal distribution of rights amongst citizen populations continues today in the former Soviet states (ethnic Russians in Estonia for example), in Malaysia regarding ethnic Chinese, in Sri Lanka—and the list continues.

Examples abound, and reality once again reveals that while the right to own property and to participate in democratic elections might appear to be the ABCs of democratic theory, in practice, the official distribution of rights *alone* is not a sufficient condition for full democratic entitlement. *Full* democratic entitlement, that is, the ability to partake in the full array of democratic rights and benefits, is a condition available to certain citizens of the polity but not to all. The question that arises is, to whom? Who qualifies for this entitlement? Who are considered and treated as full members of the democratic polity, and how is this membership defined and determined?

The exclusion of Israeli-Palestinians from the mainstream of democratic entitlement in Israel, and of African Americans from the full gamut of democratic rights in the United States indicates that full democratic entitlement, or, as defined above, membership in the polity overlaps, mostly, with membership in the nation. The exclusionary nature of national membership apparently serves democratic regimes well. Relying on the rigid and exclusive boundaries of nationality enables democracies—regimes that are committed to principles of equal and universal membership—to maintain exclusive and exclusionary entrance criteria, while at the same time maintaining a facade of democratic legitimacy.

Maintaining democratic legitimacy over time, however, requires the ability to manipulate the boundaries of the nation, thus avoiding the existence of intransigent national boundaries, marked by continued and unchanging exclusion and discrimination. To this end, democratic regimes periodically engage in both inclusionary and exclusionary actions aimed at manipulating these boundaries, and hence the membership of those entitled to the full array of democratic rights and benefits. These inclusionary and exclusionary actions raise significant and complex questions about the relationship between democracy, legitimacy, and membership. This book is concerned with this particular relationship and examines it through an analysis of the shifting membership status of African Americans in the United States and of Palestinians in Israel. Focusing on the juncture of democratic and national exclusion, the book examines different strategies of inclusion and exclusion implemented by the state, and the political and economic interests that motivate them.

The two celebrations described above attest to the fact that for significant periods in the history of both societies, severe strategies of exclusion were implemented so as to exclude the two minorities from full democratic entitlement. In the United States this took the form of almost total disenfranchisement of African Americans, while in Israel the exclusion is manifested in the partial curtailment of central civic, political, and property rights. Part 1 of this book offers an explanation of this democratic exclusionary strategy, focusing on the intimate cooperation between democratic and national values and criteria. Emphasis is placed on the ways in which definitions of nationhood interact with these membership criteria, and the role of nationality and national identity in these processes of exclusion. Maintaining exclusive membership criteria provides democracies—regimes that can employ only limited degrees of explicit coercion in maintaining order—with a low cost, and democratically legitimate mechanism for minimizing free riding. Ultimately, then, I argue that exclusive membership criteria are a necessary requirement for the stability of democratic regimes.

Hence, within the purview of this explanation, exclusion emerges not as an aberration of democratic theory and practice, but rather as an inherent and constant element therein. The stability of democratic institutions is maintained, in most democratic societies, not despite the exclusion of different groups, but rather through the maintenance of such exclusionary policies. Within this explanatory framework, therefore, *inclusion*, rather than exclusion, emerges as the more puzzling strategy. The United States maintained severe exclusionary policies for decades without paying a high cost, neither in terms of democratic legitimacy, nor in terms of the stability of its democratic institutions. Why then were inclusionary acts initiated? Why were African Americans granted voting rights in the 1960s, and why did the Kennedy and Johnson administrations fight for equality when they did? Similarly, in Israel, the national and political exclusion of its Palestinian citizens has been a fundamental characteristic of the Israeli democracy since its inception in 1948. What then motivated the Supreme Court to rule in favor of the Kaadan's after decades of denying basic rights? How should one best interpret liberal moves towards the inclusion of Israel's Palestinian citizens that occurred during the 1990s, and how have these policies impacted upon the definition of national membership in Israel?

AMERICAN AND ISRAELI NATIONAL IDENTITY

The American and Israeli cases indeed offer a unique opportunity to look at the juncture of citizenship and nationality in a comparative perspective. On the face of it, both societies share critical features. Both Israel and the United States were founded, explicitly, as immigrant, settler societies. As countries based on immigration, for long periods of their history they each manifested highly inclusionary immigration policies. Moreover, as countries and societies whose raison d'etre, and raison d'etat, was the ingathering of immigrant communities, each country placed supreme value on the construction of a shared national identity, spending vast resources on melding a shared identity from disparate cultural groups. In the United States, American identity was forged out of German, Scandinavian, and British immigrants, later augmented by Italians, Irish, and Poles, and later still by Asians, Latin Americans, and Africans. In Israel, while immigration has been limited to diverse Jewish communities, the task of assembling and then assimilating such communities from central and eastern Europe, North America, North Africa, and the Middle East has proved no less daunting.

Founded upon immigrant communities, the political system that developed in each has been fundamentally democratic. While lacking a written constitution, Israel from its establishment has maintained and supported the fundamental principles of democratic government: the equal distribution of civic and political rights amongst members of the polity, and the maintenance of open and contested democratic elections. The United States, for its part, has been the paragon of democratic rule for the past two centuries.

However, despite the fact that both societies have enjoyed widespread democratic legitimacy, at home and abroad, both have exercised severe exclusionary practices in terms of their second tier membership. Beginning their American sojourn as slaves, African Americans had no recognized legal rights, including the right to citizenship, until the institution of the Reconstruction amendments following the end of the American Civil War in 1865. In the following hundred years, despite having attained formal citizenship, African Americans suffered serious abuses of civil, political, and social rights. For the larger part of shared American history, African Americans have been outside the pale of American membership, no matter how defined.

Israel, on the other hand, extended citizenship to those Palestinians who remained within the newly established—yet still contested—sovereign state in the midst of its war of independence in 1948. Identified entirely with the Arabs with whom Israel was at war, these new citizens were perceived as a potential fifth column. Hence, immediately following this initial act of civic inclusion, they were placed under a system of military rule, which governed their daily interactions within the new state. As a result, many of their basic democratic rights were either denied or limited. The basic freedoms of association, movement, and expression were curtailed. In 1966 the military government was abolished, yet the Palestinian citizen population remained seriously disadvantaged and discriminated against. Palestinian citizens of Israel suffer from a fundamentally discriminatory distribution of fundamental rights, including the right to political association, property rights, and basic rights of membership. Moreover, this exclusion is acknowledged by both Jews and Palestinians alike.

Most theoretical discussions of nationalism have referred to both the United States and to Israel respectively as archetypes of opposing models of nationhood. The United States forms the basis for the civic or territorial model of nationhood. According to this model, membership in the nation is based on will and citizenship, which in turn is closely tied to territorial residence (jus solis). The values that inform the mainstay of American national identity are political and liberal. The American nation is seen as the civic, assimilating and inclusionary nation par excellence, embracing liberal universalistic values and principles.[4]

Israel, on the other hand, could very well serve as the exemplar of ethnic nationhood. Membership in the nation is based on lineage and religion, citizenship is granted on the basis of nationality and the values that constitute this identity are cultural and ethnic. Since Israeli nationhood is indistinguishable—both legally and politically—from Jewish nationhood, religious identity is the prime marker of national membership. Founded on myths of ancient heritage, and embracing a nationalist ethos which is blatantly exclusionary, if not racist, few national identities are seen to approximate the romantic model as closely.

If one accepts this dichotomous understanding of nationhood, the similarities listed above defy explanation. Given the inclusionary nature of American national identity, how did the United States "get away" with excluding African Americans so brutally for so long? Similarly, given the exclusionary nature of Israeli identity, how is one to interpret recent moves towards inclusion of Israeli Palestinian citizens?

Processes of inclusion and exclusion aim at the construction of political membership. This membership, is, in turn, constituted, both symbolically and legally—through a matrix of political and national symbols, and through legislation. Since legal and symbolic arenas of politics are, as yet, controlled primarily by the state and its different institutions, the state plays a pivotal role in determining this membership. How should we best theorize about this role? Why are changes initiated in the boundaries, and what particular context conditions these changes? More precisely, how are political and economic incentives informed by cultural and ideological frameworks? Thus, to properly understand the interests that motivated the acts of inclusion and exclusion within the Israeli and American contexts, an understanding of the changing notions and meanings of state sovereignty is necessary.

STATE SOVEREIGNTY AND MEMBERSHIP CONTROL

The ability to exercise control over one's own boundaries is a central element in demonstrating sovereignty. As the world enters the twenty-first century, demographic boundaries are becoming an arena no less central, no less contested, than territorial boundaries. Demographic boundaries, like territorial boundaries, delineate the parameters of membership in the polity. But demographic boundaries, unlike most territorial ones, are constantly changing, and most importantly, are multi-layered. Hence control over these demographic boundaries is not a singular activity, but in its simplest form, a two-tiered process. The first tier concerns entry into the state and into the community of residents, and involves determining who will be allowed to penetrate the community from the outside. The second tier considers the community of citizens, and refers to the circle of national membership amongst them.

As the sovereign power, the state controls membership of both tiers; in its capacity as gatekeeper, it controls immigration, and in its capacity as national leader it plays a significant role in the constitution of the nation. Historically, the process of state formation in Western Europe was epitomized by the gradual expansion of the state's capacity to do precisely this task, control membership—through taxation, the establishment of a standing army, and the devising of the population census.[5] As citizenship evolved during the nineteenth century, the notion of "control" came to embody a more reciprocal meaning. The state has come to control its citizens not merely through the implementation of rules regulating its extractive capacities (i.e., taxation, military service), but through rules that aim at stipulating, regulating, and implementing an increasingly expansive array of rights. Hence, the ability of the state to enforce rights is no less a mechanism of control than its ability to extract funds. Both can be seen as part of what Foucault has called the disciplining of society.[6]

The evolution of sovereignty has thus involved a lengthy and often painful process of membership determination. Through the gradual process of discipline, control, and regulation, a state-bound, national community was created. With the growing control and hence reliance of individuals upon the central political institutions, the local, particularist identities became increasingly devalued. At the same time, the growing importance of economic modernization to the state economy, along with its trans-local and interest-based relationships made a sense of state-bound nationhood increasingly significant and valuable. The formation of a national community bound and defined by the boundaries of the state became central to the functioning of modern politics and the political economy, as well as to the material well-being of its citizens.[7]

Hence the development of the nation in Western Europe accompanied the development of the state, greatly facilitating shared communication and mobility, the ability to partake in the project of economic modernization and the development of capitalist production.[8] The construction of both citizenship and nationhood was, and remains, a dynamic process. Indeed, the periodic inclusion and exclusion of different groups—immigrants, minorities, laborers—has emerged as both a dominant, and permanent facet of modern politics. With the advent of globalizing trends of labor and capital migration, the dynamic nature and pace of civic membership increased dramatically during the twentieth century, rendering mass migrations of populations from east to west and south to north, a commonplace feature of the emerging global economy.[9]

What holds for civic membership, holds for national membership as well. In new nations, as in established ones, membership in the nation is not static. Demands for inclusion, like those for exclusion, characterize most contemporary nations, new and old. While most obvious perhaps in "new" nations, where negotiation of membership is not merely a common, but a dominant facet of contemporary politics—see the politics of nationhood in the former Soviet states for example—over the past decade these processes of negotiation have come to distinguish the more "established" states as well, where increasingly discourses on multiculturalism dominate the relationship between majority and minority cultures in countries like Canada, Spain, the United States, and France.[10] The discourse of nationhood and of citizenship has focused, increasingly, on the identification of patterns of change: patterns whereby different groups, defined at times by religion, at times by race, and at times by ethnicity, have been included into—but more often, excluded from—from the different tiers of membership.

EXPLAINING NATIONAL INCLUSION
AND EXCLUSION WITHIN DEMOCRATIC STATES

During the past three decades, the nation and its derivative concepts—nationalism, national identity, nationality—have emerged as one of the most thoroughly discussed set of concepts in modern social science. With the publication of Gellner's *Nations and Nationalism* in 1983, and Anderson's *Imagined Communities* in 1982, the theoretical study of nationalism burst onto the academic scene from relative obscurity[11]. Nationalism was transformed from a descriptive to an explanatory category. Nationalism, along with ethnicity, now serves to shape much of western, and of late—non-western—thinking about the politics of identity and the forces that define inter- and intra-group relations. Books and journals devoted to the study of nationalism grow exponentially every year.[12]

The publication of the two aforementioned books mark the initial phase of theorizing about nationalism.[13] Two positions were staked out in that debate.

The first identified commonly as the modernist position maintains that nationalism is a condition of modernity, and that nations are essentially modern units.[14] The nation is seen to have evolved either as part of, or in response to, distinctive social and economic processes of modernization and the advent of the capitalist mode of production. These include the abrupt transformation heralded by industrialization and the consequent breakdown of traditional social units, the declining status of religion on the one hand, and the development of standardized education, the spread of communication and a growing dependency on the centralizing state on the other. Nation-building is both depicted and narrated as a process of construction, whereby national identity is not a natural component of one's identity, but socially and politically imposed.[15]

The second position, known as the ethnic or at times the primordial viewpoint, maintains that in fact modern-day nations are the political heirs of pre-existing cultural and ethnic groups whose origin can be traced back hundreds, if not thousands, of years. Not denying the significance of processes of modernization such as industrialization, the advent of modern communications, and the development of capitalism, primordialists—represented most adamantly by Walker Connor—perceive these phenomenon as accelerating agents in an historical process whose origins lay outside of these developments.[16] Thus, while modernists link the origins and hence very essence of nationalism to modernization, primordialists contextualize nationalism in a far longer historical perspective. Accordingly, nation-building is not defined as a process of *construction* but rather as one of re-emergence and refinement. The task of the scholar is likened to that of the archeologist: the national past is an unrefuted reality waiting to be discovered, and the scholar's task is to re-construct this past to the best of his or her ability. National identity is thus seen as an inherent, or *primordial* element of modern collective identity.

The discourse on nationalism and the nation was, for a long time, defined by this debate. Scholars felt it necessary to stake out a position in the debate, and were categorized according to their position. As such, the theoretical debate on nationalism was largely historical, or socio-historical. Issues of more contemporary relevance were relatively neglected. Hence, when the ethnic cleansing and violence in eastern Europe and Africa erupted in full force in the 1990s, students of nationalism were quite unprepared. Armed with the albeit impressive scholarship of Gellner, Anderson, Smith, and Connor, they were nonetheless ill equipped to discuss, let alone predict, the political dynamics of contemporary nationalism. Modern or primordial, constructed or authentic, national identity had once again proven to be the most powerful and violent political force and a source of political conflict.

This brings us back full circle to the initial question of this chapter. Why are certain nation-states more successful in peacefully assimilating minorities than others? What determines processes of exclusion or inclusion, and how can the propensity of different nation-states to include and to exclude be explained? The theoretical literature discussed above furnishes us with two contending legacies. The first argues that the original cultural and ideological context and definitions of the nation condition contemporary nationalist politics. The second posits the political and material conditions as primary, and explains processes of inclusion and exclusion, violence and assimilation, as products of political construction and engineering.

The first legacy is by far the more prevalent, and has captured the imagination of students of nationalism for its simplicity and seeming elucidatory power. This legacy, which is referred to as the ethnic-civic dichotomy, basically argues that nations (and for that matter nationalisms) can be roughly divided into two distinct types or categories which correspond to two separate models of national identity as well as to two different paths of national development.[17] The first, characteristic of both the historic development and contemporary structure of western nations (France, England, Spain, Portugal, the Netherlands) is the western, civic, or territorial model. These nations are the products of civic-political expansion, and emerged through the gradual incorporation of minorities into the growing state administration during the eighteenth and nineteenth centuries. Since these western nations expanded in conjunction with the sovereignty of the state, membership in these nations is based on territorial affiliation. In addition, the values which came to legitimize this particular process of nation-building were fundamentally legal—and liberal— and hence the bonds which solidified the nation are essentially voluntary, and political. While the national ethos came to adopt distinct cultural labels and symbols, the western or civic nation is ethnically and culturally capable of peacefully assimilating different cultural and ethnic groups into its ranks.

The second is more characteristic of the historic development and structure of central and eastern European nations, whose national development solidified later on, in the mid to late nineteenth century. This model or type is referred to as either the ethnic, the romantic, or the eastern model.[18] Historically, these nations developed in opposition to larger multinational empires, and hence not in conjunction with the administrative state, but rather in confrontation with it. Cohering around a singular ethnic or cultural unit, rather than a territorially defined state, membership in these nations emerged from an ethnic or cultural origin rather than a civic affiliation. National solidarity is thus based on the shared language, culture, and history of the ethnic group (often on a shared religion too) and the values which come to symbolically represent the nation are cultural. Since this type of nation evolved in conflict with other cultural units, it is seen as exclusionary and non-assimilating.

While these two models describe different historical processes, they are articulated as classificatory models as well. As such, they have evolved into schema which embody not merely descriptive and historical capabilities, but explanatory and analytic potential as well. Different nations and nationalist tendencies or policies are thus explained by their origins in either category. Brubaker, for example, argues that different models of citizenship, and hence different propensities for exclusion and inclusion, can be historically traced to these national understandings (or models).[19] Accordingly, modern states whose understanding of nationhood is romantic, ethnic, and cultural (like Germany and Serbia for example), will tend to develop more exclusionary tendencies. The United States, France, and Britain, on the other hand, whose national understanding can be traced to the civic model, will tend to be more inclusionary. In his comparison of France and Germany, the archetypes of two distinct understandings, Brubaker concludes:

> The distinctive and deeply rooted French and German understandings of na-
> tionhood have remained surprisingly robust. Nowhere is this more striking than
> in the policies and politics of citizenship vis a vis immigrants.[20]

Understandings which, according to Brubaker's own testimony, solidified in both countries in the nineteenth century, serve as robust explanatory variables for immigration policies adopted in Europe at the close of the twentieth century. This distinction between ethnic and territorial nations has emerged as a common explanation for different processes of nation-building, different state policies, and differing treatment of minority groups, with the ethnic conflict in the Balkans at the end of the twentieth century constituting a prime example.[21] It is easy to trace the connection between the primordial approach to nationalism and the ethnic-civic dichotomy. The act of categorizing nations according to historical development and civic orientation is premised on the understanding that what distinguishes different nations and different nationalisms is culture and ethnicity (as opposed to politics and economics).[22]

The second legacy can be traced to the modernist approach. In 1983 Terence Ranger and Eric Hobsbawm published a slim edited volume entitled *Invention of Tradition*.[23] In the introduction to this volume they stated that "traditions which appear or claim to be old are often quite recent in origin and sometimes invented." While usually linked to some historic past, often "the continuity with it is largely factitious."[24] These traditions, therefore, serve the explicitly political purpose of inculcating a sense of continuity with the past to legitimize social, economic, or political change. In other words, to the extent that collective identities are to a very large extent constituted by narratives of shared past history, this very history is, more often than not, manufactured or invented.

The appearance of this volume gave rise to an entire discourse on the nature of collective identity. Building on the modernist premise that the nation—the primary locus of collective identity in the modern era—is itself an invention (an imagination and a political construct), scholars set themselves the task of examining the very mechanisms of construction. Hence, this second legacy posits both a dissenting view of national identity—as politically constructed—as well as a dissenting view of the role of the scholar: to uncover and expose the political engineering processes. A variant on Anthony Smith's archeologist, the post-modernist nationalism scholar is the political agitator whose task is to expose the workings of modern nation-state politics.

The interest in commemoration, and the ways in which a collective memory is built upon the commemoration of key events and personages, is premised on the notion that nations constitute shared, or collective memories, and that the memories or identities shared are planned and constructed.[25] The task of the scholar is to uncover the mechanism of the memory. Both identity and memory are posited not as objective historical realities, but rather as subjective and constructed.[26] Moreover, since they are subjective, collective memories and identities are crafted out of a variety of potential existing ones. As opposed to the dichotomy legacy, where one singular, objective national identity exists, the variability of identities serves to underscore its constructed nature. As Gillis notes:

> At this particular historical moment, it is all the more apparent that both identity and memory are political and social constructs, and should be treated as such. We can no longer afford to assign either the status of a natural object, treating it as "fact" with an existence outside language. Identities and memories are not things we think *about*, but things we think *with*. As such they have no existence beyond our politics, our social relations, and our histories. We must take responsibility for their uses and abuses.[27]

Contesting the Dichotomy

Neither legacy is entirely satisfactory. While the ethnic-civic dichotomy serves as an interesting historical schema, illuminating different paths towards nationhood, the dichotomy does not serve us well when analyzing contemporary policies. First, as many post-colonial theorists have noted, the dichotomy is essentially Eurocentric, and is biased, normatively, towards the western civic model. Furthermore, most nations fit neither mold perfectly and, as with the two cases discussed in this book, so-called civic nations are often as exclusionary as ethnic nations. Both the liberalization of citizenship laws in Germany and the rise of the extreme right in France contradict the basic distinction between civic and ethnic. Since it is an essentially *descriptive* model, it offers little help in understanding exclusion in civic nations. Moreover, all nations ultimately rely on culture and common values to mobilize their ranks, and myths, symbols, and rituals (invented or otherwise) are present in all national repertoires. Finally, to say that exclusionary policies result from exclusionary nationalities is either to submit to tautology, or to overestimate the power of ideas, and to attribute far too much emphasis to ideology.

The second legacy suffers from different problems. While much of the commemoration and identity research explores the political mechanisms of inclusion and exclusion, few of these studies offer explanations. Most studies state that identities are constructed, that memories are invented, and leave it at that. Exploring the specific historic narratives that are chosen, and explaining the symbolic impact of choosing specific myths over others, leaves the larger comparative political questions unanswered. Why are specific identities constructed in the way they are? What political interests are relevant to assessing these questions? Who is to gain, and what is the specific role of political leadership? Is there a connection between regime type, and memory or identity-construction, and if so, what is it? In short, can processes of inclusion and exclusion be related to larger, more general political processes and categories?

If descriptions of political mechanisms fail to provide explanations, and if ideology provides an ultimately unsatisfactory set of explanations, how can we explain the differential inclusionary and exclusionary membership policies in different types of regime? A satisfactory explanation would have to account for a number of things. First, what is the impact of regime type upon processes of inclusion and exclusion? The simple classification of democracies as inclusionary, and non-democracies as exclusionary, is clearly inadequate. What then is the proper way to theorize about this relationship? Second, since neither a cultural nor constructivist explanation alone is adequate, a satisfactory explanatory framework would need to account for the complex relationship between culture and politics. How do political interests interact with ethnic or cultural legacies of nationhood? To what extent do these legacies condition political decision-making processes? Finally, what is the role of political agency and where does it lie? To say that the state plays a role in determining membership is not enough. In order not to reify the state, an adequate explanation must identify those institutions and actors within the state network that are responsible, and identify the particular way in which culture, ideology and nationalism impact upon them.

A theoretical approach that incorporates an explanation of state action is clearly necessary. Such recent studies as that of Anthony Marx on the making of race and nation in Brazil, the United States, and South Africa, and that of Rogers Smith on the evolution of American citizenship are excellent examples of such an approach.[28] This study contributes to this emerging direction of scholarship, providing a comparative "statist" approach to the analysis of the emergence of the boundaries of national identity.

Plan of the Book

In the following chapter I propose an alternative explanatory framework. I suggest that models of collective action and public goods provision better explain processes of national inclusion and exclusion within the democratic nation state. Exclusion and inclusion within democratic polities can best be understood as strategies aimed at ensuring public goods provision and minimizing free-riding. By arguing that the construction of collective national identities serves as a mechanism of cooperation aimed at minimizing free-riding, exclusion emerges as a sine qua non of democracies, not as an aberration from the basic mold. Hence, our attention should be directed towards those instances of inclusion. Explaining inclusion proves a far more challenging question in political contexts than explaining exclusion.

Two empirical narratives follow the theoretical discussion. One tells the story of the Palestinian citizens of Israel. Two processes are explored: their long-term exclusion from the national membership, as it is manifested in both the distribution of fundamental rights, as well as in their representation in the symbolic matrix. The second process concerns inclusion. Overtures of inclusion which took place in the second half of the 1990s are examined and analyzed. The question posed is why these overtures were initiated, given the legitimacy granted to long-term exclusion. A number of alternative explanations are examined—cultural, ideological, and political.

The other narrative concerns the shifting status of African Americans in the American national identity. Again, two processes are explored: the long-term racial exclusion is re-cast in this narrative as exclusion from the national identity. This exclusion is expressed in terms of both rights and symbols. I examine the inclusion of African Americans that occurred during the 1960s, arguing that the passing of civil rights legislation was tantamount to including African Americans in the membership of the polity. Exploring the incentives of the regime to act towards incorporation, I set out to determine what influenced the inclusion of this minority at that time. The conclusion examines the implications of the cases from a comparative perspective.

NOTES

1. The term Israeli-Palestinian refers to Palestinians who are Israeli citizens. Hence, this population is distinct from the Palestinians in the West Bank and the Gaza Strip who are refugees. This minority is referred to in the literature by a number of labels. The issue of "labeling" is dealt with at greater length below. Henceforth and throughout the book this minority is referred to either as Palestinian or as Israeli-Palestinian.

2. The Jewish National Fund was established at the turn of the century to purchase land in Palestine for the settlement of Jews. The relationship between the JNF and the Israel Land Administration will be discussed below, in chapter 4.

3. The reforms concerned the granting of citizenship to commonwealth members. See British Nationality Act of 1981 and 1983, Immigration and Nationality Directorate, British Home office, www.ind.homeoffice.gov.uk.

4. See Anthony D. Smith, *National Identity*, (Reno: University of Nevada Press, 1991), chapter 5.

5. Charles Tilly (ed.), *The Formation of National States in Western Europe*, (Princeton, N.J.: Princeton University Press, 1975), pp. 32–47.

6. Michel Foucault, "Two Lectures on Power," in *Power/Knowledge*, (New York: Pantheon Books, 1980).

7. Gianfranco Poggi, *The State: Its Nature, Development and Prospects*, (Stanford, Calif.: Stanford University Press, 1990), p. 27.

8. See Dominique Schnapper, "Beyond the Opposition: Civil Nation versus Ethnic Nation," in *Rethinking Nationalism*, ed. Jocelyne Couture, Kai Nielsen, and Michel Seymour, (Calgary: Calgary University Press, 1996), p. 222.

9. See Saskia Sassen, *Globalization and its Discontents: Essays on the New Mobility of People and Money*, (New York: The New Press, 1998); Yasmin Nuhoglu Soysal, *Limits of Citizenship*, (Chicago: University of Chicago Press, 1994).

10. Most anthologies published over the past decade now incorporate analyses of majority minority relations in both the older and new nations. See for example Geoff Eley and Ronald Grigor Suny, (eds.), *Becoming National; A Reader*, (New York: Oxford University Press 1996); Gopal Balakrishnan (ed.), *Mapping the Nation*, (London: Verso, 1994).

11. Ernest Gellner, *Nations and Nationalism*, (Ithaca, N.Y.: Cornell University Press, 1983), and Benedict Anderson, *Imagined Communities: Reflections on the Origin and Spread of Nationalism*, rev. and exp. ed., (London: Verso, 1991).

12. During the 1990s four new journals appeared with the concept of nation in the title—*Nations and Nationalism, National Identities, Nationalism and Ethnic Politics*, and *Nationalities Papers*. This brought the total number of journals aimed specifically at the study of nationalism close to ten. This of course does not include the main political science, sociology, history, and anthropological journals that publish articles about nationalism.

13. While the discourse on nationalism and the nation has by now virtually spread across the political and academic globe, its origins can be traced to the hallowed corridors of the London School of Economics, and to an internal debate between scholars in the politics, sociology, and history departments. Kicked off by Elie Kedourie's small yet seminal volume *Nationalism* published in 1960, and Gellner's terse tract on nationalism in a chapter in the volume *Thought and Change* in 1967, the debate picked up in the 1980s with Gellner's fuller account, and Anthony Smith and Kenneth Minogue joining the ranks. The sides were defined and the battle, so to speak, had begun. See Elie Kedourie, *Nationalism*, (London: Hutchinson, 1960); Kenneth R. Minogue, *Nationalism*, (London: B. T. Batsford, 1967); Ernest Gellner, *Nations and Nationalism*; Anthony D. Smith, *Theories of Nationalism*, 2d ed., (London: Duckworth, 1983); and *The Ethnic*

Revival, (Cambridge: Cambridge University Press, 1981). The story of this eclectic group of White, British male scholars who spurred debate on a concept which constituted both the essence and the downfall of the British Empire could no doubt form the basis of a fascinating feature film.

14. The first to articulate this modernist position was Kedourie in his book *Nationalism,* published in 1960.

15. This ties in with the modernization literature on nation-building. See the discussions of modernization and nation-building in for example David Apter, *The Politics of Modernization,* (Chicago: University of Chicago Press, 1965) and Reinhard Bendix, *Nation-Building and Citizenship,* (1964; reprint Berkeley: University of California Press, 1977).

16. See Rogers Brubaker, *Citizenship and Nationhood in France and Germany,* (Cambridge, Mass.: Harvard University Press, 1992); Rogers Brubaker, *Nationalism Reframed: Nationhood and the National Question in the New Europe,* (Cambridge: Cambridge University Press, 1996).

17. Kamenka (ed.), *Nationalism: The Nature and Evolution of an Idea* (London: Edward Arnold, 1976); Anthony D. Smith, *The Ethnic Revival.* (Cambridge: Cambridge University Press, 1981); Hans Kohn, *The Idea of Nationalism: A Study in its Origins and Background,* (New York: Macmillan, 1944).

18. Plamenatz was the first scholar to substitute the civic-ethnic categories with western-eastern. See Plamenatz and Kamenka, *Nationalism.*

19. Walker Conner, *Ethnonationalism: The Quest for Understanding,* (Princeton, N.J.: Princeton University Press, 1994).

20. Rogers Brubaker, *Citizenship and Nationhood in France and Germany,* p. 3.

21. See for example two very popular books on the conflict in the Balkans, Michael Ignatieff, *Blood and Belonging: Journeys into the New Nationalism,* (New York: Farrar, Straus, Giroux, 1995); William Pfaff, *The Wrath of Nations,* (New York: Simon and Schuster, 1994).

22. It is therefore no coincidence that Anthony Smith has written extensively on the historical origins of this dichotomy.

23. Terence Ranger and Eric Hobsbawm, eds., *Invention of Tradition,* (1983; reprint, Cambridge: Cambridge University Press, 1988).

24. Ranger and Hobsbawm, *Invention of Tradition,* pp. 3–4.

25. The literature on the construction of identity and memory is vast. See especially, Yael Zerubavel, *Recovered Roots: Collective Memory and the Making of Israeli National Tradition,* (Chicago: University of Chicago Press, 1995); Michael Billig, *Banal Nationalism,* (London: Sage, 1995); Pierre Nola, "Between Memory and History," *Representations,* 26 (1989): 7–25.

26. John R. Gillis, (ed.), *Commemorations: The Politics of National Identity,* (Princeton NJ.: Princeton University Press. 1994), p. 16.

27. Gillis, *Commemorations,* p. 16.

28. Anthony W. Marx, *Making Race and Nation: A Comparison of the United States, South Africa, and Brazil,* (New York: Cambridge University Press, 1998); Rogers Smith, *Civic Ideals,* (New Haven, Conn.: Yale University Press, 1997).

Chapter Two

National Identity
and Collective Action

The quest for public order and stability has long preoccupied political philosophers. Two fundamental vantage points have emerged over the years. The first, essentially Hobbesian, argues that political order can be achieved only with the institution of a strong ruler, even a political despot. Assuming individuals to be not only selfish, but also uncompromising in the pursuit of their individual interests, logic dictates that for order to be sustainable and hence stable, a strong enforcement mechanism is necessary. The alternative perspective, mostly associated with Rousseau, assumes that individuals are perfectly capable of acknowledging and promoting collective interests. Hence they are able to arrive at an orderly and stable society consensually, without, that is, the help or the intervention of an external enforcer. Political order, according to this viewpoint, is an outcome of these individuals' acceptance and internalization of fundamental unifying values and norms. Subsequently, the establishment of a cohesive community becomes a precondition for stability.[1]

In this chapter I suggest that processes of national exclusion and inclusion are best understood in the context of the efforts of the state to establish a sense of belonging or community. I argue that far from being driven by moral or ethical conceptions, the self-interested democratic state promotes a shared identity, and a political community, so as to maintain stability. I link the maintenance of stability to the ability of the state to promote collective action, and in this way secure the provision of public goods. Finally, I demonstrate that the promotion of collective action is dependent upon the construction of a shared national identity, which is by definition exclusive, and hence exclusionary.

STABILITY, COMMUNITY AND IDENTITY

The first half of the twentieth century was overcome with hyper-communitarian ideologies such as Nazism, Fascism, and Socialism. These ideologies argued that the good of the community, defined in ideological and in the first case racist (and therefore exclusionary) terms, was primary and prior to the good of the individual. Much as a result, the Roussean legacy, linking stability with community, was largely discredited.[2] During the second half of that century, the waning of the extremist ideologies and the changing scholarly and political realities made the reappearance of communitarian worldviews possible.

In the scholarly arena, one of the most crucial events that put the link between community and order at the top of the intellectual agenda was the highly acclaimed publication of John Rawls' *A Theory of Justice* in 1977. According to Rawls' veil of ignorance individuals appeared unencumbered by any cultural, moral, and historical context. The convening of society therefore, was unconditioned by a sense of previous belonging, or an underlying identity.[3] In response, a critique of this essentially liberal concept emerged which argued that the cultural neutrality of the liberal state was both historically inaccurate, and politically unadvisable. A strong sense of community, belonging, and purpose was necessary to promote liberal values, and was also essential to accomplish fundamental liberal goals such as economic redistribution. This critique, which came to be known as the "communitarian critique," reintroduced a discourse on politics that proposed a significant relationship between political stability and the promotion of a sense of belonging to the community.[4]

Similar cycles characterized the political arena. Towards the end of the 1980s the break up of the Soviet Union ushered in an unprecedented wave of democratization and a euphoric atmosphere. The thesis promoted by social scientist Fukuyama, that the ideological struggles of the century were decided with democracy and liberalism emerging as the victor, and hence marking *The End of History* was accepted with great applause and enthusiasm.[5] The gradual solidification of the European Union and the global communications revolution raised expectations of a new global era. Hence, the demise of totalitarianism was accompanied by visions of the demise of the nation state and of politics governed by sentiments of nationality as opposed to sentiments of rationality. Optimism, however, soon gave way to disillusionment when one after the other many of the newly established democracies gave way to an orgiastic release of ultra-nationalist sentiment, and to an eruption of violent ethnic politics. From Bosnia to Rwanda and to Chechnya, the end of history seemed to take on a new meaning. All of this, coupled with the continuous waves of migration (now bloated by refugees) from the South to the

North, has given an extra charge to the renewed interest in issues of identity in general and of nationalism in particular.

At the same time, the ability of international finance and capital to dictate the ebbs and flows of migration has challenged the exclusive sovereignty of the nation-state over its demographic boundaries. In the developed western countries this challenge has ironically raised expectations of the state to protect the rights and conditions of the workers within their jurisdiction. These seemingly contradictory trends have contributed to the urgency with which the interest in collective identity has emerged.

Converging with the emergent discourse on community, efforts have been made to reconcile democracy and nationalism. This modern discourse can be traced back to two nineteenth century theorists, Lord Acton and John Stuart Mill. While both acknowledged the growing appeal of the principle of nationality, each promoted a different interpretation, and a different perspective. In *Considerations on Representative Government* Mill claimed that "free institutions are next to impossible in a country made up of different nationalities."[6] The smooth functioning of democratic institutions demands a fundamental consensus on values. This type of consensus can only emanate from a shared identity, the basis for which is provided by shared culture: traditions, language, and that favorite Victorian characteristic—sensibility. All of these, for Mill, spelled out the concept of nationality. The kind of agreement which Mill deemed vital to the functioning of democracy could be found in a shared nationality.

Lord Acton's argument was built on an almost opposite rationale: that the best defense of democratic institutions lies in cultural diversity. It is the very diversity of cultures, belief systems, and customs that ensures that governments would safeguard individual liberties.[7] Echoing Madison, Acton's logic serves as a basis for Dahl's theory of polyarchy, namely that the effective functioning of democracies depends not on the rule of "the people," but rather the rule of "many people."[8] The self-regulating dynamic of diverse interest groups negotiating between themselves, the very presumption that democracies exist to promote diverse interests, and not one unitary one, is seen, in this Actonian, or Madisonian tradition, as the best democratic safeguard. Nationality, for Acton, interpreted as a representation (and defense) of shared culture, was a tragedy and a threat. A political nationality, however, representing the conglomerate of cultures necessary for democracy, all based of course, upon a shared political understanding, was a different matter. Hence, Acton supported the idea of the nation, defined politically, and hence capable of incorporating (but not assimilating) diverse cultural traditions.

Two different approaches to the same idea. For the first, cultural assimilation is a necessary condition for stability, while for the second, it is a threat to stability. For the first the shared understanding that emanates from a national identity rests on homogeneity, while for the second, this very same understanding emanates from the tolerance of difference possible only through an umbrella of a shared national identity. These two different arguments or understandings of collective identity have evolved, over the years, into two distinct approaches to the understanding of national identity and democratic politics. The first position argues that "when cultural diversity threatens to undermine a sense of belonging together, the state should pursue a policy of assimilation."[9] Assimilation policies are conducted through a wide variety of state-run institutions, in particular educational ones. This position defines the creation of a shared realm of understanding, a central political "project" in which the state takes an active role in inculcating shared understanding because the persistence of different understandings presents an obstacle to efficient democratic government. Normative theories of liberal nationalism, such as those recently promoted by political philosophers Yael Tamir and David Miller, support this position.[10] Although neither Tamir nor Miller would defend a policy of radical assimilation (whereby minority cultures are prohibited from expressing values which contradict the majority culture), both support the privatization of minority cultures, and the active role of the state in promoting the majority culture and its values.

The alternative position, supported by amongst others Bikhu Parekh and Brian Barry, claims that a shared national identity need not impose any cultural preference.[11] This position distinguishes between an identity based on culture (or ethnicity), and a strictly political identity, arguing that within democratic regimes, a shared national identity must be strictly political. Such a political identity would be based on constitutive principles, and would focus on political institutions and structures. While educational institutions play a role in the implementation of this type of national identity, more important are the political institutions responsible for distribution and inclusion themselves. The role of the state is to ensure that these main distributive institutions be inclusive for all cultures and minorities. The more inclusive, the more equal the distribution, and the more identification with these institutions is facilitated, the greater is the shared understanding. Within this framework, a shared understanding emanates from the existence of shared political practices, rather than common political socialization.

Combining both approaches, the argument linking democratic stability with the existence of a shared national identity rests on four distinct claims:

1. A shared identity fosters a commitment to the workings of national democratic institutions.
2. Liberal institutions stand little chance of long-term existence without a common national identity.

3. A national identity is a precondition for the existence of trust, which makes compromise possible.
4. National identity is a necessary condition for a "politics of the common good." Stated differently, the existence of "fellow-feeling" facilitates co-operation on common projects, and therefore makes redistribution more acceptable.

Claims one and two posit that sustaining democratic procedures (such as voting for example) requires a high degree of commitment (gathering information about the candidates, informing oneself on the issues, registering to vote, and actually going to the polls). Such a commitment can only arise out of a community, i.e., a commitment amongst members of a community towards each other. Claims three and four go one step further. They argue that the framework of rights and obligations which is established by democratic polities involves continual decisions and actions concerning distribution and redistribution. These types of decisions presume the possibility of empathy and sacrifice which in turn are possible only amongst members of a community.

To conclude, therefore, the arguments linking national identity with democratic stability might differ in their understanding of where the sense of belonging originates, but they agree on its importance. A sense of belonging promotes an understanding that these institutions are designed and intended for one's benefit, and thus facilitates identification with them. In other words, a sense of belonging to the polity entails a belief that one's interests are linked to those of the polity, and that serving one's own interests (and those of one's cultural group) is embedded in the polity's agenda. This is the essence of solidarity and trust that is essential in the maintenance of any type of group.

BELONGING TO THE POLITY:
COLLECTIVE ACTION AND PUBLIC GOODS

Many positive results ensue from the existence of such trust and solidarity. At the most basic level, they introduce regularity into inter-personal relations, i.e., the ability to predict, and hence rely on, the behavior of people other than ourselves (or at least the illusion of this). Organizations that exhibit high degrees of both solidarity and trust—police forces, where the buddy system depends on such trust; political task forces, where the intensity of the belief in a shared enemy induces levels of intense solidarity; churches, where the sense of community which emanates from deep faith invokes a feeling of brotherhood—all pride themselves in this kind of intimate knowledge.

Solidarity, however, is not limited to these types of groups. All future-oriented groups—that is, groups whose members are linked by future-oriented plans or interests—cease to function without the maintenance of at least a minimal level of trust. The logic is simple: coordinated action is dependent upon the ability of members to predict the behavior of their fellow members. In democratic polities, which are essentially voluntary and non-coercive arrangements, the existence of trust and solidarity is necessary to generate collective action which is, in turn, essential to ensure most collective goals.

Intellectual interest in the logic that underlies collective action has reemerged in the past few decades.[12] The mainstay of the debate reflects a general agreement that the modern human condition does not encourage collective action, and that modern individuals exhibit far too little collective spirit.[13] The tragedy of the shared commons is a present-day tragedy; the growing alienation which modern life entails, the availability of alternatives and the freedom of choice, and the ever-growing quest for individual profit have rendered collective action and the ability to subordinate individual interests to collective ones anachronistic.[14]

However, if we look at the frequency of the domestic and international conflicts that took place during the twentieth century (including two world wars), one might be tempted to say that an excess of collective action is a far more accurate assessment of the human condition. While the type of collective action that aims at the provision of public *goods*, such as a clean environment or the attainment of social justice, might be hard to find, collective action aimed at such public *bads*, such as ethnic cleansing, authoritarian politics, and military excess is abundant.[15] This suggests that the problem may lie not in the individuals' incapacity to act collectively, but in their propensity to promote hostile and conflictual goals, rather than socially constructive and cooperative ones.

Collective action in democracies is not limited to the international arena, nor is it limited to "grand" goals such as social justice, and global environmental safety. If we define collective action as concerted action by a group of individuals aimed at attaining certain shared goals, then in fact it would prove difficult to explain how democratic regimes can function at all *without* collective action. Banal manifestations of collective action permeate our every day and our every sphere of life, rendering the daily functioning of democratic societies dependent upon the coordinated and cooperative interaction of the many individual members of society. In its most basic form, the possibility of maintaining fundamental democratic procedures such as basic individual liberties, is dependent on the collective mutual respect of each member's autonomy. Freedoms of speech, association, and belief are dependent on the collective respect of the other's opinion; the very fact of democratic elections hinges on these fundamental acts of collective action. Adam Smith's eighteenth century liberal metaphor of the "invisible hand" can be extended far beyond the boundaries of the economic market: self-regulating cooperation governs not merely the economic, but the social and political realms as well.

Ironically, Adam Smith was among the first to recognize what Hardin has called the back of the invisible hand.[16] If the invisible hand referred to the self-regulating element of free societies, its "back" referred to those "free riders" that evaded this self-regulation; to those shirking their responsibility for attaining those shared, collective goals. The back of the hand, however, operated only in certain realms and Smith was quick to explain why. While the individualist, egotistic drive for profit is what fuels the self-regulating market (by providing for oneself, one inadvertently provides for society as a whole), this drive fails in certain areas. He writes: "it can never be for the interest of any individual, or small number of individuals, to erect and maintain [these realms]: because the profit could never repay the expense to any individual . . . though it may frequently do much more than repay it to a greater society."[17]

Hence, the "realms" which defy self interest and hence self-regulation have two essential attributes. The first is that they incorporate goods that are too expensive for any private firm, not to mention individual, to produce on their own. And the second is that the production (and provision) of these goods is dependent on the cooperation of all members of society.

The problem of "free riders" has received its more modern, and most popular, articulation by the economist Mancur Olson. Certain collectively produced goals have a particular quality that once produced and shared collectively, rational individuals have a clear incentive not to contribute to their production because they will enjoy the benefits in any case:

> Since any gain goes to everyone in the group, those who contribute nothing to the effort will get just as much as those who made a contribution. It pays "to let George do it," but George has little or no incentive to do anything in the group interest either, so . . . there will be little, if any, group action. The paradox, then, is that (in the absence of special arrangements or circumstances . . .) large groups, at least if they are composed of rational individuals, will not act in their group interest.[18]

Economists have defined those goods that attract free riders as public goods.[19] Public goods are distinguished from private goods by two basic characteristics: jointness of supply and the impossibility of exclusion. Jointness of supply means that one person's consumption of any amount of the good in question does not reduce the amount left for consumption by others, and nonexclusivity refers to the inability to prevent any one person from consuming any part of the good. Hence, as Samuelson suggests, once a pure public good is produced, it appears in the utility function of all members of the relevant society.[20] Typical examples of public goods are security (e.g. from outside threats or from domestic violence) or the beam of a lighthouse.[21] But public goods can also be material goods such as air, sewage, or radio waves. They can be, and most commonly are, intangible conceptual goods such as road safety resulting from the erection of traffic lights, physical safety resulting from effective policing, or peace resulting from conflict resolution. However, as Hardin points out, few of the more physical goods are indeed "pure" in Samuelson's sense.[22] This is because some type of exclusionary mechanism can be, and usually is, applied to exclude people from their consumption. For example, tolls are imposed on roads, payments are required to gain electricity, and filters are installed to get clean air. Hence, what distinguishes these goods from private ones is that by their very nature they meet the first (but not the second) attribute in the definition of a public good: jointness of supply. Consequently, the market will most likely fail to provide them. The exclusionary mechanisms must therefore be imposed on the good externally. The market failure type of explanation is not really applicable to conceptual goods. These are much more complex and elusive, and prove a much more robust challenge for understanding.

It is close to impossible to prevent any individual from enjoying a sense of safety—both domestic and international—once it is produced. Furthermore, with the development of the welfare state, it is increasingly difficult to prevent an individual from enjoying the sense of living in a just society generated by the provision of social services.[23] The extreme case is of course education. In most western states even illegal immigrant children are eligible for public education, and thus all can enjoy the sense of living in an educated society. Even criminals, or typical free riders like draft dodgers or tax evaders, are able to enjoy the fruits of the system while contributing absolutely nothing towards its production. Paradoxically, the production of these types of goods (often labeled "social goods") relies entirely on collective action in the form of taxation or other forms of civil participation. The central problem of all types of organization—the democratic state included—is how to generate this type of collective action.

DEMOCRACIES AND PUBLIC PROVISION

As a result of the free rider problem attached to most social goods, it is the state that assumes the responsibility for their provision. The three categories most commonly seen as falling under the responsibility of the state are national defense, public order and the administration of justice, and the elementary provision of public services. The first two, national defense and public order, are as close as one can come to the notion of pure public goods first elaborated upon by Samuelson. The production of public goods is a more complicated mission in democratic than in non-democratic regimes, because the former are both fundamentally voluntary and reluctant to exercise extreme coercion. Hence, the production of these goods depends heavily on the free will and voluntary cooperation of the members of the polity. Let us consider three typical examples involving citizens' voluntary participation in democracies in the production of law and order, security, and taxation. First, to maintain domestic order, individuals are required, on the whole, to voluntarily obey the law. Since anyone can potentially break the law and disrupt social order, everyone is potentially involved in maintaining it. And this they do. Despite the growing prison populations in most western societies, most individuals do not take the law into their own hands. On the contrary, voluntary civil associations assisting law enforcement agencies are not uncommon in these countries. Second, to maintain international security, military service is occasionally needed. Most members of democracies serve in the armed forces when called upon; indeed, military service is often perceived as a right and not an obligation, and is often demanded by minorities prevented from enlisting.

Third and finally, fundamental public services like public schools, roads, and other infrastructure-related domains are dependent upon public financing in the form of taxation. Despite widespread tax evasion, most people pay most (or some) of their taxes. In all three cases, if individuals refused to cooperate, coercion would be necessary and the regime would change its spots. To continue supplying these goods, and still remain democratic, the state must find ways to enforce public contribution towards the provision of these goods.

How do they do it? How do democratic states—committed to voluntary participation—overcome the problem of collective action, i.e., free riding? The answer of course is simple. They do this by providing members of society with a series of negative and positive incentives, that are contingent upon the behavior of the contributing individuals. Negative incentives are attached to non-cooperation, and positive incentives are awarded for cooperative behavior. In the context of state action, these incentives can be best defined as political mechanisms.[24] Two types of such mechanisms are available to the state: those utilizing coercion and those inducing cooperation.

Mechanisms of coercion are indeed a widespread and central means of promoting collective action: they were invented long before Hobbes' *Leviathan* and have clearly survived him. Laws that institutionalize contribution and make non-participation punishable, and policing systems that enforce these laws, all ensure that individuals contribute towards the production of these goods. Police forces, armies, park rangers, street cleaners, dog catchers on the one hand, and judges, courts, and law books on the other, can all be seen as members of a national team-force whose raison d'etre is to ensure the consistent production of law and order. If order, security, and social services are the sine qua non of life in a free society, then the existence of these institutions help to force us, to paraphrase Rousseau, to be free.[25] Indeed, most people obey the law, at least those laws which they are likely to transgress, because of their unwillingness to bear the cost of punishment and the simple rational calculation that the benefit accrued from disobeying the law is not worth the price paid for transgression.

Fear of punishment, as strong and deep as it may be, is however an insufficient explanation for the extent of the order which characterizes most democratic societies. The question of political obedience has generated numerous theories and explanations as to why individuals tend to obey the law. As far as the laws which most of us are unlikely to transgress—those that prohibit violent crimes for example—our unlikeliness is usually due to some moral framework that exists outside of the law—some source of ethical conduct, be it religious, philosophical, or inherent. Hence, most of us do not perform crimes of violence not because of our cost benefit calculation, but because of one or another internalized system of morality.

The mundane laws, those that govern daily activity, and focus on activities about which most of us have no moral or ethical qualms, are the more difficult case. While most of us may occasionally jaywalk, cheat on our taxes, run the stop light, or even refuse to show up for military duty, most of us do not transgress most of the time. The only plausible explanation lies in the existence of additional, cooperation-inducing mechanisms employed by the state, which must therefore be non-coercive. Modern states thus combine mechanisms of coercion with mechanisms of cooperation to enforce a collective contribution towards the provision of public goods.

MECHANISMS OF COOPERATION

Different types of states and regimes rely on different measures of coercive and cooperative mechanisms. Let's imagine a spectrum of regime type that runs from most democratic to most authoritarian. As regimes move along the spectrum (from least democratic to most), the degree to which they can legitimately employ coercion to enforce contribution to the provision of public goods decreases. As they approach the democratic side of the spectrum, they must rely less and less on coercion, and more and more on the consent of their members. Hence, the democratic and democratizing state must find ways to induce and strengthen the spirit of voluntary contribution and consent.

Democratic societies, therefore, are characterized not merely by the implementation of mechanisms of coercion, but by mechanisms of cooperation as well. Indeed, democratic regimes can be defined as regimes that rely on mechanisms of cooperation for the joint production of public goods. Obeying the law, paying ones taxes, in short—being a good citizen—has become a relatively pervasive social norm that guides most peoples' social actions.[26]

In most societies, one public good that ensures that agreements are honored is a precursor of all others.[27] The concept of the "social contract", for example, reflects this notion of a prior or meta-agreement based on the consent of the members and aimed at ensuring that all further agreements among them were to be honored. In general then, to ensure future gains (no matter how these gains are to be defined or understood) in the veil of uncertainty and fundamental lack of trust among the sides to agreements, the pre-arranged mechanism would be called for. This mechanism would then be used not only to facilitate trust and thus induce cooperation amongst the members, but also to reduce uncertainties by making sure that all sides meet their obligations. Hence, this mechanism of cooperation provides members of a group or organization with an agreed framework whereby their cooperation is ensured by inducing other members to cooperate. Such a mechanism of cooperation, if properly and efficiently instated, could provide at least a partial solution to a prisoner's dilemma situation, by ensuring that all sides recognize that cooperation is the accepted norm of behavior, and that if followed all will gain.[28] If some decide to violate the agreement, then there are punitive measures, of course.

Contracts represent *formal* agreements, and by their very nature they serve as legal mechanisms of cooperation. Solidarity organizations, which inspire a collective identity, represent a more *informal* type of mechanism. This distinction between formal and informal means of inducing cooperation is important because it reflects the spectrum of alternative options available to regimes in their pursuit of their goals. Seen in this light, constitutions and legal codes that set down the rules of cooperation within a society constitute the former formal method, while religions, diverse ideological social movements, and shared culture writ large constitute the latter, informal ones.[29]

Thus religions, perhaps the original solidarity organizations, manifest an extremely high degree of cooperation. Collective action, therefore, within religious organizations, actually precludes the free rider problem. The faith of religious people is fundamentally what maintains and constitutes the religious organization itself. People maintain their faith to no small degree because other people maintain exactly the same faith. They know that their faith is shared. Religious belief is an inherently collective affair. Members of the same religion are willing to cooperate with one another, and also to pray today, because they are never sure what they might need tomorrow. Prayer is like a contract which ensures that in case of need, the dividends can be cashed in.

Cooperative mechanisms help create amongst individual members the understanding, or perception, that future cooperation is possible because their interaction is insured, so to speak, by the feelings of solidarity that each member experiences. Feelings of solidarity may enhance the capacity of individuals to engage in "other-related" activities: if the level of identification amongst members is high (a defining characteristic of solidarity), then actions aimed at helping promote the goals of others are seen as contributing to one's own welfare. Thus, within solidarity organizations, the production of public goods is more successful than in non-solidarity organizations, because the motivation to free ride is reduced.

Indeed, collective action is common and relatively unhindered within religious organizations, ideological movements, and intensely solidarity professional organizations such as the police force. By creating a solidarity association that is loosely linked to the state association, democratic governments create a type of mechanism of compliance.

Solidarity associations create, and then maintain, an ethic according to which solidarity in itself, and national solidarity in particular, is perceived not merely as a natural, essential, or fundamental part of one's identity, but also virtuous, admirable, and a source of pride and envy. In essence, the establishment of solidarity associations attached to the state help to transform what Olson termed latent groups into small groups. According to Olson, free riding was prevalent within large-scale latent groups which are socially atomized.[30] This experience of atomization discourages fellow feeling and hence nourishes the kind of selfish individualistic calculations which give rise to free riding in the first place. Free riding, therefore, while a product of rationality, must be understood contextually—that is, in the context of atomized societies. Individual motivations within other contexts, smaller or less alienated groups, are different. In these types of groups, it is easier for individuals to recognize the connection between their own interests and those of the group. Attaching a solidarity association to the state enables the free rider problem to be bypassed by circumventing that specific type of rational individual motivation. As sociologist Pierre Biernbaum notes, free riding can be avoided once "the actors do not mobilize in the hope of enjoying specific rewards, for individual and collective gain are here the same."[31]

Mechanisms of cooperation based on solidarity render individual and collective gain indistinguishable. As ethical or ideological commitment becomes increasingly mixed up with self-interest, collective action emerges.

COLLECTIVE NATIONAL IDENTITY
AS A MECHANISM OF COOPERATION

Collective national identity constitutes such a mechanism of cooperation. The identity bestowed upon a group by the nation inspires in its members a sense of belonging, and a sense of cooperation which manages to transcend individual differences of class and often even culture. Two elements are considered as essential, or basic, to a national identity. The first is this sense of belonging, or of community, whereby members of the nation intuitively feel (often despite empirical evidence to the contrary), that communication and understanding are more natural and free-flowing amongst members of the same nation, and this is because of some shared (and often vague) worldview.[32]

Hence, the nation is often a paradoxical unit. It rests upon a shared understanding that the group is unitary and homogeneous, while in fact more often than not, members of the nation share no more with each other—economically, socially, and even culturally—than members of cross-cultural association. What they do share is the belief in their commonality, in their implicit understanding of each other, and in the imagining of a free-flowing communication amongst members of the nation.

The second element concerns politics. Amongst members of the nation these shared understandings and worldviews are implicitly related to the notion of sovereignty. As Benedict Anderson said, "A nation is an imagined community that imagines itself as bounded, and as sovereign." The critical element that distinguishes a shared national identity from other shared identities, both in history and in contemporary politics, is that this identity lays claims to an autonomous political organization, and views this political organization as essential to its very existence.[33] A symbiotic relationship has evolved between the nation and the state whereby each is dependent upon the other for the "true" expression of its essence. The nation is dependent upon the state for the institutions of governing (essential for the nation to be "self determining.") The state, in turn, is reliant upon the mutual communication and understanding implicit in the community of nationals. As Brian Barry has noted,

> Loyalty to a nation . . . tends to grow out of a habit of cooperation between different groups within the nation, which gives rise to stable expectations about their future behavior, and especially to some degree of trust that concessions made today without a precise quid pro quo being specified will be reciprocated at some future time when the occasion arises.[34]

Propagating a collective national identity intensifies solidarity feelings amongst members of the community and enhances the willingness of members of that community to contribute towards the provision and production of collectively desired public goods. The sense of solidarity, which itself presumably inspires the members with a sense of collective spirit and purpose, is a critical component of the maintenance of society: these members are less prone to act against the regulations or the collective ethos.

Thus, the values and norms are not in and of themselves mechanisms of cooperation. Rather, it is the association created, the communal sentiment which facilitates communication, and which in turn establishes the necessary basis for shared interests, which promotes cooperation.[35] In a fundamental sense, then, nationalism in general, and national identity in particular, can be seen as an elaborately staged mechanism of cooperation.

The sentiments of affinity and identification resulting from the forging of a collective memory, which always goes hand in hand with a collective future, are indispensable tools for political leadership—be it democratic or totalitarian. However, for the democratic government, the sense of identification that emerges from such relatively simple devices such as the arousing of national sentiment, are a legitimate and low-cost means of enforcing so-called voluntary contribution.

And here lies the most fundamental explanation for the investment of democratic regimes in the promotion of a shared national identity. A shared national identity encourages collective action and thus minimizes free riding on basic collectively produced public goods such as domestic stability, international security, and public works. The promotion of trust amongst members of the nation is essential to the redistributive capacity of the state. Different individual members—or even groups—within the boundaries of the identity (i.e., members) trust that they are equally eligible for state support by virtue of their membership. Excluded groups lack this trust, and hence have no a priori expectations from the state.

EXCLUSIVITY AND EXCLUSION

Because public goods once produced cannot be divided and cannot be awarded to people in accordance with their proportional contribution to their production, no one can be excluded from consumption. Hence, non-exclusivity, i.e., the inability to exclude non-contributors from consuming the public good, is one of two characteristics that distinguishes public goods from private goods. This is, of course, what allows for free riding and defines the basic paradox involved in their provision.

Consider the sense of public satisfaction that emerges because the government conducts a just social policy. The belief that we all live in a fair and just society in Rawls' terms is indeed indicative of successful public policy. This could be obtained as a by-product of the implementation of various social programs. No member of this hypothetical "just society" can be denied a share in this indivisible sense of pride generated by being included in such a society. But to sustain this sense of pride and to keep the costs of social service provision at a manageable level in this attractive society, its external boundaries must be defined. Hence, the property of non-exclusivity may apply to the internal affairs of the members of society but not to outsiders who also wish to join. This is because the rational members would rather sustain their sense of pride and level of contribution to the costs of social service provision and not share them with additional people. The production of public goods may thus generate incentives not to expand the size of the group of benefactors by defining the boundaries between insiders and outsiders. Outsiders would be excluded so long as they cannot assure that their contribution to the production of public goods is greater than the benefits incurred by joining the group. As discussed above, the boundary between citizen and non-citizen is one mechanism of limiting membership, but it has emerged as insufficient. Modern democratic polities require additional delimiting boundaries—i.e., exclusionary mechanisms—amongst citizens of the state. Both the coercive and cooperative mechanisms employed by the state to encourage collective action aimed at the production of public goods always exclude non-members, and hence constitute democratically legitimate, exclusionary mechanisms.

In modern democratic societies these mechanisms are the responsibility of the state. However, as the discussion above indicated, the very mechanisms provided by the state to minimize free riding on public goods, are themselves public goods upon which citizens (or members) can free ride. The question then arises—how can the state impose exclusivity upon the very mechanisms which are aimed at solving problems of public goods production.

In the case of coercive mechanisms this is clearly a mute point. No rational individual has an incentive to free ride on imprisonment or fines. The problem is a relevant one for the cooperative mechanisms. The solution to the free riding problem lies in the very nature of the mechanisms themselves. All contracts and associations are limited in their membership. This is true by definition, and is trivial. An association is judged by its membership, and membership, to be effective in any sense, must be limited. This leads us to the simple axiom: state produced mechanisms of cooperation are, by definition, exclusive. Hence all shared identities produced by the state (democratic and otherwise) must be exclusive, and hence exclusionary.

According to the logic of public goods provision, since the potential consumers of order, security, and services are inclusionary (i.e., include the entire set of individuals residing or even passing through the boundaries of the state), the cooperative mechanism, aimed at persuading individuals to contribute towards the production of the good, must somehow be able to impose an exclusionary device. National identity is such an effective exclusive and exclusionary devise. It offers its members solidarity, a sense of belonging, and a certain sense of identification with the goals of the state. As members of this identity, their incentive to contribute towards the maintenance of order and security is greater. But as members of this identity, the commitment of the state to their well-being is also greater and entails higher costs for the state. Therefore, democratic regimes will include new members when, and only when, excluded groups or individuals threaten the continued provision of the public good. Inclusion thus imposes two costs: first, by expanding the membership in the national identity, its effectiveness as a mechanism of cooperation weakens, and secondly, inclusion entails responsibility, which entails costs.

Inclusion is thus a means of cooption. Including new groups in the national identity provides them with a means of identifying with the state, with its institutions, and of sharing in its self-image. Reducing alienation from the core of society should also reduce the incentive to free ride and encourage collective action towards the provision of domestic order.

MAPPING INCLUSION AND EXCLUSION

This discussion has shown that the question—why exclude—is somewhat misguided. Democratic regimes always exclude groups or individuals from the membership boundaries of their shared national identity. They do this to maintain the exclusivity necessary for the identity to function as an efficient mechanism of cooperation. The relevant question that emerges is not why exclude, but rather, why, and when, will a democracy include new groups into the national membership.

The answer to this question is largely an empirical one, and results from the political and economic calculations of the relevant state actors. In the two cases studied in this book, I narrate two separate stories of exclusion and inclusion. Both cases involve long-term exclusion of a minority group from membership in the shared national identity. In both cases the excluded group enjoyed the status of citizen but suffered severe exclusion nonetheless.

In the first case, that of African Americans in the United States, I argue that despite the establishment of citizenship rights for African Americans during Reconstruction, African Americans were, for all intents and purposes, excluded from the boundaries of national membership. I illustrate their exclusion through both legal and symbolic indicators. The inclusion of this group occurred one hundred years later, during the 1960s, in the Civil Rights era. The explanation for inclusion lies in the analysis of a series of regime incentives, both domestic and international, but basically comes down to the fact that the costs of exclusion, at that point in time, exceeded those of inclusion.

The second case, that of Palestinian citizens in Israel, is less clear-cut. After demonstrating their exclusion from national membership, I argue that the advent of the Oslo accords in 1993 ushered in a number of changes and introduced new incentives for the Israeli state. Whether or not, and the extent to which these incentives will lead the state to full-fledged inclusion is not clear, especially in light of the unstable course of the negotiations. Moreover, as I demonstrate, the propensity for inclusion is, to a certain extent, also a function of the different types of demands voiced by the minority itself.

In both narratives, I focus on two basic indicators of inclusion and exclusion: symbols and legislation. These, I argue, are the two axes of identity. Legislation is the indicator of distribution, and is an essential component of membership in the national community. As I have argued above, within democratic societies only members enjoy the entire gamut of rights and benefits provided by the state. These rights and benefits are distributed through a wide array of mechanisms, the most important of which are legal. In both cases the exclusion of the minority was deeply entrenched in the legal code of the society, which managed to bypass the democratic notions of equality before the law. In the American case, the strongest indicator of inclusion was the passing, in 1964 and 1965, of legislation which secured the political rights of African Americans. In the Israeli case, the debate which developed in Israel during the 1990s surrounding key exclusionary legislation, such as the Law of Return and the property rights laws, were a clear indication of a possibility of inclusion.

Inclusion and exclusion begin with laws, but they are supported and entrenched in the very stuff that identity is made of: symbols. As countless scholars of nationalism have already established, inclusion in the national identity enables sharing in the common imagination, and in the self-image of the rest of society. Self-image and the shared imagination are elaborated upon, by both the state and society, through the construction of symbols that are transmitted through a variety of channels. These channels are rituals that celebrate holidays, anthems, flags, monuments which commemorate heroes, and of course written texts which tell the shared history of the nation. In the cases I look at, I demonstrate the exclusion of both the Palestinians and African Americans through a careful analysis of both commemorative texts (rituals, monuments, museums) and written texts. In the American case, the exclusionary texts of the pre-1960s are compared with those of the post-1960s, and inclusion is evident in all symbolic avenues. In the case of the Palestinians, a more careful assessment is made of any potential shift in symbolic representation. The ambivalence of the symbolic representation is itself taken as an indication of the ambivalence towards inclusion.

NOTES

1. For a discussion of the problem of social and political order in the context of stability, see Brian Barry, "John Rawls and the Search for Stability," *Ethics* 105 (July 1995): 874–915.

2. See for example the interpretation of Rousseau in J. L. Talmon, *The Origins of Totalitarian Democracy* (London: Mercury Books, 1961 (1952)).

3. See Rawls, *A Theory of Justice* (Oxford: Oxford University Press, 1971).

4. For a collection of the main arguments in the communitarian-liberal debate see Shlomo Avineri and Avner de-Shalit, eds., *Communitarianism and Individualism* (Oxford: Oxford University Press, 1992).

5. Fukuyama Francis, *The End of History and the Last Man* (New York: The Free Press, 1992).

6. See John Stuart Mill, *Considerations on Representative Government* (Oxford: Oxford University Press, 1975). The citation is taken from Andrew Mason, "Political Community, Liberal-Nationalism, and the Ethics of Assimilation," *Ethics* 109 (January 1999): 261–86.

7. See Lord Acton, "Nationality," in *Mapping the Nation,* ed., Gopal Balakrishnan, (London: Verso, 1996): 17–39.

8. See Alexander Hamilton, James Madison and John Jay, *The Federalist Papers*, ed. Clinton Rossiter (New York: New American Library, 1961), number 10, pp. 77–84. Robert Dahl, *Polyarchy, Participation and Opposition* (New Haven, Conn.: Yale University Press, 1977).

9. Andrew Mason, "Political Community," p. 266.

10. David Miller, *On Nationality* (New York: Oxford University Press, 1995); Yael Tamir, *Liberal Nationalism* (Princeton, N.J.: Princeton University Press, 1993).

11. Bikhu Parekh, "Defining National Identity in a Multicultural Society," in *People, Nation and State: The Meaning of Ethnicity and Nationalism*, ed., Edward Mortimer (London: I. B. Taurus, 1999), p. 70; Brian Barry, "Self Government Revisited," in *The Nature of Political Theory*, ed. David Miller and Larry Siedentop (Oxford: Clarendon Press, 1983), pp. 121–55.

12. There is a large literature on collective action. See in particular Mancur Olson, *The Logic of Collective Action* (Cambridge, Mass.: Harvard University Press, 1965); Russell Hardin, *Collective Action* (Baltimore: Johns Hopkins University Press for Resources for the Future, 1982); Jon Elster, *The Cement of Society; A Study of Social Order* (Cambridge: Cambridge University Press, 1989).

13. See for example Russel Hardin, *One for All: The Logic of Group Conflict* (Princeton, N.J.: Princeton University Press, 1995).

14. "The tragedy of the commons develops in this way. Picture a pasture open to all. It is to be expected that each herdsman will try to keep as many cattle as possible on the commons. Such an arrangement may work reasonably satisfactorily for centuries because tribal wars, poaching, and disease keep the numbers of both man and beast well below the carrying capacity of the land. Finally, however, comes the day of reckoning, that is, the day when the long-desired goal of social stability becomes a reality. At this point, the inherent logic of the commons remorselessly generates tragedy.

As a rational being, each herdsman seeks to maximize his gain. Explicitly or implicitly, more or less consciously, he asks, 'What is the utility *to me* of adding one more animal to my herd?' This utility has one negative and one positive component.

The positive component is a function of the increment of one animal. Since the herdsman receives all the proceeds from the sale of the additional animal, the positive utility is nearly +1.

The negative component is a function of the additional overgrazing created by one more animal. Since, however, the effects of overgrazing are shared by all the herdsmen, the negative utility for any particular decision-making herdsman is only a fraction of –1. Adding together the component partial utilities, the rational herdsman concludes that the only sensible course for him to pursue is to add another animal to his herd. And another. . . . But this is the conclusion reached by each and every rational herdsman sharing a commons. Therein is the tragedy. Each man is locked into a system that compels him to increase his herd without limit—in a world that is limited. Ruin is the destination toward which all men rush, each pursuing his own best interest in a society that believes in the freedom of the commons. Freedom in a commons brings ruin to all." Garrett Hardin, "The Tragedy of the Commons," *Science* 162 (1968): 1243–48.

15. See Russel Hardin, *One for All*.

16. Russel Hardin, *Collective Action*, pp. 14–15.

17. Despite the fact that the scope of services and benefits now expected from the democratic state has expanded, the three categories of "realms" which lay beyond the reach of the invisible hand are still relevant and inclusive. Smith defined them as national defense, the administration of justice, and the maintenance of "certain public works and certain public institutions." Adam Smith, *An Inquiry into the Nature and Causes of The Wealth of Nations*, ed. J.C. Bullock (New York: P. F. Collier and Sons 1901).

18. Mancur Olson, *The Rise and Decline of Nations* (New Haven, Conn.: Yale University Press, 1982), p. 18.

19. The classic expositions were made by Samuelson in the 1950s. See Paul A. Samuelson, "The Pure Theory of Public Expenditure," *Review of Economics and Statistics* 36, no. 1 (November 1954): 387–89. And "Diagrammatic Exposition of a Theory of Public Expenditure," *Review of Economics and Statistics* 37, no. 1 (November 1955): 350–56. More recent, and more political analyses of public goods include Olson, *Logic*; Hardin, *Collective*; and Elster, *Rational*.

20. See Peter O. Steiner, "The Public Sector and the Public Interest," in *Public Expenditures and Policy Analysis*, ed. Robert H. Haveman and Julius Margolis (Chicago: Markham, 1970).

21. See Steiner, "The Public Sector," p. 34.

22. See Paul A. Samuelson, "The Pure Theory of Public Expenditure," p. 387.

23. William H. Riker, "Public Safety as a Public Good," in *Is Law Dead*, ed., Eugene V. Rostow (New York: Simon and Schuster, 1971), p. 370. According to Riker, an orderly and non-violent society is the "primary and compelling" example of a public good. On public goods that construct, or condition our environment, see Duncan Snidal, "Public Goods," *International Studies Quarterly* 23, no. 4 (December 1979): 539.

24. On political mechanisms see James Q. Wilson, *Political Organizations* (Princeton, N.J.: Princeton University Press, 1995) (originally published by Basic Books, 1974), and Jon Elster, *Political Psychology* (Cambridge: Cambridge University Press, 1993).

25. Jean-Jaques Rousseau, *On the Social Contract*, trans. Judith R. Masters (New York: St. Martin's Press, 1978), p. 55.

26. Foucault's understanding of power greatly influenced the way in which we now perceive and understand the role of the state in constituting the "good citizen." See, Michel Foucault, *Power/Knowledge* (New York: Pantheon Books, 1980).

27. Michael Laver puts this as follows: "A system which leads to the honoring of commitments would thus be a public good in itself, since the benefits would be available to all participants. Such a system, would not be a pure public good, since it is possible to exclude people from its benefits." Michael Laver, *Private Desires, Political Action*, (London: Sage Publications, 1997), p. 37.

28. On the role of trust in the prisoner dilemma see Hardin, *Collective Action*, 1981.

29. See William Baumol, *The Economics of the Performing Arts*. For more recent attempts at theorizing about the role of culture in the modern state, see George Steinmetz ed., *State/Culture; State-Formation after the Cultural Turn* (Ithaca: Cornell University Press, 1999); Victoria E. Bonnell and Lynn Hunt, eds., *Beyond the Cultural Turn* (Berkeley: California University Press, 1999).

30. See Olson, *The Logic of Collective Action*, chapter 2.

31. Pierre Birnbaum, *States and Collective Action: the European Experience* (Cambridge: Cambridge University Press, 1988), p. 18.

32. A number of theorists have emphasized the importance of shared communications to the essence of national identity. See in particular Karl Deutsch, *Nationalism as Social Communication* (New York: MIT Press, 1966) and Gianfranco Poggi, *The State; Its Nature, Development and Prospects* (Stanford: Stanford University Press, 1990).

33. Two different theoretical takes on nationalism share this assessment of the importance of politics—or sovereignty—to national identity. Benedict Anderson, *Imagined Communities* (London: Verso, 1983), and Ernest Gellner, *Nations and Nationalism* (Oxford: Basil Blackwell, 1983).

34. Brian Barry, "Self Government Revisited," in *The Nature of Political Theory*, eds., David Miller and Larry Siendentop, (Oxford: Oxford University Press, 1983), p. 137.

35. Most public goods theorists shy away from accepting that shared values and norms play a role in social interaction and are significant in any independent way. See Paul V. Warwick, *Culture, Structure or Choice? Essays in the Interpretation of the British Experience* (New York: Agathon Press, 1990), pp. 25–57. Few however, would deny that norms and values exist, and if they could be enforced in a utility maximizing fashion, would function as significant mechanisms of cooperation.

Part Two

The Political and Legal Construction of Collective National Identity

As representative of relatively young, immigrant societies, both the Israeli and the American collective national identities can be seen as the product of self-conscious and purposeful construction. Both societies have contended with extensive waves of immigration seeking to assimilate into the emerging national identities. The Israeli identity, however, was constructed upon the foundation of the historic Jewish national identity. Hence, most of the emerging debates concerning this collective identity focused on the relationship between religion and nationalism and the differing cultural and political impacts of the successive waves of immigration. The American national identity, on the other hand, was fashioned out of abstract political principles. Hence, the development of this identity involved debates surrounding the particular nature of these values. At the same time, both identities need to forge a new, integrated identity on the one hand, while preserving the distinct cultural legacies on the other.

In this context, the two excluded minority groups, African Americans and the Palestinian citizens, have posed significant challenges to the construction and definition of each identity. Moreover, to a large extent, the construction of these two groups as *minorities* should be properly understood in the context of the development of the contours of the collective identity. In both cases, because of the history of deep rooted exclusion, the boundaries of the debate surrounding membership as well as the membership itself, have been constituted through a legal discourse.

Given the fundamentally democratic nature of each society, how was exclusion treated within the ideological articulation of the identity? What types of changes can be observed in the contours of the different identities? In this part I present the evolution of the two collective national identities as narratives. As narratives, I sketch the main ideas and events that constitute them, focusing on the political, legal, and social contexts that have impacted upon the creation and then maintenance of both minority groups as minorities. Finally, I discuss the ways in which the excluded minorities fit into the narrative of identity.

Chapter Three

Representing American National Identity: the Shifting Status of African Americans

During the course of American history, African Americans have followed a variety of paths of inclusion: from slave into freeman, from non-citizen to citizen, from second class citizen to first class citizen. Documenting these paths, scholarship over the past two decades has variously described the exclusion of African Americans as exclusion from the "political community," from the "American legal community," from "American political culture," and from "American civic culture."[1] In this chapter I argue that more than anything else, the path of inclusion from second class citizenship to first class citizenship has been the path of inclusion into the American collective national identity. For much of American history, African Americans were not considered (although they often considered themselves) to be fully-fledged members of the American nation.

The different paths of inclusion were paved by different events in the course of American history. I suggest that the path towards national inclusion was determined and defined by the landmark 1964 Civil Rights Act and 1965 Voting Rights Act. More than any other events in the history of African Americans, acquiring the equal right to vote and the right to de-segregated public accommodations have determined their full membership in American society in general, and in the American national identity in particular.

This chapter is comprised of two sections. In the first I discuss the contours of American national identity, demonstrating the centrality of political principles—particularly that of equality and citizenship—to the constitution of this identity. In the second part I trace the legal history of the African American community in the United States, explaining the special significance of the 1960s legislation.

THE AMERICAN NATIONAL IDENTITY

Benedict Anderson's definition of the nation as an imagined community has achieved canonical status. Referring to the nation in terms of imagination, captured a certain quality of nationhood that had previously eluded scholars.[2] Nonetheless, as alluring as the term might be, it is actually the *second* part of the definition—i.e. community—which highlights a far more crucial, if not essential, element of nationhood. Real or imaginary, nationhood is constructed through the establishment of a community; a community based upon a perception of things shared. Regardless what these "things" are, the basic cement of a national community is the fact that its members imagine that they are related to each other through shared memories and heritage.

What constitutes the basis for the American shared imagination? From what is the American collective national identity comprised? This in itself is not a simple question to answer because the discourse on American nationhood is usually an implicit one. Constituting a haven for a wide range of European refugees—religious, economic, and political—American society, from its inception, lacked a coherent ethnic or cultural core. While the religious, ideological, spiritual, and economic diversity that characterized the first waves of settlers was underlined by a fundamental Anglo-Saxon cultural homogeneity, each successive wave of immigration introduced new cultures, new traditions, and new histories, vastly expanding the cultural breadth of American society. American national identity over the eighteenth, nineteenth, and finally twentieth century became increasingly culturally diverse.

Hence from the outset, the idea of an American nation had to be imagined in terms very different from its European counterparts. The concept of the nation however, as discussed above, is an essentially European concept, and in its European imagining it refers most basically to a group of people bound by a shared culture (imagined, constructed, or not). This absence of a common cultural core has posed a unique problem to students of American national identity. How does one approach an identity whose main identifying characteristic is missing?

While addressing the concept of American identity, it should come as no surprise that few scholars employ the term "nation" or "national." They prefer, instead, to use more culturally or politically neutral terms such as the American political culture, or the American community to describe the American national identity.[3] Further testimony to a fundamental unease with these topics is the fact that often scholars use these terms interchangeably and rather inconsistently. They may begin a discussion with the term identity, moving onto the notion of national identity and culminating with the more general political community.[4] The fact that American scholars feel inherently uneasy using the term nation is, in itself, a meaningful aspect of American nationhood. In the American political culture, nationalism is seen as a manifestation of romantic, elemental, and intense political feelings, and as such foreign to the American ethic and sensibility. This, as I show, expresses itself in the reluctance to openly associate an American national identity with cultural and ethnic notions, preferring the more neutral, and seemingly "rational" political values and ideas.

Nevertheless, despite this reluctance and ambivalent relationship, an American nation clearly exists, and along with it boundaries that both constitute and define its membership. The fact that the American national identity lacks a coherent cultural core in the ethnic sense, does not make it less national; it merely implies that the content and boundaries of this national identity are articulated in different terms.

The articulation of a national identity defined in abstract, and not in cultural terms, makes the role of the historian (and intellectual)—an already central one in defining national identities—even more critical.[5] In the following discussion I elaborate on different expositions of American national identity in an effort to stake out both its contours, and its content.

THE CONVENTIONAL NARRATIVE: AN IDENTITY DEFINED BY IDEAS

Most contemporary discussions of American national identity begin with reference to Alexis de Tocqueville. In *Democracy in America,* Tocqueville identified the "equality of conditions" as America's defining characteristic.[6] This fundamental equality (born out of the fact that America, unlike Europe, lacked a feudal social structure) generated a civic identity associated more with the free exercise of civil rights than with a particular history, ethnicity, or cultural tradition:

> Picture to yourself . . . if you can, a . . . people differing from one another in language, in beliefs, in opinions; in a word a society possessing no roots, no memories, no prejudices, no routine, no common ideas, no national character, yet with a happiness a hundred times greater than our own . . ."[7]

For Tocqueville, writing in the mid-nineteenth century, when nationalist rhetoric born of the French Revolution permeated most political and historical writings, the absence of a shared culture and heritage was tantamount to the absence of a national character altogether. It was this spirit of equality, pervading most spheres of American public life, that Tocqueville believed to be the source of American happiness, and therefore of their collective identity. American identity was fundamentally political, defined by shared beliefs in liberty, equality, and the participatory nature of society.

This thesis constitutes the founding assumption of the conventional narrative of American nationhood.[8] While most notably expanded upon by Swedish sociologist Gunnar Myrdal and American political scientist Louis Hartz, it has been shared almost uncontested by scores of American political scientists writing in post–World War II America.[9] This conventional narrative follows the Tocquevillian tradition and constructs the American national identity on two foundations. The first is the general representation of the identity as a conceptual identity, defined and described by abstract values, and not by any specific, or historically concrete (or tangible) characteristics. Discussions of American national identity tend not to elaborate upon specific individuals—not of "simple" Americans nor of "heroic" ones. Discussions of the American community are abstract and rather lofty. As one historian has put it, ". . . the [American] people are timeless, beyond the contingencies of history, a . . . fabricated and highly generalized community of men guided by nature and reason . . ."[10]

The second foundation is the emphasis placed upon the specific values that constitute the identity. In the seminal political study of the development of the American nation, *The First New Nation*, written in 1963 by political sociologist Seymour Martin Lipset, values are almost the only show in town. The American nation celebrates neither ancient struggles nor brilliant achievements. It celebrates a political doctrine:

> When Americans celebrate their national heritage on Independence Day, Memorial Day, or other holidays of this sort, they dedicate themselves anew to a nation conceived as the living fulfillment of a political doctrine that enshrines a utopian conception of men's egalitarian and fraternal relations with one another.[11]

This gordian knot connecting between the essence of the American national character and the vibrancy of its political regime, is echoed twenty years later by Samuel Huntington, one of the leading political scientists of his generation. In a discussion of American national identity he notes, ". . . destroy the political system and you destroy the basis of community, eliminating the nation. . . . In other countries one can abrogate the constitution without abrogating the nation. The U.S. does not have that choice."[12]

Defining American nationality as fundamentally political, based in shared beliefs, rather then in shared culture, tradition, or ethnicity, conveniently allowed for the maintenance of parallel ethnic identities which gained in prominence following World War II. During this period, the hyphenated American was not projected as a lesser American, on the contrary: the hyphen in itself has emerged as a source of national pride.[13] The study of ethnicity has therefore been an integral field of study within the general study of American identity. Beginning in the 1950s studies of ethnicity have contributed to the articulation of American national identity as an identity fundamentally comprised of a plurality of cultures, both complementing and defying the metaphor of the melting pot. The need to entrench American identity in a basis of shared beliefs rather then shared cultures was clearly related to the expanding immigrant nature of American society, and the pressures of assimilating such a myriad of cultures, traditions, and backgrounds. As Harvard political scientists Nathan Glazer and Daniel Moynihan embarked on their series of studies of ethnicity in America, examining the different ways in which ethnic identity interacted with the larger national identity in America it became clear that American studies, as an intellectual discipline, was to be taken over, for a while, by the study of ethnicity. Harvard gradually emerged as an influential intellectual center that impacted on the public conception of American national identity as much as it documented and studied it. This perception tended to highlight the inclusive dimension of the American national identity. Indeed, few studies of American identity up until today refrain from quoting the following entry on American identity from *The Harvard Encyclopaedia of Ethnicity*:

> A person did not have to be of any particular national, linguistic, religious, or ethnic background. All he had to do was commit himself to the political ideology centered on the abstract ideals of liberty, equality and republicanism. Thus the universalistic ideological character of American nationality meant that it was open to anyone who willed to become an American.[14]

This last sentence pointed to the interesting fact that American nationality was not merely perceived as based on shared ideas, but that entry and inclusion into the community was based solely on will and volition, recalling the civic and ethnic models of nationality referred to in the introduction. The entry cited above could be read as a description of the civic model of nationality. Hence, one could argue that regardless of whether American nationality fit the model of civic nationality, American intellectuals narrated the identity as a civic identity par excellence. The problem, however, was that not everyone who willed entry gained it. The continued disenfranchisement of African Americans, and their blatant exclusion from the boundaries of this community posed a continual problem that refused to disappear, and that posed a serious threat to this civic, inclusive, and liberal image of American nationality.

Gunnar Myrdal, a non-American like Tocqueville, was one of the first scholars to tackle this discrepancy head on in his influential book *An American Dilemma* published in 1944. The values of equality, liberty, and individualism formed what Myrdal termed the American Creed. Myrdal, writing specifically about the race issue, focused on the gap between the level of belief and the level of practice. He identified this gap, however, as being fundamentally *outside* the Creed and an expression of aberrant and marginal forces in American society. Hence, despite Myrdal's focus on the racism that seemed to challenge the hegemony of the Creed, his basic understanding of American national identity remained firmly entrenched within the conventional narrative. Most Americans, according to Myrdal, believed in liberal values. The racism which caused the denigration of African Americans was seen as the expression of irrational impulses most characteristic of the "poor and uneducated white" people in the "isolated and backward" rural areas of the South.[15] Even they, however, were aware of the superior morality of the Creed, and it was a question of time until these irrational impulses were overcome by reason.

At this time, American intellectual elites began looking at the idea of American identity in a different manner, and Myrdal had a strong impact on this change. Testimony of this impact is a 1947 report compiled by President Truman's Committee on Civil Rights entitled *To Secure These Rights*.[16] The report adopted the analytical and terminological framework of *An American Dilemma* almost entirely, declaring racial segregation inconsistent with traditional American morality and the American Creed. Of minor significance in terms of policy, the report had an important symbolic impact. The establishment of the committee and the analysis presented ushered in an era in which the "gap" ceased to be politically invisible.

Ironically, while Myrdal failed to solve the dilemma for American society, he succeeded far more in terms of American intellectuals who narrated and hence represented American national identity. Myrdal had discovered a way to maintain the image of a liberal and fundamentally national identity, while at the same time acknowledging and even documenting the racist and exclusionary attitudes and perceptions toward African Americans. Most scholars writing on American identity since Myrdal, and through the 1960s and 1970s, adopted his approach. When African Americans and their status were confronted, it was seen as an "aberration", not directly bearing upon the cohesion of American identity. Indeed, most discussions of American identity during this period do not incorporate the discussion of Blacks as part of the coherent whole, but rather reproduce social segregation in their segregated discussions (this strategy is reflected in the Israeli discussions of Palestinians as well).[17] The status of African Americans was seen as a direct and exclusive outcome of the institution of slavery, which, as a southern institution, never aspired to the more sophisticated and universal liberal discourse of citizenship. Hence, the ideology of racism, which underpinned the exclusion of African Americans, did not contradict the universality of the American civic identity, but was exogenous to it. This outlook allows scholars to criticize the racist and exclusionary attitudes, while maintaining their image and discussion of American civic identity. Thus, Lipset can characteristically note in his epilogue that "American egalitarianism is, of course, for white men only. The treatment of the Negro makes a mockery of this value now as it has in the past," but still maintain that the "First Nation" is constituted by the values of liberty and equality.[18]

To summarize then, the picture drawn from these discussions is of an ideational national identity, fundamentally static and non-changing. Political events seem to have no impact on the contour or content of the identity, and its fundamentally liberal and equal essence remains untarnished by changing social and racial trends, by political and economic discrimination, and by a gradually changing public consciousness. The American national identity that emerges incorporates a People, without designating any concrete mechanisms that determine who are these People.

DEFYING CONVENTION: THE EMERGENCE OF A NEW NARRATIVE OF IDENTITY

The recent preoccupation with identity politics and multiculturalism has generated renewed interest in American identity in general, and American national identity in particular. This contemporary discussion of American identity focuses upon the excluded and the un-represented: women, native Americans, the economic under-class, and of course, African Americans. In this debate, the premise of the conventional narrative is challenged: how can an identity constituted by liberal values of inclusion remain unchanged and intact within a political, social, and economic context of exclusion and inequality. Hence, these discussions insist, in different ways, on integrating the "digressions" from the Creed into the Creed itself. Exclusion, rather then inclusion, becomes central, rather then peripheral, to the fabric of identity.

Kenneth Karst for example, a leading legal scholar, supports the conventional narrative insofar as the essential meaning of American identity is concerned. This meaning, argues Karst, is adherence to the Creed, but not merely in belief but in behavior as well. The implementation of the values is the real test of the Creed: "Among full members of the community, the ideal of equality prevails; as outsiders, the issue of equality seems irrelevant. Equality and belonging are inseparably linked: to define the scope of the ideal of equality in America is to define the boundaries of the national community."[19]

Within this paradigm, the active and concrete manifestations of civic identity—political participation, distribution of rights—are the real indicators of the American national identity. By introducing the manifestations of civic ideals the contours of American identity are personalized. Once personalized, membership—as the representation of values—becomes a focus of both analysis and discussion. Prominent scholars of American society such as Shklar and Fuchs, for example, argue that membership, or belonging, is deeply connected to political participation, and the active involvement in a shared political association. Unequal ability to participate because of limited access to the main channels of political participation have typically been markers of exclusion from the political community.[20]

Taking exclusion seriously has led other theorists to reconsider the Tocquevillian tradition. Higham's pathbreaking studies of the impact of nativist and racist ideologies on the construction of American identity are a case in point.[21] Recent studies of immigration and citizenship in the United States have argued that for most of American history, the legal system in fact excluded more people then it included, both in terms of eligibility for citizenship, and, as citizens, for full benefits.[22] In fact, eligibility for citizenship, and access to the full gamut of benefits, was not based on a person's liberal beliefs, but rather on ascriptive characteristics such as race, gender, and ethnicity. Clearly this type of historical perspective engendered a revised conception of the bases of American identity. Hence, according to Smith,

> American politics is best seen as expressing the interaction of multiple political traditions, including liberalism, republicanism, and ascriptive forms of Americanism, which have collectively comprised American political culture, without constituting it as a whole.[23]

The multiple tradition thesis maintains that seemingly contradictory attitudes can (and have) been maintained simultaneously; that African Americans and other ethno/racial/gender categories were perceived and then treated both as members and non-members. The implication being, for any discussion of national identity, that while African Americans were granted citizenship and civic status (a precondition for membership), they were, nonetheless, excluded from the identity.

These contemporary studies reveal a deep shift in the way in which American identity is theorized. The conventional narrative presented the American nation as constituted by a static and idealized vision of liberalism. Partaking in the national identity was presented as a matter of choice and volition, detached from both public policy and politics itself. The contemporary discourse differs both in its conception of the content of the American nation, as well as the means of its representation. The nation itself is portrayed as constituted only partially by liberalism. Hence, different ideological traditions such as nativism and republicanism are seen as part and parcel of the American national tradition and not outside of it. More significantly however, partaking in the national identity is presented not merely as an act of personal agency, but is acknowledged as deeply constrained by the political practices of the time. This emphasis on practices naturally shifts the focus from the center to the periphery, or from the majority of White Americans, to the large pockets of diverse minorities. The shift from ideals to practices is expressed in the conclusion of Karst's study:

> if Black people were to think of themselves as belonging to America, the nation must make a reality of the ideal expressed in the motto on the Supreme Court Building: Equal Justice under Law.

This brings my discussion full circle. The shift that emerged in intellectual thinking about American identity is clear; the growing recognition of the need to acknowledge the gap between values and reality led to the growing emphasis on the status of the different minorities, and specifically that of the African American minority, within the contours of the American identity. Clearly, the gradual shift in thinking in itself reflected a significant change. What were the key events that instigated this change? In what way were these events, and these intellectual processes related to shifts in the status of the minority itself? If indeed the American national identity is constituted not merely by a static expression of liberal values, but by the interaction of these values with concrete public and political policy, the question remains: at what juncture could African Americans "think of themselves as belonging to America?" The answer to this question cannot be detached from the history of the status of African Americans within American society. The history of African Americans within American society, and within the contours of American national identity is to a large extent a legal history, marked by key events in the evolution of American legal and constitutional history. In the following section I outline the main events which led to the shift in the status of African Americans vis-à-vis American national identity.

AFRICAN AMERICANS AND
THE AMERICAN NATIONAL IDENTITY

At the time of U.S. independence, with the writing of the Constitution, African Americans were considered to be property. As such, they were denied the rights afforded to citizens of liberal democracies, as well as the basic *human* rights secured for the average citizen of the new federation. They had no protection under law, save the protection accorded to property. The three provisions in the Constitution regarding African Americans exemplified their status as property: firstly, Congress was prohibited from abolishing the import of slaves for twenty years. Secondly, the fugitive-slave clause required states to return fugitive slaves to their owners, and thirdly, each slave counted as three-fifths of a vote in the determination of each state's representation in the House of Representatives.[24] As the infamous *Dred Scott* Supreme Court decision stated, seventy years later, African Americans, during the post-revolutionary years, "had no rights which the white man was bound to respect."[25]

As "property", there is no argument as to whether African Americans were, at the time of the writing of the Constitution, members of the newly-founded American nation. Now, more than two hundred years later, it is equally uncontestable that they are. On the whole, they are considered by others, and consider themselves, to be "hyphenated" Americans: African Americans.[26] As such, they are equal members of the American corporate national identity. When did this act of inclusion occur?

It clearly did not occur during the first ninety years of independence. Until the Civil War, African Americans had no rights to speak of. In the south they were slaves and as such continued to be the legal property of their owners. In the north their status was not much better. First of all, they constituted only 1% of the entire population of the north. Moreover, legal disenfranchisement was the norm. In New York for example, property qualifications for White voters were eliminated in 1821. At the same time, they were raised for Black voters to $250. In Pennsylvania, Black voting was all but eliminated in 1837, when the Pennsylvania Supreme Court declared that while Blacks were "citizens of the state" they need not be admitted "into political partnership."[27] By 1860, five separate northern states had prohibited the entrance of African Americans into their region.[28] All in all, being a northern Black was not an entirely enviable status.

The Civil War and Reconstruction, which produced the celebrated Thirteenth, Fourteenth, and Fifteenth Amendments to the Constitution, and in essence the drafting of a radically different constitutional document, appears to mark inclusion of African Americans into the American identity. The said amendments respectively abolished slavery, established a national citizenship, and granted African Americans the right to vote. The first reconstruction in effect established a new political reality which foreshadowed the political reality established one hundred years later, with the second reconstruction: the establishment of a centralized nation-state, with significant sovereign power to the federal government. The federal government emerged stronger, with increased powers and responsibilities. In this changed capacity, the federal government took on a new role, that of "custodian of freedom."

The empowerment brought about by Reconstruction was, however, short-lived. By 1873, the Supreme Court was active in reversing the changes ushered in by the new amendments. The first instance was in the *Slaughterhouse* cases of 1873. This case involved a claim that states could not constitutionally create a private monopoly in the slaughtering trade. The claim, made by independent butchers, relied on the privileges and immunities clause of the Fourteenth Amendment arguing that in creating the monopoly the state was abridging their privileges as citizens of the United States. Though unrelated directly to civil rights, the Court, by narrowly circumscribing the privileges and immunities clause was aware of the implications in the arena of civil rights. In 1883, the Civil Rights cases invalidated an 1875 Act of Congress prohibiting racial discrimination in public accommodations, through a very narrow interpretation of the Fourteenth Amendment, thereby sanctioning the rights of the state to legal segregation. [29] The 1896 *Plessy v. Ferguson* decision represented the final death blow. In this case, the constitutionality of a Louisiana law which demanded segregation in the railroads was considered. By upholding the law, the Supreme Court gave final official legitimization to racial segregation by declaring that racial segregation did not violate the equal protection clause of the Fourteenth Amendment. This done, the southern states could proceed unchecked in annulling the Reconstruction amendments, and entrenching what came to be known as Jim Crow: de facto and de jure racial segregation in all walks of life—political, social, and economic.[30] Thus, while Reconstruction initially seemed to promise the inclusion of African Americans, it was a promise that was broken.

From the turn of the century, Jim Crow was alive and flourishing in the south. African Americans were totally segregated from Whites, and for all intents and purposes, disenfranchised. Disenfranchisement was largely achieved through the implementation of measures like the poll tax, and property and literacy requirements. While poor illiterate Whites also fell under the purview of these measures, it was African Americans who were most affected and in whose case the measures were largely enforced. In 1901 the last Black southern Congressman left office and no Black resumed office until more than a quarter of a century later.[31] African Americans in the north of America did not fare significantly better. Economic depression subsequent to World War I hit the already poor northern Black community particularly hard. The unemployment rate of African Americans was double that of Whites in the north, at 38.9 percent in 1937.[32] And finally, the Supreme Court and Congress remained silent on all issues relating to civil rights and racial equality for the ensuing half century.

World War II, with its reliance on Black fighters and its commitment to fight racism abroad, ushered in a new era. Roosevelt, who was the African American man's hero as the initiator of the New Deal, and who brought economic relief to millions of poor White and African Americans, took a passive stance on racial issues. Truman, the border state president, seeking a coalition between liberal democrats and Black voters, was more active, de-segregating the military in 1948 and initiating a series of civil rights commissions. Of particular importance was the *Brown vs Topeka Board of Education*, the most significant civil rights ruling since Reconstruction. The *Brown* decision declared the separate, but equal ruling in the *Plessy* case to be unconstitutional, thereby paving the way for the de-segregation of the school system. More than establishing a legal right, the majority opinion in *Brown* took a stand on the question of the membership and status of African Americans: "Segregation generates a feeling of inferiority as to their status in the community that may affect their hearts and minds in a way unlikely ever to be undone." [33] Indeed, the *Brown* decision is often referred to as the single most important decision in the history of the U.S. Supreme Court.[34]

Nonetheless, de facto integration was slow in coming as a result of *Brown*. In fact, research on school integration in the south illustrates that de facto integration had to wait ten years (until the 1964 legislation giving the federal government enforcement capacities) for substantial integration to take place. Statistics are telling: in 1960, six years after *Brown*, just over 15 percent of Black schoolchildren were attending school with Whites. This had risen by a mere 1.2 percent by 1964. In 1968–69 the figure was 32 percent; by 1972–73 it stood at 91.3 percent.[35] In 1960 Jim Crow was still alive and kicking, leaving the Black American unrepresented and hence excluded. Public opinion was similarly unaffected. In July 1959 a 5 percent increase in public support for the *Brown* decision was recorded (from 54 percent to 59 percent).[36] What *Brown* did achieve was a violent counter-reaction in the south, with southerners taking an even more conservative stance on anything to do with racial issues. In addition, the minimal and limited civil rights acts of 1957 and 1960, aimed at protecting voting rights, lacked appropriate enforcement clauses. Together, they did not add even one new Black voter to the southern registration rolls.[37] Ironically, as demonstrated below, this adverse effect had much to do with the passing of the 1960s legislation which made inclusion possible.

Finally, the 1960s ushered in a new era. The civil rights movement had become a mass movement, mobilizing increasing numbers of African Americans and whites to its cause as its struggles became more visible and provocative. From the sit-ins in Georgia and Alabama, through the freedom rides from Washington D.C. to Louisiana, more and more participants joined in, culminating in the Freedom Summer Project in the summer of 1964 when thousands of northern white student volunteers went down south to join the voter registration drive. The movement heralded two landmark pieces of legislation: the 1964 Civil Rights Act and the 1965 Voting Rights Bill. The purview of both pieces of legislation was all-encompassing. Most importantly, together they gave the federal government sufficient leeway to effectively enforce desegregation through the ability to withhold federal funding for segregated facilities (schools and other public institutions) and quick recourse to federal courts.

The Civil Rights Act of 1964 ultimately included eleven sections. Its most significant sections pertain to voting rights and public accommodations. Regarding the former, denial of the vote was prohibited to anyone on account of "race, color, religion or national origin," and all prohibitive clauses such as the poll tax or complicated literacy tests were eliminated. The second section, which pertained to public accommodations, prohibited discrimination on the basis of "race, color, religion or national origin" in any type of public accommodation (from motels to soda fountains to gasoline stations). Most importantly, it "authorized aggrieved individuals to file suit in federal court to seek relief against discriminatory practice; permitted the attorney general to intervene in such suit or to initiate a civil action when a pattern or practice of discrimination is believed to exist."[38]

The remaining sections, relating to public faculties, public education, commissions on civil rights and equal employment opportunity, equalized the status of African Americans and White Americans before the law. Most significantly, however, the act "permitted a three-judge federal court to hear voting rights cases if requested by the attorney general or the defendant."[39] When this proved insufficient to enable significant numbers of African Americans to register in the south, the 1965 Voting Rights Bill was passed which ended Black disenfranchisement for good. The 1965 Bill contained "an automatic triggering mechanism that suspended literacy tests and permitted voter registration by federal registrars if voter registration or voter turnout fell below 50 percent of the voting-age population in 1964. This covered the states of Alabama, Georgia, Louisiana, Mississippi, South Carolina, Virginia, and sections of North Carolina."[40]

The most notable change heralded by this act was the emphasis upon the right of the federal government to enforce these laws in cases where the individual state governments failed to do so. Thus, the significance of this civil rights act compared with those that preceded it lies in both its scope and its specific content—it not only formally recognized African-Americans as equal, but allowed for the necessary enforcement capacity of this equality. With the passing of these acts, African Americans could no longer be denied the right to vote, nor the right to any other civic and property right afforded to other White—or other—Americans.

It is no small matter that both Kennedy and Johnson, in their efforts to promote the civil rights acts, spoke consistently in terms of the inclusion of "fellow Americans," emphasizing the shared national identity of Blacks and Whites. Kennedy, when introducing the draft legislation for 1964, stated that "The heart of the question is whether all Americans are to be afforded equal rights and equal opportunities, whether we are going to treat our fellow Americans as we want to be treated."[41] Johnson, one year later, announced: "Their cause must be our cause too. It is not just Negroes, but it is all of us . . . the issue of equal rights for American Negroes is . . . a challenge to the values, the purposes and the meaning of our nation."[42]

Hence, the 1960s debate over the civil rights legislation which sought to grant the population full rights of citizenship, can be read simultaneously as a debate over the definition of a specifically *White* American nationality, as opposed to the more inclusive "multi-racial" American nationality. The debate took place, and to some degree still takes place, in terms of who properly is a member of the American nation, and who is not.[43] The passing of these landmark pieces of legislation rendered African Americans, one hundred years after their attainment of citizenship, members of the American national identity.

NOTES

1. Michael J. Klarman, "How *Brown* Changed Race Relations: The Backlash Thesis" *Journal of American History* 81 (June 1994): 81–118, for example, uses the term "American political community" as does Samuel Huntington in *American Politics: The Promise of Disharmony* (Cambridge, Mass.: The Belknap Press, 1985). Rogers Smith, on the other hand, prefers the term "American political culture". See Rogers M. Smith, "Beyond Tocqueville, Myrdal and Hartz: the Multiple Traditions in America" *American Political Science Review* 87 (1993): 549–66. Legal scholar Kenneth L. Karst, *Belonging to America: Equal Citizenship and the Constitution* (New Haven, Conn.: Yale University Press, 1989) uses the "American Legal Community," while Leonard H. Fuchs, *The American Kaleidoscope: Race, Ethnicity, and the Civic Culture.* (Hanover: Wesleyan University Press, 1990), adopts the term "American civic culture."

2. Benedict Anderson, *Imagined Communities* (London: Verso, 1991), p. 3.

3. See note 1 above.

4. See for example Rogers Smith, "Beyond Tocqueville," the different usages on pp. 549, 550, 551; Leonard Fuchs, *The American Kaleidoscope*, pp. 10, 15, 22; and Kenneth Karst. *Belonging to America*, pp. 34, 37, 38.

5. See Anthony D. Smith, *Nations and Nationalism in a Global Era* (Cambridge: Polity Press, 1996), p. 176.

6. Alexis de Tocqueville, *Democracy in America* (New York: Knopf, 1951).

7. Quoted in Jacob P. Mayer, *Prophet of the Mass Age: A Study of Alexis de Tocqueville*, (New York: Arno Press, 1979), p. 30.

8. Rogers M. Smith employs the term "conventional narrative" in his 1993 article.

9. See for some examples, Louis Hartz, *The Liberal Tradition in America: An Interpretation of American Political Thought Since the Revolution* (New York: Harcourt, Brace and World, 1955); Gunnar Myrdal, *An American Dilemma: The Negro Problem and American Democracy* (New York: Harper and Row, 1944); Samuel Huntington, *American Politics: The Promise of Disharmony* (Cambridge, Mass.: The Belknap Press, 1985). Seymour Martin Lipset, *The First New Nation: The United States in Historical and Comparative Perspective* (New York and London: W. W. Norton and Company, 1963, 1979.) Walter Dean Burnham, *The Current Crisis in American Politics* (New York: Oxford University Press, 1982); Theodore Lowi, *The End of Liberalism: The Second Republic of the United States*, 2d. edition (New York: W. W. Norton, 1979).

10. Yehoshua Arieli, *Individualism and Nationalism in American Ideology* (Cambridge, Mass.: Harvard University Press, 1964), p. 39.

11. Seymour Martin Lipset, *The First Nation*, p. 75.

12. Samuel Huntington, *The Promise of Disharmony*, p. 11.

13. See Michael Walzer, "What Does It Mean to Be an 'American'?" *Social Research* 57 (1990): p. 591.

14. Philip Gleason, "American Identity and Americanization," in *The Harvard Encyclopedia of Ethnicity*, edited by William Petersen, Michael Novak, Philip Gleason (Cambridge, Mass.: Harvard University Press, 1980).

15. Gunnar Myrdal, *An American Dilemma*, p. 552.

16. Stephen Thernstrom and Abigail Thernstrom, *America in Black and White: One Nation, Indivisible* (New York: Simon and Schuster, 1997), p. 91.

17. Telling examples are offered by doyen American political scientist Robert Dahl in his two classics of American democratic theory, *Who Governs* (New Haven: Yale University Press, 1964), and *A Preface to Democratic Theory* (Chicago: University of Chicago Press, 1956).

18. Seymour Martin Lipset, *The First Nation*, p. 330.

19. Kenneth Karst, *Belonging to America*, p. 15.

20. See Leonard Fuchs, *The American Kaleidoscope*, and Judith Shklar, *American Citizenship: The Quest for Inclusion*, (Cambridge, Mass.: Harvard University Press, 1991).

21. John Higham, *Strangers in the Land* (New Brunswick: Rutgers University Press, 1955); and *Send these to Me*, (New York: Atheneum, 1984).

22. James Kettner, *The Development of American Citizenship, 1608–1870*, (Chapel Hill: University of North Carolina Press, 1978); Rogers M. Smith, "Beyond Tocqueville," in *Civic Ideals: Conflicting Visions of Citizenship in U.S. History* (New Haven, Conn.: Yale University Press, 1997).

23. Rogers M. Smith, "Beyond Tocqueville," p. 550

24. Foner, Eric, "The Blacks and the Constitution," *New Left Review*, No. 183, (Sept/Oct 1990): 63–75. See also, Constitution, art. IV, sec. 2.

25. The *Dred Scott vs. Sanford* Supreme Court decision from 1857 declared African Americans to be noncitizens. See 163 US at 558–559, 563.

26. The label "Afro-American" was initiated, formally, by Jesse Jackson at a 1988 news conference, where leaders of seventy-five Black groups came to discuss a new Black agenda. In it Jackson declared that members of his race preferred to be called "African American." This replaced the label "Black" which had been introduced over twenty years earlier by the Black Power movement. See Ben L. Martin, "From Negro to Black to African American: The Power of Names and Naming," *Political Science Quarterly* 106, no. 1 (1991): 83–107.

On name-labeling, Huntington aptly notes that the first word designates one's "ethnic" or "cultural" identity, and the second, one's political identity. This seems an accurate assessment of the orientation of most American ethnic groups today. See Huntington, *American Politics: The Promise of Disharmony* (Cambridge, Mass.: The Belknap Press, 1985), p. 27.

27. Cited in Judith N. Shklar *American Citizenship: The Quest for Inclusion* (Cambridge, Mass.: Harvard University Press, 1991), p. 34.

28. All cases cited in Eric Foner, "The Blacks and the Constitution," pp. 67–8.

29. For discussions of the *Civil Rights* Cases and the *Slaughter House* Cases see Kenneth Karst *Belonging to America*, pp. 58–59

30. The term Jim Crow evolved as a paternalistic term used to describe African Americans as simple minded, happy go lucky, and content with their lot.

31. Anthony W. Marx, *Making Race and Nation*, pp. 141; For a history of southern politics see V. O. Key, *Southern Politics* (New York: A. A. Knopf, 1949).

32. Michael J. Klarman, "How *Brown* Changed Race Relations: The Backlash Thesis," p. 12; Neil A. Wynn, *The Afro American and the Second World War* (New York: Holmes and Neier, 1993), note 20 p. 39.

33. Kenneth Karst, *Belonging To America*, p. 18. On the *Brown* decision see Richard Kluger, *The History of Brown v. Board of Education and Black America's Struggle for Equality* (New York: Vintage Books, 1977); Andrew Kull, *The Color Blind Constitution* (Cambridge, Mass.: Harvard University Press, 1992). On the controversy surrounding the impact of *Brown* see David J. Garrow "Hopelessly Hollow History: Revisionist Devaluing of Brown v. Board of Education" *Virginia Law Review* 80 (February 1994): 156; Michael J. Klarman, "How *Brown* Changed Race Relations: The Backlash Thesis"; Michael J. Klarman, "Brown, Racial Change, and the Civil Rights Movement." *Virginia Law Review* 80, no. 4 (February 1994). Rosenberg, Gerald N. *The Hollow Hope: Can Courts Bring about Social Change?* (Chicago: University of Chicago Press, 1991).

34. Michael Klarman, "How *Brown* Changed Race Relations"; Mary L. Dudziak "Desegregation as   Cold War Imperative" *Stanford Law Review* 41, (November 1988): 6; "The Little Rock Crisis and Foreign Affairs: Race, Resistance, and the Image of American Democracy" *Southern California Law Review* 70 (September 1997); Kenneth Karst, *Belonging to America*; Harvie J. Wilkinson III, *From Brown to Bakke: The Supreme Court and School Integration, 1954–1978.* (New York: Oxford University Press, 1979).

35. See Michael Klarman, "How *Brown* Changed Race Relations," p.3.

36. Ibid., p. 78.

37. The acts were so ineffective that Thurgood Marshall, Chief Attorney for the NAACP, is quoted as saying: "It would take two to three years for a good lawyer to get someone registered [to vote] under this bill." Quoted in Stern, *Calculating Visions: Kennedy, Johnson and Civil Rights* (New Brunswick, N.J.: Rutgers University Press, 1992), p. 148.

38. *Civil Rights Act of 1964*, title 2.

39. *Civil Rights Act of 1964, Public Law* 88–352, Title 1.

40. Michael Stern, *Calculating Visions*, p. 223.

41. Quoted in Charles and Barbara Whalen, *The Longest Debate: A Legislative History of the 1964 Civil Rights Act*, (New York: New American Library, 1985), p. xxi.

42. Quoted in Stern, *Calculating Visions*, p. 226.

43. This formulation relies on the argument presented in Kristin Couper, "Immigration, Nationality and Citizenship in the UK," *New Political Science*, No. 16/17 (fall/winter 1989): 91–101.

Chapter Four

National Identity in Israel: being a Palestinian in a Jewish State

As early as 1891 Achad Ha'am, the founder of Cultural Zionism, made the following observation:

> Abroad, we are accustomed to believe that Israel is almost empty; nothing is grown here, and that whoever wishes to buy land could come here and buy what his heart desires. In reality, the situation is not like this. Throughout the country it is difficult to find cultivable land which is not already cultivated. . . . Abroad, we are used to believe that the Arabs are all desert people, and like a donkey they can neither see nor understand what goes on around them. This is a great error. Like any other human being, the Arab has a sharp mind and is calculating.[1]

This quote is often retrieved, much like the rabbit out of the magician's hat, during debates concerning Zionism's early perception (or lack of it) of the indigenous inhabitants of Palestine. It is, indeed, very revealing. It teaches us that some Zionists were aware, quite early on, of the inherent conflict between the two peoples—Jewish and Arab—and their respective national aspirations. However, there is a more subtle point to be discerned from this quote: that even those more astute observers who recognized the inherent dilemma of Zionism, perceived the inevitable conflict as one over *territory*. Both from the Arab and Jewish sides, that aspect of coexistence which seemed the most intractable, and hence which formed the focus of debate, was the issue of territory.[2] While the issue of territorial boundaries remains central today, it has become intricately intertwined with the issue of demographic boundaries, i.e., the boundaries not merely of the territorially sovereign states, but of the political communities themselves. The boundaries of identity do not fit neatly into the territorially compartmentalized states established as the outcome of colonialism and conflict. In the case of Israel, Palestinians live not only outside of Israel proper, but right in the heartland so to speak: thus, with citizens being both Jewish and Palestinian, how is one to define (or negotiate) the boundaries of the Israeli political community?

The tension between the undefined boundaries of Israel's political community, and the boundaries of Israel's collective national identity is encapsulated in the anomalous identity of the Palestinian minority in Israel. In 2000, out of Israel's total population of 6.4 million, 1.2 million were Palestinian—close to 19 percent, with the remaining 81 percent being Jewish.[3] Hence, the Palestinian citizens constitute at once a religious minority, and, according to Israel's own domestic registrar, a national minority. However, while these citizens are classified as belonging to a separate nationality (Arab), Israel is not a binational state, and grants no formal rights of cultural or political autonomy to this minority (religious autonomy is albeit relatively protected). Moreover, despite the rapprochement between Israel and the Palestinian authority at the end of the twentieth century, the conflict between the Palestinian nation and the Israeli nation is as yet unresolved. At the same time, since membership in the Israeli nationality is limited to members of the Jewish faith, Palestinians have no possibility of assimilation. Hence, Palestinian citizens of Israel exist in a no-man's land of national identity: denied the rights of their own national identity, and prevented from assimilating into a national identity that is confined to Jews alone, the Palestinians in Israel are surely the only group in this world of nation-states who constitute neither a minority nor a majority nationality.

Being a non-Jew and a Palestinian to boot in the Jewish state is however, far from an existential dilemma. As a Jewish State, the primary "Public" whose welfare the state is committed to, is defined exclusively as Jewish. While formally Israel distributes rights equally to all its citizens, Israel's Jewish bias is reflected in the policy of most of its primary socio-economic institutions.[4]

A cursory sampling of indicators paints a gloomy picture. Over 25 percent of Palestinian-Israeli families live below the poverty level: Palestinians constitute a vast majority of the two lowest income percentile ranks, and are absent from the highest two percentile ranks.[5] While the Palestinians constitute over 18 percent of the population, they own only 3.5 percent of the land, and while they grew sixfold since the establishment of the state, the land they owned has remained constant. Close to 65 percent of the Palestinian male work force are employed in blue-collar jobs, as compared to 40 percent of Jewish men. Eight percent of the Palestinians, as opposed to 17 percent of the Jews are employed in the public sector.[6] Of 1,310 high-ranking government positions, only 17 belonged to Palestinians, and amongst the 4,000 members of different government boards of directors, there is only one Arab member. In the one sector which generally accepts Palestinians, that of public health, still out of all the doctors of the largest public health care organization, (Kupat Holim Klalit), only 2 percent are Arab. Politically, there have been no Palestinian members in any cabinet, and they have thus been excluded from every single ruling coalition.[7] This despite the fact that as the years go by, their support of Labor candidates is decisive in securing Labor victories.[8] What these statistics reveal is that beyond being discriminated against, Palestinians in Israel are invisible: they are virtually excluded from the core of Israeli social, political, and economic life.

This chapter opens the discussion of membership in the Israeli identity with an analysis of the ideological and political construction of national identity in Israel. The second part of the chapter focuses on the political evolution of the Palestinian minority in Israel.

COLLECTIVE NATIONAL IDENTITY IN ISRAEL

Collective national identity in Israel records two parallel histories. The first builds upon the history of the Jews, from its mythic biblical origins, and through its different migrations in Europe and North Africa. This history recounts selective phases of Jewish existence, constructing a narrative which is at once national and shared by Jews from both West and East.[9] The second emerges from the contemporary political history of the state, and reflects and recounts the history of national sovereignty since its establishment in 1948. The former transcends territory and geography and follows the story of a constructed community. The latter is territorially bounded, and thus potentially released from the confines of the boundaries of the historical community.[10] In other words, one narrative is defined by and confined to the history of the Jews, while the other is not. Israeli collective national identity straddles these two courses.

This duality lies at the core of the main dilemmas and difficulties posed by both the analysis and reality of Israeli collective national identity. The establishment of the sovereign state of Israel in 1948 incurred a deep transformation in the contours of this identity. First, it introduced political boundaries that at once elevated the national aspect over the religious one. Thus, if the identity and existence of the Jewish community throughout history was as a religious community with national elements, the advent of political independence transformed the identity and existence of that community into a political community with religious elements. Second, it established territorial boundaries that raised the saliency of the relationship between Jews within the boundaries and Jews outside of them, as well as between Jews and non-Jews within those boundaries. The central debates concerning the nature of Israeli national identity are all derived, in one way or another, from this fundamental transformation.

Established in 1948 as the political outcome of the efforts of the Jewish national movement—Zionism—the self-declared nationality of the state was automatically defined as Jewish. In the formal identification cards issued by Israel's Ministry of Interior one must choose between either Jewish, or, in the case of Arabs—Arab nationality.[11] More importantly, the values and meanings attributed to the collective national identity in Israel are almost entirely associated with the Jewish nation and Jewish history. Indeed, Israeliness as an attribute of identity is commonly seen as lightweight, as lacking in historical legitimacy and as a superficial common bond. In a classic study of political culture in Israel, the author concludes the following: "Without Jewish identification, life in Israel would derive its significance merely from the residence of Israelis here during a few decades—a somewhat meager significance."[12]

Nonetheless, insofar as an Israeli body of citizens exists, and an Israeli nation-state exists, then a potential community of Israelis, or Israeli nationals, exists as well. Furthermore, shared political and social experiences drawn from the albeit short national history of the state, have begun to shape a shared political and social community. Increasingly surveys conducted amongst Jewish citizens of Israel indicate a growing percentage of respondents identifying themselves first as Israelis, and only then as Jewish.[13] For the Jewish population of Israel, this in many cases is indicative of the expanding ambivalence towards the Jewish religion. One of the central debates surrounding Israel's national identity concerns the status of religion. Since in Israel there is no separation between religion and state, the religious parties enjoy inordinate influence over the way in which public life is conducted. Limitations on secular lifestyles, such as the lack of public transportation on Saturday, and the control of the Rabbinical courts over all personal issues (marriage, birth, divorce) coupled with the growing amount of public subsidies for religious educational institutions have inspired some of the most ardent and intense public protests.

However, the growing preference for Israeli over Jewish, coming from an anti-religious point of view, does not question the legitimacy of the Jewish cultural and historical attributes of the Israeli national identity. Hence, despite the fact that many younger generation Jewish Israelis might identify themselves as Israeli, the content and membership of this national identity still refers back to Jewish history, and encompasses only Jews.

ISRAELI NATIONAL IDENTITY: THE FOUNDING NARRATIVE

Modern Jewish nationalism emerged at the turn of the nineteenth century as part of an overall attempt to normalize Jewish national existence.[14] This understanding of normalization dictated the acquisition of land, and hence the transformation of the Jewish nation into a modern, nineteenth-century European territorial nation. Traditional Jewish existence and identity was based upon an intermixture of national and religious tenets, with the religious elements dictating both the content and form of Jewish life. The religious coherence, however, was maintained through the proto-nationalist yearning for Zion. The collective Jewish memory was very much defined through the yearning for the lost golden age in which both national and religious existence were satisfied.[15]

At the same time, and perhaps precisely because of the forced external suppression of the national aspects of Jewish life, there was no tension or conflict between the religious and national aspects of identity. Since the Jew was not free to choose his or her preferred mode of identity, the national and the religious components formed an integral part of the whole, and together composed the essence of being a Jew.

It was only with the dawn of the enlightenment that an element of choice, and hence conflict, came into existence. Jews could now choose between an orthodox religious existence, potential national assimilation into host countries, a reformed religious existence, or, perhaps, a national Jewish life. Assimilation and reform constituted the two dominant responses; nationalism, the third and from the outset, the least appealing. This last option asserted the dominance of nationality over religion, and the conscious decision to construct a single, homogeneous national community from the culturally disparate and geographically distinct Jewish communities. Indeed, the only shared characteristic was the adherence to the Jewish faith, and this thus served as the mobilizing formula of the Zionist movement.

Hence, Zionism constructed an unequivocal response to the dilemmas of the enlightenment: the Jews are a territorially bounded ethnic-nation, who were exiled from their territory, and are now reclaiming their national identity by reclaiming the land.[16] Accordingly, the narrative of identity proposed by Zionism was that the Jews constitute a nation (albeit religiously defined), which, with increasing national education, and gradual migration to Palestine, will become a nation like all other nations. Jewish national identity will then embody a religious element, but its existence will be no less "national" for it.

As would be expected, as Zionism gained adherents, and power, the breadth of its ideological diversity grew. Zionists ranged from orthodox to secular atheists; from cultural autonomists to ardent statehood revisionists, and they all quarreled heatedly about both the final objectives of the movement, as well as on the methods of achieving those goals. The ideological diversity was acute and entailed often violent political controversy over both means and ends of the Zionist endeavor. Indeed in its most extreme manifestations, the ideological cleavages led one group of Zionists to denounce others to the British Mandate authorities, which at times even led to their death.[17]

Nonetheless, there existed a fundamental coherence, which linked them all: the coherence and unanimity with which they perceived both the essence of Jewish national identity, and the understanding that the state, once established, would be the political vehicle of this nation. These tenets were shared by all ideological variants of Zionism, and can be seen as constituting the conventional narrative of Israeli national identity. For all Zionists, from the religious Zionists led by the Rav Kook, through the Labor and Revisionist Zionists, and including the left-wing Communists, the Jewish nation was constituted by members of the Jewish religion whose national revival marked the redemption of their exile. As Horowitz, a prominent representative of the traditional Zionist historiography notes, "A firm consensus existed . . . concerning the commitment of the individual to the national collectivity . . . the New Yishuv was a product of Zionist ideology and . . . this ideology formed the common value basis of the entire Yishuv."[18]

In fact, the sheer unanimity of consensus is perplexing given the intensity of conflict amongst the divergent Zionist sects. Both the political and social goals of the movement were highly contested and engendered political rivalries that in their extreme form brought about not merely argument but violence. Discussions concerning Jewish identity were limited, however, to the transformation of the individual Jew.[19] Hence, the differences in ideological orientation were expressed in differing visions of *the Jew*: the Jew as agriculturist, the Jew as industrialist, the Jew as orthodox, and the Jew as a western cosmopolitan.[20] Implications concerning the transformation of Jewish collective identity were entirely derivative from these individualist assumptions.

Hence, what I have called the conventional narrative, establishes three central points. The first is that the establishment of the state of Israel represents the political victory and rebirth of the Jewish nation. The second is that this nation is constituted by members of the Jewish religion *everywhere*, and that while its membership criteria is adherence to the Jewish faith, its collective memory draws upon the nationalized and secularized Zionist version of Jewish history. The third and final point is that the legitimacy of both the nation and its state is drawn from the eternal and universal Jewish people.[21] This conventional narrative forms the basis, up till today, of the official, and dominant version of Israeli national identity. It permeates the educational curricula, political policies, and dominant intellectual viewpoints.

CONTESTING THE TRADITIONAL NARRATIVE: ALTERNATIVES IN THE POST-INDEPENDENCE ERA

Alongside the deep consensus that existed amongst Zionist activists and ideologists concerning the nature of Jewish national identity, a small number of alternative approaches emerged and even garnered significant support during the years that directly followed independence. Amongst these alternatives, what has come to be known as the Canaanite approach, and the approach propagated by former resistance commander Hillel Kook represent the basis of much of the recent debates concerning Israeli national identity. While ultimately both positions proved politically ineffective, they lay the basis for the future debates.

The Canaanite movement emerged initially as a literary movement in Paris in the early 1920s. The political movement was established in 1944 and was called the Committee for the Formation of Hebrew Youth.[22] According to Canaanite thought, the Zionist settlers in Palestine were unrelated historically to the Jewish people. These settlers, who later established the sovereign Israeli state represented a new nation—distinct in all possible ways from the historical national-religious community called the Jewish people. Accordingly, the Jews are not a nation, but, a "faith community, a religion-ethnic group, international and extraterritorial in nature."[23] The community which developed in Palestine (later to become Israel) constituted the new Hebrew nation. This Hebrew nation represented a continuation of the Hebrew existence in western Palestine from the pre-biblical times and was linked to the ancient Canaanites.[24] They were all united by the same Semitic language, Hebrew, and by a common culture. This cultural and linguistic unity was recreated in modern Palestine and has become politically viable with the establishment of the state of Israel. However, for this recreation to succeed, Israel must reestablish herself as a secular state, not a theocratic Jewish state as the Zionist ideology would have it. As a secular democratic state it would embody, and assimilate, the various indigenous minorities—Maronite Christians, Copts, Kurds, Cherkassians, Druze, Alawites, Shiites, and Armenians. Together they would compose the new Hebrew confederation and nation.[25]

The Canaanites perceived of themselves as the "Hebrew Nation"—speaking and living Hebrew both linguistically and culturally. The Hebrews are sharply distinguished, according to the Canaanites, from the Jews of the Diaspora on all levels: culturally, politically, and perhaps most significantly, religiously. The culture that will emerge in this new state would be a new mixture, combining Arab, Hebrew, and Jewish elements. The history of the nation would be the history of the territory.[26]

The second alternative approach came from an off-shoot of the Irgun organization, the Hebrew Committee for National Liberation (HCNL). Established in Washington, D.C., in late 1944[27] by former commander of the Irgun[28] and political activist Hillel Kook (alias Peter Bergson), the Committee was active in Washington, D.C., in its efforts to gain recognition and support for the establishment of the state of Israel. While politically ineffective, nonetheless, Hillel Kook, a political activist and critical political thinker, has undoubtedly had a seminal impact upon all forms of dissenting post-Zionist thinking in Israel today.[29]

The fundamental political principle espoused by the committee concerned the distinction between individual and national self-determination, claiming the right of individual Jews to decide for themselves whether or not they need, or desire, to exercise their right to national self-determination. This led to a gradual distinction between Jews who, as individuals, would exercise this right, and those Jews who chose to remain in their own countries and hence implicitly accepted the national identity of their "host" society.

Kook and his colleagues were guided by what they called the fundamental questions of identity:

> [First is] the question of the status in the world of those Jews who are citizens of free countries and who do not desire to move to Palestine, and [the second is] the general question of the relations between the Jewish religion and the proposed Jewish Commonwealth.[30]

The political circumstances dictated the need to distinguish between those Jews for whom a Jewish state in Palestine is a necessary and desired goal, and those for whom the objective of statehood is but a symbol. The Jews who have chosen the path of nationalism, and who have decided to lead their lives in a newly established state have accepted the nationalization of their identity. Those who have opted to remain in their respective country of origin, have, for all intents and purposes, relinquished the *political* definition of their Jewish identity. The fundamental issue lies in "the fundamental difference that exists between the terms "Hebrew" and "Jew," in the light of political realities of the world . . . is the difference between a nationality and a religion."[31]

The renewed nationalization of Jewish identity is manifested in the renewed Hebrew Nation. This nation, while forever connected to the Jewish people through ties of heritage, history, and religion, is, nonetheless, a politically distinct entity. The Jews who opt for their respective countries (American, Canadian, or British Jews), have themselves fully adopted, with the establishment of the State of Israel, a separate political-national identity, while not for a moment having to relinquish their cultural, religious, or historical identity as Jews.

CONFRONTING THE
TRADITIONAL NARRATIVE: LATER ALTERNATIVES

The alternative conceptions of both the collective national identity in Israel, and its relationship to the Jewish people were short lived, and produced no significant impact on the dynamics of collective national identity in Israel for roughly the first forty years of independence. Moreover, the political agenda they addressed was dictated by concerns about the relationship amongst Jews, and between the Jewish religion and Jewish nationality. Hence, both Kook's and Ratosh's radical alternatives focused on the implications of distinguishing between religion and nationality for the Jewish community. Although the implications for the non-Jews in Israel were clear, the identity of the ethnic Palestinians in Palestine/Israel was of secondary significance for them.

By the end of the 1980s, a new wave of both political and academic thinking about national identity in Israel emerged. This new wave posited a different interpretation of the contours of collective national identity, and while it addressed the issue of Israel-Diaspora relations, most of the focus was on the implications of identity for the relationship between Jewish and non-Jewish citizens of the state.[32] This was of course clearly a reflection of the changing political agenda of the Jewish community in Israel. If the issue of Jewish relations was at the forefront of Jewish concerns in the immediate post-war era, with the aftermath of the extermination defining every aspect of reality and the reality of Israeli inter-ethnic relations a distant concern, fifty years later the tables were turned. With the break-up of the Soviet Union, the last major wave of Jewish immigration arrived in Israel. The relationship between the "Diaspora" and Israel was an increasingly academic—or abstract—concern. On the other hand, the implications of what I call the conventional narrative on the national status of Palestinians in Israel, and hence of relations between Jews and Arabs in Israel became a reality few could choose to ignore.

Hence, understandably the discourse surrounding Israeli collective national identity found much of its focus on the relative status of non-Jewish minorities within this identity. Two critical positions can be identified. The first, labeled neo-Zionist, offered a critique of the traditional narrative, while maintaining the essential elements of it. The second post-Zionist position, constituted a far more radical critique, and offered a revision of the basic Zionist principles. Since these two positions are elaborated at length below in chapter six, a brief discussion of each will suffice.

The neo-Zionist position has two fundamental concerns. The first relates to the politicization and hence orthodoxy of the Jewish religion in the Israeli political culture, and the consequent growing alienation and revulsion of younger generation Israeli Jews from the religion. The claim, as it was espoused by such leading intellectuals as Nissim Kalderon, Nimrod Aloni, Amnon Rubenstein, and Yael Tamir is that Judaism is not only a rigid religious doctrine, but is also a culture and a heritage.[33] Through publications, the establishment of colleges, and public lectures this group promoted an understanding of Judaism that is neither religious nor particularly nationalist, but essentially cultural. Politically they suggested the separation between religious institutions and political institutions but the maintenance of a Jewish nationality in a much softer, and liberal version. Thus while espousing equal rights for non-Jews, and the elimination of sources of discrimination from the legal code of Israel, they supported the maintenance of Israel as a Jewish state. Their revision thus proposed a more tolerant Jewish national identity which would allow for alternative national identifications, and even possible assimilation. Defining Judaism as culture would, presumably, allow for non-Jews to assimilate into the Jewish cultural milieu.

The post-Zionist position suggested a far more radical re-assessment of collective national identity. At its extremes, it called for the de-nationalization of Israel, and the establishment of what is called in Israeli parlance, "a state for all its citizens." Thus while post-Zionism included a certain array of distinct claims, the position as a whole is united by the insistence of its critique of the traditional narrative of Zionism as an essentially and fundamentally racist discourse, which in its insistence on a rigid nationalist definition of collective national identity both implicitly and explicitly discriminates against non-Jews. Philosopher Joseph Agassi for example, a disciple of Hillel Kook, proposed the establishment of an Israeli nationality which would be entirely distinct from the Jewish religion, and hence allow for the assimilation of non-Jews, and the equalization of conditions. Others, such as political scientist Ilan Pappe and historian Amnon Raz propose the total secularization of Israel, and the elimination of exclusionary national identifications altogether.

Thus, the different alternatives to the Zionist narrative have emphasized the centrality of the status of the Palestinian citizens of the state, and the need to incorporate a discussion of their predicament in any discussion of Israeli identity. As was clear in the discussion of American identity, the shift in the perception of Israeli identity, and the growing acknowledgement of the centrality of minorities to the definition of the identity, reflected changes in the political and legal environment. In the next section I turn to a discussion of this environment, in what I term the invention of the "Israeli Arab" minority.

THE INVENTION OF THE "ISRAELI ARAB"

As a national minority, the Palestinians in Israel—as even their name indicates—are something of an anomaly. They evolved as a distinct political entity in the midst of the 1948 war. On the eve of the war, estimates of the Arab-Palestinian population of Palestine range from 860,000 to 1.3 million. By the end of 1949 (after the cessation of open hostilities) the number had fallen to 160,000 (by that time 13.6 percent of Israel's total population).[34] After conducting a first census in November 1948, the Israeli provisional government granted Israeli identification cards (later to become citizenship papers) to those Arabs who remained.[35] In 1952, with the passing of the Nationality Law, their status as citizens was formalized. Their identification papers read: Citizenship: Israeli; Nationality: Arab. Thus it happened that an indigenous group changed, almost overnight, from a majority to a minority, from Palestinians to "Arabs" and "Israelis", and thus the hyphenated "Israeli-Arab" was born.

In January 1949, before the end of the war, the reborn Israeli Arabs joined the rest of the Jewish citizens of the state, and voted for representatives to the Constituent Assembly (later to become the first Israeli parliament) and by implication of course, for the government that imposed upon and then maintained military rule over them for sixteen years. This act, which combines the perverse duality of empowerment and disempowerment, is metaphoric of the relationship between Jews and Arabs in Israel, as it has been molded by the policies and attitudes of the Israeli authorities: democratic rights on the one hand, and discrimination and exclusion on the other. In no other sphere is this ambiguity more evident than in the sphere of identity. The peculiar problematic surrounding identity is reflected in the ambiguity concerning categories and labels.

The category of "Israeli Arab" was constructed by the Israeli authorities. As it indicates, this category assumes and constructs two levels of identity. The first is that of Arab. Local Palestinians who remained in what became Israel were designated as Arabs rather then Palestinians. This category refers to the realm of culture and ethnicity and not, clearly, politics. The official, government intention was for the "Arab" to designate culture or ethnicity, and the "Israeli"—to designate the political identity. That level of identity which the minority is said to share with the rest of the citizens of the state.[36] Interestingly however, in common discourse up until the end of the 1990s most people, when employing the category "Israeli" implicitly referred to the Israeli Jews, despite the fact that few if any explicitly employ this category. Bizarre situations result from this overlapping, as is manifested in the example of a eulogy conducted by a high ranking officer in the military at a memorial service for two soldiers killed in the same incident. In his eulogy the officer refers to the two as "two soldiers, one Israeli, and one Druze."[37]

It was only with the emergence of a critical discourse concerning the non-Jewish citizens of the state that Israeli Jews have begun to distinguish between "Israeli" and "Jewish Israeli" implicitly acknowledging the existence of non-Jewish Israelis. In addition to the category of Israeli Arabs, other categories include "the minorities" and the "Arab sector," or, in certain circles the more cryptic appellation of "our cousins." The use of these labels denies the existence of any type of political or national identification, and the use of "minority" even denies them a distinct cultural identity. With the emergence of a more critical discourse, as I explore below, the categorization expands to include Israeli Palestinians, Palestinians in Israel, Palestinian Arabs, Israeli Palestinian Arabs, the Palestinians of 1948, and so on.[38]

ISRAELI POLICY TOWARDS ITS
PALESTINIAN CITIZENS—MILITARY RULE

During the course of the war and directly following it, four-fifths of the Arab Palestinian population left, and overnight they became a minority in the country. Palestinian society and economy disintegrated: the mainstay of the economic, political, religious, and intellectual elite population dispersed, leaving behind a largely agricultural and rural population. Families were divided, and the urban centers were largely evacuated or abandoned.[39] The economic infrastructure of their community had been shattered: no marketing concerns, Arab-owned industry, or newspaper or publishing houses remained. There were no political parties or labor unions. Out of Palestinian Arab villages— 121 remained intact. There remained a shattered periphery, with no center.[40] Before the war, 50 percent of employed Palestinians worked in agriculture, leasing farmland which belonged to absentee landlords. Much of the land was confiscated by the state, leaving few other channels of employment. This resulted in endemic unemployment.

In terms of policy regarding the Palestine Arabs, the new government of Israel followed in the footsteps of the Yishuv and Zionist leadership. As such, no clear policy was developed. During the pre-state era, the relationship between Jews and non-Jews was not discussed in the context of national membership. While there existed a vast political discourse concerning Jewish-Arab relations, it was external to the ideology of the movement.[41] The Jews' relationship with the local Arabs was conceived of as a matter of the relationship of the movement with outsiders. As Eisenstadt notes: "The relations with the . . . Arabs . . . constituted the focus of the 'external' political relations of the Zionism movement and of the Yishuv . . ." As such, it was undifferentiated from the Jews' relationship with their general environment.[42]

Until the mid-1930s, when the Jews still constituted a distinct minority, parity was introduced by David Ben Gurion and other leading figures in the Zionist movement as the ideal basis for co-existence. Ben Gurion even discussed the idea of a canonization of Palestine.[43] However, as the percentage of Jews started growing the notion of parity and other consociational arrangements became more and more remote.[44] The emphasis shifted towards a more abstract notion of cooperation, and away from distinct ideas of sharing. This shift culminated in Ben Gurion's denial of the existence of an independent Arab nation in Palestine.[45]

From the outbreak of World War II, and especially since 1942 when the Biltmore program demanding statehood as the formal goal of the movement was consolidated, less and less attention was paid to the future institutional relationship between Arabs and Jews. The energy was directed towards elaborating and fulfilling the notion of Jewish sovereignty, and more precisely towards establishing Israel as the homeland of the Jewish people. However, what became increasingly clear, as sovereignty became imminent, was that the Zionists had no clear program—neither ideological nor practical—which would provide a way of resolving the conflicting goals and demands of the two populations—Jews and Arabs.

Nonetheless, military and political events dictated the inevitable development of a policy towards the local Palestinian population. The policy that emerged was one dictated by the hegemonic status of the value of security and was implemented primarily by the different security forces—the military, the General Security Forces (Shabak), and the police. In general, an atmosphere of confusion, ambivalence, and basic neglect surrounded the efforts at formulating any kind of comprehensive and consistent policy towards the Arab population. As some commentators have noted, much of the government policy towards the Arabs represented a process of "muddling through," and was dictated by a "non-policy" attitude.[46]

From 1948 to 1966, the Palestinian population was subject to Military Rule.[47] Military Rule meant that management of the Palestinian population was delegated to the military administration and generals, who had already been in charge of the Arab populated areas since the outbreak of the war. These areas included Nazareth, western Galilee, Ramle-Lod, Jaffa, and the Negev. No significant guidelines were handed down to the military officials from the political level. This resulted in the delegation of important policy decisions to the bureaucratic and administrative levels which produced haphazard, ad hoc, and somewhat arbitrary decisions.[48] Legally, the Military Administration drew its power from the British emergency regulations of 1945–1946, and covered most aspects of daily life. Two elements are usually cited as the most critical. The first was the defining of closed areas, and thus linking travel within the country to obtaining travel-permits. By severely restricting and monitoring the movement of the Arabs, the officials hoped to minimize security offenses. The second was the subjection of all forms of organization—from political parties to sports clubs, to the authorization of the Military Governor.[49] Most of these organizations were forbidden under the rationale that any organization might induce the politicization and nationalization of the Arab identity.[50]

Underlying the policies of the Administration was the perception, shared by the political elite and the population at large, of the local Palestinians as a potential fifth column. Throughout the 1950s this anxiety and fear was reinforced by the tension on the borders, and the appeals by the Arab governments to the Palestinian population in Israel to revolt against the Jews. Palestinians who had either fled or were expelled to neighboring Jordan, attempted to cross the border, in efforts to retrieve whatever remained of the possessions they had been forced to leave behind. These incidents were consistently represented by the security officials as "terrorist infiltrations" aimed at perpetrating violent crimes against the Jews in Israel. The Palestinian border villages were thus perceived, by the administration, as "bases for infiltration, spying, and smuggling."[51] The destruction of homes, the confiscation of lands, and the expulsion of Arabs from their villages continued, largely justified by this security excuse.

Most of the popular, political, and intellectual discourse surrounding the relationship between the Jewish and Palestinian citizens of the state is defined by what can be seen as the security paradigm. This paradigm dictates what appears as self-evident to most Israeli Jews and to the Israeli government: that despite the fact that the Israeli Palestinians were granted citizenship and are citizens of a democratic state, they are still seen as an integral part of the larger body of the Arab people with whom Israel is at war. Hence, from the outset, the Israeli Palestinians were perceived as potential enemies. The security parameter has defined both the terminology and the content of the discourse concerning the relationship between these two separate populations of the state of Israel: hence the emergency regulations imposed upon them; hence the Military Rule; hence the perpetuation of significant civic, educational and economic inequalities between the two groups; hence the political and national restrictions placed upon them. And of course, hence the unwillingness of the Israeli authorities to allow them membership in either the Israeli or the emerging Palestinian national identity.[52] The conclusion to the classic *Israeli Society* by S. N. Eisenstadt, a prominent Israeli sociologist is characteristic and revealing:

> In many ways the possibility of a fuller and freer encounter between the Arab minority and the Jewish majority in Israel contains important possibilities, not only of political arrangements, but also of variegating the components of Israeli identity. *The complexity and tragedy of the situation lies in the fact that these possibilities and potentials are greatly limited by the international political situations.* [Italics mine, R. K.][53]

The abolishment of Military Rule over the Israeli Palestinians in 1966 engendered many institutional changes regarding the treatment of the Palestinian population, but it was not, as I explore in detail below, to change this fundamental paradigm.

ISRAELI POLICY TOWARDS ITS
PALESTINIAN CITIZENS—BEYOND MILITARY RULE

Less then one year after the formal dismantling of the system of Military Rule, Israel occupied the West Bank and the Gaza Strip. For many of Israel's Palestinians, the opening of the gates between the West Bank and Israel meant reunification with family members and with an entire Arab community which had been cut off from them for close to twenty years. The end of Military Rule, along with the "opening" of the green line, had a significant impact on all dimensions of Palestinian life—economic, social, and political. Economically and socially, the lifting of the restrictions was translated into a slowly rising standard of living. From the beginning of the 1970s the government began allocating more funds towards education and development, which resulted in higher income levels, lower levels of infant mortality and higher levels of education. Nonetheless, the discrepancy between Jewish and Palestinian average standards of living has remained inordinately large.

Politically, removal of the strict restrictions on freedom of association resulted in the gradual evolution of an authentic Palestinian political life. Over the course of thirty years, Palestinians have organized a wide range of political parties and social movements that have mobilized large segments of the Palestinian population. Despite the persistence of severe mechanisms of control that survived the abolition of Military Rule, by the end of the twentieth century Palestinian society created a new generation of political, intellectual, and social elites and leaders. The candidacy of Azmi Bisharah in the 1999 elections for Prime Minister is but one example of many of the growing sense of political empowerment.[54]

The question remains, however, how has this changing political and social reality impacted upon the status of the Palestinian minority within Israeli society as a whole, and Israeli national identity in particular. Undoubtedly, the critical act of the government towards the Arab population was the granting of citizenship early on in the game, and with citizenship came the potential benefits of living within a western-style democratic welfare state. Interestingly, while this act is perplexing given the prevailing attitude toward the Palestinian population, and given the fact that they were denied most other democratic rights during the period of Military Rule, little has been written about the circumstances that surrounded the decision to grant the Arabs citizenship.[55] Apparently, the decision to grant citizenship was based upon the Declaration of Independence which avows equal treatment of all individuals within the state—although the declaration is largely a symbolic document and embodies no legal status. In the period directly preceding the 1949 elections, intense efforts were made by all the major Israeli-Jewish parties to woo Arab voters, mainly through the cooption of major Hamula (extended family) leaders, who would assure the votes of their clan.[56] It therefore seems that the main motivation to grant the Israeli Arabs citizenship was to provide the political leadership of the then-ruling Mapai party with additional sources of voters.[57]

For most of the Zionist establishment, the creation of the state did not represent the entire fulfillment of the goals of the movement. The leadership did not see a need to restructure or even rethink its nationalist and ideological goals, nor it's raison d'etre.[58] The twin goals of "ingathering of the exiles", and "redeeming the land" constituted not only the leading ethos of the state, but its dominant political orientation as well. With only a minority of the Jews in Israel and with the constant threat of enemy invasion, neither the leadership, nor the people, saw a need to reevaluate the goals of the state, and its relationship with non-Jews. The attitude towards the Arabs within became the same as that which was held towards the Arabs without; they were enemies of the state, and as such should be treated with suspicion and utmost prudence. The policies of the new government pointed to the fact that the overall purpose was to "control the Arab community in Israel rather than to eliminate, integrate, absorb or develop it."[59]

The crucial questions and issues upon which the success of maintaining a national or ethnic minority within a democratic nation-state were, by and large, avoided by the government decision-makers. Such potential questions might have included whether they should be integrated as an autonomous minority community, or should be assimilated. Should their culture be fostered, or should they be encouraged to emigrate? Towards which channels should their political identities be focused?

The inability or unwillingness of the Zionist leadership to confront these questions stemmed from a much deeper inability—that of confronting the contradiction which was embedded into their own ideological identity.[60] The Zionist leadership quickly realized that the establishment of Israel as a Jewish state would eventually raise the question of the meaning of the implications of such a state for the Jewish people at large. Such issues as the future relationship of world Jewry with the Jewish State loomed heavy on the horizon. Initiating a substantial, ideological debate concerning the status of a non-Jewish minority in a Jewish state would invariably raise these questions as well. For the most fundamental of these questions is one and the same: who are the core members of the state of Israel: the Jews (worldwide), or, as is the more common practice in modern democracies, the citizens of the state. The movement's and then the state's leadership have chosen to delay the debate indefinitely.

The following chapter examines the legal status of the Palestinian citizens in Israel today, focusing upon those laws which serve to restrict the implementation of equality vs a vs this population. The discussion illustrates the dynamic nature of the Palestinians membership, as it is illustrated in the legal discourse in Israel.

NOTES

1. Ahad Ha'am, "Ha'emet Me'eretz Yisrael," [The Truth from Eretz Israel], in *Kol Kitvei Ahad Ha'am* [Writings of Ahad Ha'am] (Jerusalem, 1946), p. 256.

2. For a survey of early opinions concerning the Arabs, see D. Harden, *Contemporary Jewish National Thinking*, (Jerusalem: World Zionist Organization Publication, no. 5, 1970), (Hebrew); also, Neville J. Mandel, *The Arabs and Zionism before World War I* (Berkeley: University of California Press, 1976); E. Rubenstein, "Zionist Attitudes in the Arab-Jewish Dispute to 1936," *The Jerusalem Quarterly* no. 22 (winter 1982). This latter author proposes that far from evading the question of the Arabs, the early Zionists dealt with the Arab question incessantly, and were intent and sincere in attempting to find a resolution to the conflictual demands. They were, however, unsuccessful, hence the "myth" of the Zionist evasion. On the focus on territory see, Baruch Kimmerling, "The Impact of the Land and Territorial Components of the Jewish-Arab Conflict on the Building of Jewish Society in Palestine," (Ph.D. diss., The Hebrew University, Jerusalem, 1975) [Hebrew].

3. Israel Central Bureau of Statistics, 31 December, 2000. (http://www.cbs.gov.il/305/2000). Among the Palestinians, approximately 80 percent are Muslim, 9 percent Druze, and 11 percent Christians.

4. See "After the Crisis: New Directions for Government Policy towards the Arab Minority in Israel," an emergency report written by an inter-university team of scholars. (On file with author).

5. Alouf Hareven, *Retrospect and Prospects: Full and Equal Citizenship?"* (Jerusalem: Sikkuy, 1998), p. 48.

6. "After the Crisis."

7. Aziz Haidar, *Social Welfare Services for Israel's Arab Population* (Boulder, Colo.: Westview Press, 1990); Nira Reiss, *The Health Care of Arabs in Israel* (Boulder, Colo.: Westview Press, 1990).

8. A number of works have studied the socio-economic gap between the Jewish and Arab populations of Israel. See particularly, Noah Lewin-Epstein and Moshe Semyonov, "Ethnic Group Mobility in the Israeli Labor Market," *American Sociological Review* 51 (June 1986): 342–51; Aziz Haidar, *Social Welfare Services for Israel's Arab Population*; Nira Reiss, *The Health Care of Arabs in Israel*. The statistics cited

here were quoted in David Grossman, *Present Absentees* (Tel Aviv: Hakibbutz Ha'Meuchad, 1992) [Hebrew]; and in Atallah Mansour, "On Integration, Equality and Co-Existence," in *One out of Every Six Israelis*, ed. Alouph Hareven (Jerusalem: The Van Leer Jerusalem Foundation, 1981), [Hebrew].

9. On the construction of this national narrative see Gabriel Peterberg, "The Nation and her Narrators: National Historiography and Orientalism," *Theory and Criticism* 6 (spring 1995).

10. For the duality of Israeli identity see Dan Segre, *A Crisis of Identity* (Oxford: Oxford University Press, 1980), p. 45. For a discussion of the symbols of Israeli nationalism, see Charles Liebman and Eliezer Don-Yechiye, *Civil Religion in Israel* (Berkeley: University of California Press, 1983).

11. Non-Arab Christians indicate country of origin. For details concerning the Supreme Court relevant rulings, see chapter 5.

12. Eva Etzioni-Halevy (with Rina Shapira), *Political Culture in Israel* (New York: Praeger Publishers, 1977), p. 161. See also S. N. Eisenstadt, *Israeli Society* (New York: Basic Books, 1965); or Michael Curtis and Mordechai Chertoff, eds., *Israel: Social Structure and Change* (New Brunswick: Transaction Books, 1973), where the terminology used is Israeli society, and Jewish nation or nationality. It is interesting to note that while they describe classic "nation-building" and integrative processes, they stop short of both describing the process as one in which an Israeli nationality is cohering, as well as calling the national community within Israel -Israeli. See also David Schoenbrun, Robert Szekely, and Lucy Szekely, *The New Israelis* (New York: 1973); Yacov Rubin, *Partners in State-Building: American Jewry and Israel* (New York: 1969); S. N. Eisenstadt, Rivka Bar-Yoseph, and Chaim Adler, eds., *Integration and Development in Israel* (London: Weldenfeld and Sons, 1970). Of course the classic definitive statement was given by Eisenstadt in his article "Israeli identity: Problems in the Development of the Collective Identity of an Ideological Society," *The Annals of the American Academy of Political and Social Science* 370 (March 1967): 116–23. In this article there is no mention of non-Jews, and Israeli identity is dealt with solely in the context of the development of Jewish identity.

13. For a detailed analysis of this survey, as well as a study of Israeli nationality, see, Joseph Agassi, Judith Buber Agassi, Moshe Berent, *Who is an Israeli*, (Tel Aviv: Kivunum, 1991); For other works concerning the emergent Israeli community see a special issue of *Politika* on this topic, *Politika*, 2, no. 8 (1988); see also Alouph Hareven, ed., *On the Difficulty of Being an Israeli*, (Jerusalem: The Van Leer Foundation, 1983); More recently, see Azmi Bishara, ed., *Between "I" and "We": The Construction of Identities and Israeli Identity* (Jerusalem: Hakibbutz Hameuchad, 1999); Fania Oz-Salzberger, *Israelis, Berlin* (Jerusalem: Kefer, 2001). For an example of where the existence of an Israeli nationality is an implicit assumption see Erik Cohen, "Citizenship, Nationality and religion in Israel and Thailand," in *The Israeli State and Society: Boundaries and Frontiers*, ed. Baruch Kimmerling (Albany: State University of New York Press, 1989), p. 66–93.

14. On the notion and centrality of normalization amongst the Zionists see especially the introduction in, Arthur Hertzberg, *The Zionist Idea* (New York: Meridian, 1960), pp. 1–100; In his introduction he provides a good survey of Zionist thinking,

as well as an explanation of the centrality of normalization to the Zionist movement. See also, Ben Halpern, *The Idea of a Jewish State* (Cambridge, Mass.: Harvard University Press, 1961); Y. Gorni, *Collective Identity*; Bernard Avishai, *The Tragedy of Zionism: Revolution and Democracy in the Land of Israel* (New York: Farrar Straus Giroux, 1985).

15. See, Jacob Katz, *Jewish Emancipation and Self-Emancipation* (Philadelphia: Jewish Publication Society, 1986); idem., *Out of the Ghetto: The Social Background of Jewish Emancipation, 1770–1870* (New York: Schoken Books, 1978); Heinrich Graetz, *The Structure of Jewish History and Other Essays* (New York: The Jewish Theological Seminary of America, 1975); Eliezer Schweid, "The Attitude Toward the State in Modern Jewish Thought Before Zionism," in *Kinship and Consent*, ed. Daniel J. Elazar (New York: University Press of America, 1983), p. 127–51; Simon Dubnow, *Nationalism and History: Essays on Old and New Judaism* (New York: Atheneum, 1970).

16. Again, for an explanation of this response see Hertzberg, *The Zionist Idea*; Also, David Vital, *Zionism, the Formative Years* (Oxford: Clarendon Press, 1982); and Walter Laqueur, *A History of Zionism* (London: Weidenfeld and Nicolson, 1972). It should be noted that the notion of "territorial" nation is not used here in the theoretical sense expounded upon by Anthony Smith and explained elsewhere in this work. By territorial the meaning is that the notion of a specific territory is central to the essence of the particular nation.

17. This of course refers to the battle between the Irgun and the Haganah, known as the "saison" of the "season" during the late thirties. Irgun members were betrayed to the British by members of the rival, and more establishment underground organization, the Haganah. See, Yaacov Shavit, *The Season of the Hunt: The "Season"—The Confrontation between the "Organized Yishuv" and the Underground Organizations, 1937–1947* (Tel Aviv: Hadar, 1976) [Hebrew]. Also see J. C. Hurewitz, *The Struggle for Palestine* (1950; reprint, New York: Schoken Books, 1976).

18. From Dan Horowitz and Moshe Lissak, *Origins of the Israeli Polity* (Chicago: University of Chicago Press, 1978), p. 134–37. As to the issue of who constitutes the Jewish people, the matter was not quite so simple. Indeed, Herzl's definition of Zionism—"the Jewish people in the making" merely highlights the fact that for many of the Zionist leaders, the question of who constitutes a member of the Jewish people was a fluid issue. It is important to note in this context that following the so-called "ethnic revival" in Israel during the late sixties, and mid-seventies, when the Jews of African and Arabic (so-called Sepharadi Jews) descent began to organize themselves politically, and demanded recognition of Israel as an ethnically divided society, one of the mainstays of their attack upon the Israeli establishment was that since the inception of Zionism, they were excluded from the definition of "who is a member of the Jewish people." Zionism, thus, was the national movement of the European, Ashkenazi Jewish people. For relevant references on the ethnic problem of Israel see chapter five, note 37.

19. The images of the Zionist Jew differed: most dominant in the Israeli collective memory today are those of the Socialist Zionists, since, not surprisingly, they were politically dominant prior to the state, and in its first years, and hence their symbolism

dominated. The new Jew was promoted as young, agricultural, tall, blond, secular, and muscular: the anti-thesis of the ghetto Jew. The content of the nationalist symbols was mixed due to the at times strange intermingling of socialist/marxist ideology, with nationalist ideology.

20. See A. D. Gordon, "People and Labor," in Hertzberg, *The Zionist Idea*, pp. 372–75; for the Jew as humanist, see Martin Buber, "Hebrew Humanism," Hertzberg, *The Zionist Idea* p. 453–57; for visions of religious Jewry see Yehiel Michael Pines, "Religion is the Source of Jewish Nationalism," Hertzberg, *The Zionist Idea* p. 412–14. See also chapter on Uri Zvi Greenberg in Shlomo Avineri, *The Making of Modern Zionism* (New York: Basic Books, 1981).

21. The lack of attention paid to this central issue has been explained by the circumstances that accompanied Israel's establishment: both the reality and memory of World War II. The Jewish leadership at the time was surely overwhelmed by the nightmare of extermination, and by the ensuing immediate war for independence. Many of the initial state-building functions and planning were performed in a rather ad-hoc fashion. See Horowitz and Lissak, *Origins of the Israeli Polity*, and Eisenstadt, *The transformation of Israeli Society*.

22. They were also known as the Young Hebrews—emulating the nationalist movements of the nineteenth and early twentieth century—the Young Turks, the Young Italians etc.

23. See James Diamond, p.2.

24. The historic Canaanites were a composite group composed of Amorites, Moabites, Ammonites, Pheonicians, Israelites (from whom the Jews are descended) and others.

25. The critique of this version of history is that whether or not it is history or imagination, the peoples who were "carriers of the Hebrew culture"—asides from the people of Israel—have disappeared from the world. Therefore, the whole argumentation is irrelevant. For the substance of the historiographic critique, see Shavit, *From Hebrew to Canaanite*, chapter 8.

26. Politically, they were what would today be called Hawkish, claiming the boundaries of the Hebrew state to be "from the Prat to the Hidekel" (the biblical borders—from the shores of the Mediterranean, to the boundaries of Iraq)—encompassing, and assimilating, the entire population in a newly established nation.

27. This committee followed a number of previous political committees, amongst which were "The Emergency Committee to Save the Jews of Europe," and "The Committee for a Jewish Army of Stateless and Palestinian Jews," all organized by Kook and his colleagues as part of the political lobby to put pressure on the American administration. On the efforts of the Emergency Committee much has been written. See especially, David S. Wyman, *The Abandonment of the Jews* (New York: Pantheon Books, 1984).

28. The Irgun was a Hebrew resistance movement established in 1933 to fight the British control in Palestine. In time the Irgun became associated with the political movement Betar, established by Zionist leader Ze'ev Jabotinsky, and later with the right wing Herut party established by Menachem Begin.

29. On the subsequent development of Bergson's (Kook's) ideas and activities, numerous articles, and a few books, have been written. See, Joseph Agassi, *Between Re-*

ligion and Nationality (Tel Aviv: Papyrus, 1984); Hillel Kook and Shmuel Merlin, "A Proposal for a National Debate," *Haaretz*, April 18, 1975; Louis Rapaport, *Shake Heavan and Earth* (Jerusalem: Geffen Press, 1999).

30. Peter H. Bergson, "A Blueprint for Hebrew Freedom; a letter to Dr. Ch. Weizmann," *Answer*, April 1945, p. 4.

31. Bergson, "A Blueprint," p. 6.

32. See, Joseph Agassi, *Between Religion and Nationality*; S. N. Eisenstadt, *The Transformation of Israeli Society* (London: Weidenfeld and Nicolson, 1985); Baruch Kimmerling, "Between the Primordial and the Civil Definition of the Collective Identity: Eretz Israel or the State of Israel?" in *Comparitive Social Dynamics*, ed., E. Cohen, M. Lissak, U. Almagor, (Boulder, Colo.: Westview Press, 1985), pp. 262–83;

33. See for example, Amnon Rubenstein, *From Herzl to Rabin and On*, (Jerusalem: Schoken 1997) [Hebrew]; Nissim Kalderon, *Pluralists Despite Themselves*, (Tel Aviv: Haifa University Press, 2000) [Hebrew]; Yael Tamir, *Liberal Nationalism* (Princeton, N.J.: Princeton University Press, 1995); Nimrod Aloni, *Lehiot Adam* (Tel Aviv: Hakibbutz Hameuchad, 1998) [Hebrew].

34. The so-called "battle over numbers" represents a highly contested issue. See the different figures presented in the following: Groman (1995), p. 31 (an official Israeli civics textbook), and those in Sabri Jiryis, (1976), appendix 1.

35. Qualification was dependent upon certain specific residence requirements. Residency in a specific area, during a specific time interval before and during hostilities, in order to qualify as a resident. There are many sources. See for example, Uzi Benziman and Atallah Mansour, *Subtenants; The Arabs in Israel—their status and Israeli policy towards them* (Jerusalem: Keter, 1992), chap. 8; and David Kretzmer, *The Legal Status of the Arabs in Israel* (Boulder, Colo.: Westview Press, 1990).

36. Azmi Bisharah describes the "Israeli Arab" as describing a reality in which Arabs lack the ability to be "full" Israelis, with the Israeli Arab being "half" an Israeli. See Azmi Bisharah, "The Arab Israeli: Discussions in a Fragmented Political Discourse," in *Between I and We: The Construction of Identities and Israeli identity*, ed. Azmi Bisharah (Jerusalem: Hakkibutz Hameuchad), pp. 169–90 (p. 180).

37. The Druze are recruited in the military and serve the compulsory three year service. They are citizens of the state, and as such, are Israeli.

38. This is for the simple reason that a. due to the definition of corporate Israeli identity, they do not belong, and b. the expression of Palestinian or Arab national identity is taken as an act of support of enemy forces. See Dan Rabinovitz, "Eastern Nostaligia: How Palestinians became Israeli Arabs." *Theory and Criticism* 4 (autumn 1993): p. 141.

39. In Jerusalem, for example, there were 75,000 people before the war, and 3,500 after; in Jaffa, 70,000 before, and 3,600 after; in Haifa, 71,200 before, and 2,900 after. See Jiryis, *The Arabs in Israel*, chap. 3.

40. The bulk of the population, 90,000, was centered in the Galilee, 31,000 in the little triangle in the center, and the remaining 13,000 in the south. The rest were scattered in the cities which emerged from the war with a predominantly Jewish population. The religious breakdown was Moslems, 70 percent, Christians, 21 percent, Druze and Circassians, 9 percent. See Zureik, *Palestinians in Israel*, chap. 5.

41. One exception, of course, was the course suggested by the proponents of bi-nationalism. The bi-national plan suggested the establishment of a state which would serve as the national home for both the Jews and the Arabs. Hence, while this plan did not suggest any formal change in the nature of the collective Jewish identity, it did try to account for the relationship between the two national groups. The plan suggested that the state take into consideration the national distinction and divide up political power between the two groups based on separation and cooperation at the same time. This was the formal plan of MAPAM until the unification with MAPAI in the 1970's. An additional alternative view, though far less popular, was that proposed by the idealist group "Brit Shalom." The group consisted of several Hebrew University Professors and operated during the 1940s. See Ilan Peleg and Ofira Seliktar, eds., *The Emergence of Binational Israel* (Boulder, San Francisco, and London: Westview Press, 1989).

42. Eisenstadt, *The Transformation of Israeli Society*, 136. Of course, attention was paid to the threat posed by the Arabs to the security and safety of the Jews. Two tentative explanations might be provided for this quite striking point: the first is that the core ideological Zionist writings remained, long after substantial emigration arrived in Palestine, the European writings of Herzl, Hess, Borochov, Gordon and Jabotinsky. The raison d'etre of Zionism remained the anti-Semitism of the gentiles, and hence their context was Europe and not Palestine. The second point is that political independence was declared as a formal goal of the movement as late as 1942. The hesitancy to declare sovereignty as the formal goal of the movement may partially explain why the Zionists did not apparently see any dire need to discuss the national/political relationship of the Jews and the Arabs.

43. See Don Peretz, *Israel and the Palestinian Arabs* (Washington, D.C.: The Middle East Institute, 1956); Moreover, up until the late thirties and early forties, the Labor Zionists had no clear picture of what precisely the national home for the Jews would consist of. Hence, there was no necessary contradiction between Jewish settlement in Palestine and Arab settlement (aside from the conflict over land). Indeed, any program short of political sovereignty would not necessarily require a rethinking of the definition of the sovereign nation and its relationship to a non-sovereign national minority. See Gorni, *The Quest*, chapter 4.

44. In 1917, the Jews constituted approximately 10 percent of the general population. In 1930, only 17 percent, but by 1940—33 percent. See Shlaim, *The Partition of Palestine*.

45. See Rubenstein, 1982, p.124–28.

46. In particular, see Peretz, *The Palestinians in Israel*, conclusion.

47. A comprehensive and chronological account of the formation of early policy towards the Arab citizens is difficult to come by. A good recent account is provided by Benziman and Mansour, *Subtenants*, particularly chaps. 3 and 4.

48. Benziman and Mansour, *Subtenants*, chap. 2. It should be noted that many of the high ranking military officials saw in the imposition of Military Rule a policy which was aimed at facilitating the daily lives of the Arabs themselves.

49. For details of the various capacities of the Military Governor, and its affect on the daily lives of the Arabs see Jiryis, *The Arabs in Israel*, chap. 4.

50. One of the reasons, interestingly enough, for the ease with which the Palestinian population was neglected was the common belief that most of the Palestinians had fled during the war, and that that was basically the end of the problem. In a book published in 1950 the author succinctly presents this mind set:

"As a result of the war and the flight of the Arabs, Israel has become a state with an ethnically almost homogeneous populations. . . . The culture of the State is Jewish, the government administration, the army . . . are almost exclusively Jewish. It would be folly to resurrect artificially a minority problem which has been almost eliminated by the war. "Israel and the Arab Refugees" (1950), pp.12–13; quoted by Gabbay, *A Political Study of the Arab Jewish Conflict*, 292.

51. Lustick, *Arabs in a Jewish State*, p. 55.

52. Indeed, many Israelis perceived, and still perceive today, the Israeli Arabs as first and foremost, constituting a 'hostile minority'. See, Al-Haj, 1991; Sami Smooha, "Existing and Alternative Policy Towards the Arabs in Israel," *Ethnic and racial Studies* 26, 1 (January 1982): 71–99; Smooha, *Arabs and Jews in Israel: Conflicting and Shared Attitudes in a Divided Society*, Vol 1, (Boulder, Colo.: Westview, 1989), introduction.

53. Eisenstadt, *Israeli Society*, p. 406.

54. For detailed statistics see, Sami Smooha, *Arabs and Jews in Israel; Change and Continuity in Mutual Tolerance*.

55. Even such scholarly and evenhanded discussions as those of Aloni and Segal fail to illuminate this issue. See, Shulamit Aloni, *The Citizen and his State* (Tel Aviv: Ministry of Defense, 1985); Ze'ev Segal, *Israeli Democracy; Constitutional Law* (Tel Aviv: Ministry of Defense, 1988).

56. On the history of Mapai and its initial campaigning efforts see, Yonatan Shapiro, *Achdut Ha'avodah Hahistorit* (Tel Aviv: Am oved, 1975); On the general conditions surrounding the first election see, Asher Arian, *The Choosing People: Voting Behavior in Israel*, (Cleveland: Press of Case Western Reserve University, 1973); Horowitz and Lissak, *Origins of the Israeli Polity*.

57. See Yoseph Agassi, *Between Religion and Nationality*, 2d. ed. (Tel Aviv: Papyrus, 1992). Not surprisingly, indeed the majority of the Arab votes went either to Mapai or to the satellite parties established by them.

58. A rather banal, but telling indication of this mindset is the fact that the Zionist Congresses, held every two or three years since the establishment of the Zionism Movement in 1896, continued following Independence with the same numbering: apparently the establishment of a Zionist State did not seem to warrant the re-formulation of the goals, institutions, or even organizational regulations of the World Zionist Organization.

59. Lustick, *Arabs in a Jewish State*, p. 64.

60. See Peretz, *Palestinians in Israel*, p. 91.

Chapter Five

The Legal Construction
of Membership in Israel

"Even if we discover that the principle of equality was abused, and that differential treatment was granted to equals, it is not always the case that this is wrongful discrimination, because the principle of equality is not an absolute, but a relative value. In other words, if it becomes necessary to compare the principle of equality with some other principle, a situation may arise where it is more important to defend some other interest, and then equality will get hurt . . ."

—Israeli Supreme Court Ruling 5394/92

According to the mainstay of democratic theory, political equality, which is one of its primary defining characteristics, is most fundamentally manifested in the legal code of the society. This is, of course, merely the formal and overt manifestation of political equality, and indeed, only with a consideration of the many social and economic dimensions of pubic and private life can an accurate assessment be made of the extent of political equality within any given society. Nonetheless, the equality of a society's legal code is considered to be the pillar of democracy; it is the foundation upon which the equalization of conditions within society rests. Given inequality in the legal code, inequality is sure to follow in all other political institutions.

The problematic of Israeli society is the problematic of democratic theory: how does one weigh the relative importance of the principle and value of equality? Presuming democratic societies to be societies of equals, how does it happen that differential treatment is accorded to different groups, and how can one justify unequal opportunity, and unequal achievement? As the above quote states, equality in Israel is a principle of relative value. From the establishment of the state onwards, the relative value of equality has been contested in the face of competing values, in particular, the value of a Jewish state. There is no arena in Israeli society which is free from this contestation, the legal arena being no exception. This chapter looks at the way in which the legal arena manifests this contestation.

The chapter analyses three fundamental laws of the Israeli legal code. It demonstrates how these laws clearly reveal the boundaries of the Israeli collective national identity by formally distinguishing between members and non-members of this identity. These three laws are 1) the Law of Return and the attached Law of Nationality, 2) the Law governing public land ownership, and 3) an amendment to the Basic Law: the Knesset. These three laws demonstrate a discriminatory distribution of both fundamental civic rights (the right to political assembly and to citizenship), and property rights (through qualification for ownership of public lands) that is written into the formal Israeli legal code. As other facets of society, however, the legal code is a dynamic and not static institution. In this discussion the shifts and changes reflected in this code are examined as well.

A preliminary comment on the legal discussion is necessary. The existence of both covertly and overtly biased treatment of the non-Jewish citizens of Israel has been widely acknowledged and documented by non-Israeli and Israeli scholars alike, Palestinians and Jews.[1] My discussion is limited to those sources of discrimination which emanate directly from the definition of the collective national identity, and which are overtly manifested in the national legal code.[2]

BACKGROUND TO THE ISRAELI LEGAL CODE.

Despite the fact that the declared purpose of Israel's first legislative assembly (the Constituent Assembly) was to draw up a constitution, Israel until today has no written constitution. The Constituent Assembly was disbanded and renamed the First Knesset the same day it was established, and the writing of a formal constitution was delayed indefinitely.[3] In lieu of a written constitution, it was decided that a constitution would be enacted gradually, by a series of "Basic Laws." These refer to fundamental institutions such as the Knesset itself, the military, and the government. However, as Kretzmer notes, "in the absence of a law giving the Basic Laws superior normative status, the Supreme Court has held that the Basic Laws have no inherent superior status,"[4] and therefore they do not really have equivalent constitutional status. Thus, the Knesset has the authority to pass any law which it sees fit. Moreover, in the absence of any written bill of rights, "even statutes which offend basic civil rights, or contradict principles enshrined in the Declaration of Independence, such as the principle of equality, will not be struck down on this account by the Supreme Court."[5]

The commitment to the principle of equality is manifested in several leading opinions written by Supreme Court judges, in which the principle of equality is clearly the guiding principle in the assessment of disputes, particularly between Jews and non-Jews.[6] It is strongly emphasized, in a number of central rulings, that any practice which discriminates on the basis of religion or national affiliation in issues relating to employment and housing for example, is to be understood as both illegal and immoral.

Key political and social events occurring during the 1990s—the Oslo Peace Accords, the growing politicization of the Palestinians in Israel, and the rising tension between the religious and more secular political parties— placed the absence of a written constitution and a bill of rights high on the public agenda. The tension between the values of democracy and those of the Jewish state generated a debate on the meaning and potential of equality. The so-called "Judicial Revolution" which occurred in 1992 should be properly understood within this debate. The cornerstone of this revolution was the passing of two new Basic Laws: the first was "Basic Law: Human Dignity and Freedom," and the second "Basic Law: Freedom of Occupation." These two laws were supposed to form the basis of an Israeli bill of rights, which in turn was supposed to form the basis of a written constitution. This attempt to form the basis of a written constitution marked one stage in a campaign— public and political—which was launched in the early 1990s for a major reform of the Israeli political structure. The campaign, headed by leading legal scholars in Israel, supported by leaders of the American Jewish community and backed by key Israeli politicians, formed a three-prong program: the drafting of a written constitution, the reform of the parliamentary electoral system, and the institution of direct elections for Prime Minister. The second element, the reform of the parliamentary electoral system, was abandoned at the outset, and the last feature, the direct elections for Prime Minister, was adopted in 1992 and implemented in 1996 only to be withdrawn five years later.[7]

The first feature, that of the constitution, was adopted in piecemeal fashion. The plan was to draft a number of additional Basic Laws that would constitute a written bill of rights, as a prolegomena to the constitution. The larger package of basic laws was to include a law on human dignity and freedom, freedom of occupation, judicial rights, freedom of association and expression, and finally on social rights. Only the first two were passed. The first, concerning human dignity, is of particular interest and was heralded at the time as the most significant legal breakthrough in Israel's fifty year history.[8]

This law is aimed at promoting the fundamental civil rights: the preservation of life, body, honor, property, and freedom. Clearly, such a basic law held much promise for those who were keenly aware of the inequality inherent in the Israeli legal system, and as manifested primarily in Israel's Law of Return, Law of Property, and Basic Law: the Knesset. However, the aim of the law, as articulated in clause "1a" has tempered expectations of this law:

> The purpose of this Basic Law is to protect human dignity and liberty, in order to anchor in a Basic Law the values of the State of Israel as a Jewish and democratic state.[9]

It empowers the Supreme Court to overturn Knesset laws that are incompatible with the rights articulated in the law: the right to dignity, life, freedom, privacy, property, and the right to leave and enter the country freely. (It does not include equality as one of these rights).

Once again, the complex dialectic characteristic of the past decade manifests itself in this Basic Law. On the one hand, the Basic Law exhibits a most obvious tendency towards inclusion and liberalization and makes clear that the preservation of rights is inherent in man *as man*. At the same time, defining the goal of the law as the entrenchment of the values of the state as a Jewish and democratic state makes the Jewish character of the state even more clear and official, and in that sense intractable. Finally, the avoidance of any reference to the principle of equality is central in the quite limited capacity of the law to serve as a defender of the equal rights of the Palestinian population.

Lacking a firm constitutional defense of equality, certain key laws (including some Basic Laws) which enshrine an unequal treatment of Israel's non-Jewish citizens have until recently received little objection. Thus, any reform of the Israeli legal *system* so as to make it more equitable would necessarily have to incorporate a reform of the legal *code* which embodies within it certain laws which are testimony to the message of the Declaration of Independence, namely, defining Israel as a "Jewish state."[10]

THE LAW OF THE RETURN: FROM LEGITIMIZING PRINCIPLE TO BOUNDARY MECHANISM

In terms of concrete implications concerning equality of rights within Israel, the Law of Return has minor ramifications. In another sense, however, it is this law which is most fundamental in determining the discriminatory nature of rights distribution within Israel. It is this law which most explicitly spells out the inherent connection between the state of Israel, as a legal entity, and the Jewish people, and in establishing the legal bridge which Israel was supposed to represent, between world Jewry and itself. It remains until today the primary symbol of Israel as a Jewish state.

The Law of Return was drafted in 1950, two years after the declaration of Jewish political independence. In its first version, it stated: [section 1]: "Every Jew has the right to come to this country as an Oleh." Section 4 describes the scope of the law as follows:

> Every Jew who has immigrated into this country before the coming into force of this law, and every Jew who was born in this country, whether before or after the coming into force of this law, shall be deemed to be a person who has come to this country as an Oleh under this law.[11]

Thus, in this law, the most fundamental "right" of all is the natural right not of citizens of the state, but of Jews: this is the right of belonging, of fundamental and natural membership.

At the time the law was passed, its significance for the new emerging state was central. This was because citizenship was already granted to non-Jews, the formal enemies of the Jewish community, in 1949. Hence, the different ways in which citizenship was attained, and the differing legal reasons adopted for each category, caused some legal complications.[12] Nowadays, however, these distinctions have largely been amended. Consequently, the distinction in the manner of acquiring citizenship is no longer as central. However, even now, the ability to attain citizenship which is equated with true membership in the nation is possible only for Jews, since this type of membership is equated with the act of "returning" to the homeland.

To fully comprehend the ramifications of this type of membership one must consider an accompanying bill to the Law of Return, namely, the Nationality Law, passed in 1952.

> The special feature of a people gathering from its dispersion in its historical homeland is expressed in this law by the provision which grants the absolute right of Israeli nationality to an Oleh under the Law of Return, that is to every Jew who comes to settle in Israel, and to every Jew who was born there.[13]

This is the legal basis of the nationality distinction discussed above which appears in Israeli identification cards designating each citizen according to nationality: Jewish, Arab, and other.

An interesting case was that of Brother Daniel. Up until World War II, Brother Daniel was born and raised as a Jew in Poland. During the war, he was saved by a Catholic Carmelite Monastery, and subsequently converted and became a Catholic monk. Following the war, he came to Israel, and although a practicing monk, claimed citizenship under the Law of Return, stating that while he was Catholic by religion, he still maintained his Jewish nationality, belonging, as he felt he still did, to the Jewish people. In 1962, the Supreme Court ruled against him in the famous case of *Rufheisen vs. the State of Israel,* stating, along with the religious parties, that having converted, he was no longer a Jew.[14]

An additional case is the Shalit case. Shalit, an Israeli Jew, married a non-Jewish woman. They had two children, and wished to register their children as Jewish, at least by nationality. The National Religious Party-led Ministry of Interior denied them this request. A consequent Supreme Court appeal was won, and it was ruled that they should be registered as members of the Jewish nationality. Much in response to these two cases, the Knesset in 1970 amended the clause in the Law of Return referring to *who is a Jew* to specify that only those (1) born to a Jewish mother and (2) are not of any other religion, can be considered Jews eligible under the Law of Return. The third child of the Shalits was consequently denied Jewish nationality.[15]

In many ways, the history of the Law of Return reflects the impact of Zionist ideology on social and political issues in Israel. When first legislated in 1952, the Law of Return, as I quoted above, was clearly seen as the law that legitimized and constituted the essence of the state of Israel as a Jewish state. It encapsulated the entire ethos and moral impact of establishing a state which would come to serve as a safe haven, as a refuge for persecuted Jews. The in-gathering of the exiles—and hence the Law of Return—is considered to be the central legal pillar of the state and its related institutions. It was seen as both compensation and retribution for centuries of anti-Semitic discrimination, and the essential powerlessness of the Jews. If nothing else, Israel's Jewishness was to be forever entrenched in this guarding of the gates.

When the law was first amended in 1970, by Prime Minister Golda Meir, the issue at hand was the fear of the more religious members of the parliament and government that the vague and open-ended language of the law would dilute the religious purity of the state. This can be seen as a turning point in terms of the perception of the role of the law: from a law which was to constitute the ruling ethos of the state, aimed at entrenching a legitimizing political principle, to a law whose central purpose is to define and dictate the membership boundaries of society. The central cases which prompted the demand for change were the two mentioned above, those of Shalit and Rufheisen.

The debate concerning the Law of Return resurfaced in the late 1990s, linking once again the wording of the law, and the question of membership in Israeli society. The late 1990s marked the end of the decade which witnessed the influx of close to one million immigrants from the former Soviet Union. The specific trigger was the fact that by the end of that decade, the Ministry of Interior revealed that a growing percentage of the immigrants were in fact not Jewish. By 1998 the percent was estimated at 32.1 percent, and resulted in a total of approximately three hundred thousand non-Jewish immigrants.[16]

The mechanism which allowed this vast non-Jewish immigration is precisely the law whose purpose was to ensure the Jewish nature of the state. The breakdown of the Soviet Union was quickly followed by a mini-mass exodus. The particularly liberal wording of the Law of Return made Israel one of the most accessible choices for immigration. Moreover, the fact that the Israeli government not only accepted these immigrants with open arms, but also provided them with a package of aid and benefits acted as further incentive. Consequently, entire families whose Judaism was determined by the religious identity of a distant relative passed the immigration criteria and immigrated under the Law of Return.

One of the consequences of this phenomenon has been the emergence of the most radical and far-reaching debates surrounding the law since it was passed in 1951. Spurred on by differing agendas, politicians and groups from both the right and the left of the political spectrum started to question the rationale as well as the efficacy of the law. In its newly emerging function as a central boundary mechanism, the fact that non-Jews managed to permeate that boundary was indicative of a dysfunctioning of the law. While the ultra-orthodox demanded increased control through the inclusion of a clause defining a Jew as one who is a Jew by halachic law, others were quite willing to abandon the entire enterprise. The reason behind this logic was that doing away with the law entirely would remove authority from the Ministry of Interior to determine *who is a Jew*, and return it to its rightful owner, the Ministry of Religion (always controlled by a member of one of the religious parties).

On the left, the willingness to discuss the abolishment of the law was spurred on by a different agenda. Increasingly sectors within the electorate have developed quite articulate secular interests. These range from former-Soviet immigrants, to traditional labor Zionists who despair of the intense right wing religio-nationalist politics of the Likud. The growing tendency of the right wing to rely on the religious parties for support led, between 1977–1992 to a gradual encroachment on the quasi-secular nature of society. Secular Israelis became increasingly militant in their demands and their tactics. Their eventual support for doing away with the law was sure to come.

The most ardent support however for this demand came from the Israeli-Palestinian politicians themselves. In December of 1999, MK Muhammad Baraka from the Hadash Party (a communist, Jewish-Arab list), submitted two legislative proposals, the first was to cancel the Law of Return, and the second was the proposed Basic Law: Equality of the Arab Population.[17] The bill calls for recognition of the rights of the "Arab citizens of Israel," based on the principle of equality. It includes sections which refer to equality and the banning of discrimination, national identity, and affirmative action. In addition it calls for the right of the minority to "promote its Arab-Palestinian national identity," and to base Arab education on "the values of the Palestinian, Arab, and human culture." While the main message of the proposed bill is to strengthen the legislative principle of equality, the particularistic viewpoint of the law—identifying and singling out a specific ethnic group—is tantamount to acknowledging the fact that Israel is a multicultural and not uni-national state. Moreover, acknowledging the special rights of Palestinians in a Basic Law is a reflection of those special rights of the Jews enshrined in the Law of Return. The absence of any reference to Israel as a Jewish state is blatant and obvious, and the very fact that this type of proposal was not banned is further proof that a specific limitation on the rights of political participation is not enforced.[18]

PROPERTY RIGHTS: WHOSE LAND IS IT?

The establishment of a Jewish state was premised upon two goals: defining and securing mechanisms to allow for Jewish immigration, and to secure the ownership of the land which was intended to house the immigrants. If the first premise was later institutionalized and politicized through the Law of Return, the latter was made possible first through the acquisition—and later through the expropriation—of land, as well as defining the legal mechanisms for securing perpetual ownership. The acquisition of land, as political geographer Oren Yiftachel writes, represents the primary mechanism of the "Judaizing project."[19] Part and parcel of the Zionist project, from the outset, was not merely establishing a safe haven for Jews, but establishing a Jewish homeland. Nationalism presented itself as the savior: saving the Jewish soul from assimilation in non-Jewish societies, saving the Jewish body from the violence of anti-Semitism, and saving the very land upon which the Jews were to be settled. "Geulat hakarakh" (redemption of the land) evolved into a central Zionist slogan, in its campaign to purchase land for the purpose of Jewish settlement. The mere act of acquisition was hence put not merely in commercial terms of transaction, but sanctified: purchasing land became a central nationalist mission. Thus, the varying processes which together brought about the massive transfer of land from Palestinian ownership to Jewish ownership was uni-directional and final.[20]

Hence, control over the land of the state of Israel was seen, in both the pre- and post-independence phases, as a national goal of primary importance. With the signing of the armistice agreement in 1949, however, Israel gained sovereignty over the land but did not attain ownership. This paradoxical situation resulted in extensive land expropriation by the state authorities.[21] It is beyond the scope of this study to deal with the important issue of land: however, much excellent scholarship has recently emerged on the subject.[22] There are a number of legal statutes which were used in order to expropriate Arab land. These include, primarily, the Absentees' Property Law of 1950 and the Land Acquisition (Validation of Acts and Compensation) Law of 1953. Also utilized were certain British Mandatory Laws such as the General Land Expropriation Law passed in 1943 as well as Emergency Regulation 125.[23] All in all, it is difficult to arrive at an accurate figure which denotes exactly how much land was expropriated; the figures range from three hundred fifty thousand dunams to one million. With the help of these laws, the state of Israel managed to recreate a reality in which, in addition to sovereignty over the land, they gained ownership as well. Indeed, today, more than fifty years after the war of 1948, the state still owns more than 90 percent of land in Israel. This, incidentally, implies that neither Arab nor Jewish citizens of the state own much of their own land; as I explain below, even Jews are reduced, in most cases, to the status of lessees of land in their own country.

The various emergency regulations with which Israel expropriates land are used almost exclusively against Arab claims of ownership. While employed extensively during the first years of independence, during which most of the land was attained, periodic expropriation continues up until today. This type of expropriation relies mainly on the security clause. Two examples should suffice.

In 1976 the Israeli government announced its intention to expropriate roughly one hundred thousand dunams of land in the heavily Palestinian-populated region of the upper Galilee. The area was called "area 9." The announcement resulted in violent conflict between the army and the Palestinian residents. Six Palestinians were killed and dozens wounded. As a result of the public uproar a compromise was reached. The event, however, has been commemorated by Palestinians in Israel ever since as "Land Day," and is observed every year with mass demonstrations. Indeed, Land Day was created as the first separate day of commemoration devised exclusively by Palestinians in Israel. The first ever Israeli Palestinian monument was erected in Sakhnin to commemorate those killed in the demonstrations.[24] Largely in response to the emotional intensity aroused by this incident, the Israeli government ceased its policy of massive land expropriation.

My second example illustrates, however, how massive land expropriation was merely replaced by a more piecemeal expropriation, as well as by an implicit policy refusing authorization of any additional building or expansion of existing Palestinian villages and towns. This example concerns the planned expropriation of a few thousand dunams adjacent to the Palestinian city of Um el Fahm in the Wadi-Ara region. As in Sakhnin, the land was officially expropriated for military purposes. However, rumors abounded about the intention of the Ministry of Housing to build a new Jewish town (Iyron) on the land—as part of the government plan to "judaise" Wadi-Ara. The announced expropriation as well as the above mentioned rumors prompted Palestinian leaders to stage a peaceful demonstration on the land for a number of weeks. During a scheduled demonstration on September 27, 1998 the violence escalated, and in their effort to quell the demonstration the Israeli police wounded hundreds of Palestinians, and arrested hundreds more. The excessive violence was evident in the shooting at a school which led to the wounding of a number of children.[25]

The different emergency regulations which grant the Israeli state the legal backing in the majority of these cases of expropriation, are, as I argued, almost exclusively enacted against Palestinian claims. Nonetheless, they are not, in and of themselves, institutionally discriminatory. In other words, the emergency regulations accord the state freedom to expropriate land (and also housing, means of transportation, etc.) from any citizen of the state under the rationale of "security emergency." They do not, however, accord the state the legal right to discriminate between Jewish and non-Jewish citizens in terms of land and property. This right is accorded to the state by the charters of the so-called national institutions: the Jewish Agency, the World Zionist organization, and most particularly, the Jewish National Fund.

Israeli Collective National
Identity and Differential Property Rights

The Jewish National Fund (JNF) was established in 1901 to purchase land in Palestine for the purpose of Jewish settlement. It was established initially as an official organ of the Zionist Movement, but was later on registered as an official company. While in the beginning it purchased land from the Ottoman Empire, following World War I and the dismantling of that Empire, land was brought from private and communal Arab owners for the express purpose of Jewish settlement. However, in line with the collectivist sentiment of the Zionist Movement at the time, the land purchased was not transferred to Jews in the form of private property, but rather, it was to be "the perpetual property of the Jewish people" and was thus parceled out through a system of leasing. In the first years of the state, in addition to the land that had been purchased by the JNF prior to independence (approximately 936,000 dunams), the government sold much of the land it had appropriated from the Arabs both during and after the war, to the JNF. In 1949, 101,942 dunams were sold (98.5 percent of which were rural—agricultural—lands); in October 1950, 1,271,734 dunams were sold (again, most was agricultural land). By the end of 1951, the JNF had acquired over three and a half million dunams of land.[26]

In 1953, the Jewish National Fund Law was passed which transferred title to these lands to an equivalent Israeli company called the Keren Kayemet

Le'Israel. These lands were to be administered in the spirit of the charter of the JNF which clearly stated that all lands were held "for the purpose of settling Jews."[27] This has long been interpreted as meaning that no Keren Kayemet land would be leased out to non-Jews. By the late 1950s, along with the Keren Kayemet lands, the state owned over 90 percent of the land of Israel.

In 1960, a law was passed whereby all land in Israel was to be administered by the Israel Land Administration (including, of course, the JNF lands). After this law was passed, a formal covenant was signed between the government and the JNF which established the terms under which the land was to be administered in the future. According to this covenant,

> All state lands must be administered according to the principle that land is not sold, but is leased according to the land policy fixed by the Israel Lands Council. JNF lands must also be administered in accordance with the memorandum and articles of association of the JNF.[28]

By the end of the year 2000, approximately 80 percent of Israeli land administered by the Israel Land Administration (ILA) was originally JNF land.[29] As such, it was (and remains) administered "in accordance with the articles of association of the JNF," the implication being that these lands cannot be leased out to non-Jews. This has severe implications for the Palestinian citizens of the state.

First, none of the formerly Jewish National Fund lands can be leased to Palestinians. Thus, to illustrate, the Palestinian population of Israel, which constitutes 18 percent of the population, owns less than one million dunam, less than half of what is owned by the Jewish agricultural settlements, which constitute 5 percent of the population. Moreover, owners of private homes built on Jewish National Fund lands cannot sell their houses to non-Jewish buyers. Each sale must be authorized by the ILA and, in the case of non-Jews, the right to sell (or actually the right to transfer the lease) is denied.

In addition, the majority of the remaining land is owned by the state and administered by the ILA. The leasing of this land to Palestinian citizens, while permissible, is intensely problematic. Many of the guidelines that regulate the leasing of public lands to individuals, for both settlement and agricultural purposes, are ideological. Given the ideological emphasis on "salvation" and "redemption," it is not surprising that since the establishment of the state in 1948, despite the sixfold increase in the Palestinian population, no new Palestinian rural or urban settlements have been established. Hence, Palestinian municipalities control less than 2 percent of all land controlled by municipalities in Israel.[30] The Israeli authorities are also very quick to apply the unrealistic regulations concerning building expansion in existing settlements, and to apply these regulations in a clearly discriminatory fashion.

Thus, for example, in the 1990s, 96 percent of the buildings destroyed by the state as a result of illegal construction were owned by Palestinian citizens.[31]

To conclude, the significance of this clause goes far beyond the amount of Israeli land administered by its terms. The right to ownership, included in the list of natural rights by most classical theorists, has long been acknowledged as one of the pillars of democratic society. Indeed, it has often been seen as the primary motivation for establishing democratically run societies. This natural right is also hailed by the Zionist movement as central. For this reason, the non-Jewish citizens of Israel, being excluded from the primary core nation, are denied the natural right to equally free ownership of property.

By the end of the 1990s the judaising project reached a curious crossroads. On the one hand, acts of expropriation continued. The above-mentioned case in Um el Fahm is but one example. Expropriation, the refusal to authorize building expansion, and additional Palestinian settlements, as well as the continued refusal to acknowledge the right of return of even the very publicized and accepted cases of the border villages of Biram and Ikrit are all testimony to the continuing judaising project.[32] At the same time, the turn of the new millenium witnessed a surprising series of events that could be seen as heralding a different approach.

At the beginning of the year 2000, the foreign policy of Israel was involved with two issues of great significance to the question of land. The first was the question of what seemed to be the imminent signing of a peace treaty with Syria, and the second was the withdrawal of Israeli military forces from the security zone in southern Lebanon. In the first case the promised peace treaty had not been signed by the year 2000, and fears concerning a possible withdrawal from the Golan Heights had not materialized. In the second case, the withdrawal took place ahead of time, amidst general mayhem and confusion, and resulted in the influx of approximately six thousand soldiers from the South Lebanese Army.[33] These two events served to highlight the issue of land and land ownership.

During the same period when Israel seemed to be in the process of consolidating its physical boundaries, the Israeli political institutions were engaged in opening up venues for a dual-directional process of land ownership transfer. I said earlier that the process of transferring land ownership from Arab (Palestinian) to Jewish hands which began at the turn of the century and accelerated greatly after 1948, was strictly uni-directional, and, for that matter final. In 2000, this finality began to exhibit signs of flexibility.

In general, the project of judaizing the land had become so totally internalized politically as to seem entirely congruent with the project of "nationalizing" the land. In other words, the dedication of land to exclusive Jewish settlement, and the stifling of any attempts to expand the settlement of Israeli Palestinians on this land was understood, by the Jewish citizens of Israel as equated with the notion of nationalizing land, or promoting national development. This of course is merely one manifestation—albeit a prominent one both materially and symbolically—of the interchangeable nature of Jewish and Israeli. As I mentioned above, the discrepancy between Arab and Jewish ownership of land remained high, as did (does) the inherently unequal recognition of Palestinian interests as valid in defining and articulating the settlement and building policy of the state.

At the same time, certain events defy the narrative described up till now. Most significantly, the Supreme Court, on March 5, 2000, reached a pathbreaking decision concerning the right to purchase land, and the status of the principle of equality. In the case of *Kaadan vs the Yishuv Katzir*, the Supreme Court, led by Supreme Court Chief Justice Aharon Barak, in a majority 4–1 decision, ruled that the state of Israel is forbidden to discriminate between Jews and Arabs in the allocation of its lands, even if the discriminatory allocation is done through the Jewish Agency and not directly through the Israel Land Administration.

The ruling referred to the specific case of the Kaadan couple who, in 1995, approached the settlement of Katzir, and applied to purchase a plot of land there. The settlement was established, by the Jewish Agency, as part of the seven star plan to judaise the Wadi Ara area on land that it received from the Israel Land Administration. In accordance with the ideological goals of the Jewish Agency, the Katzir settlement accepted only Jews. When the Kaadan couple applied, their application was denied on the grounds of their national identity. In their case against the state, the Kaadan's argued that under these types of discriminatory conditions, the allocation of land to the Jewish Agency by the state is illegal, because it discriminates against the Palestinian citizens. The Jewish Agency argued that the proclaimed goal of judaising areas in which Jewish settlement is "diluted"—i.e., predominantly Arab—constitutes a legitimate goal, and is, moreover, entrenched in the law and in the contract between the agency and the state. The court defined the dilemma as follows:

> The state allocated land to the Jewish agency. The agency established a settlement on this land (rural community settlement). This was done through the establishment of a communal association. The agency aims to settle Jews in Israel. The association accepts only Jews. Hence, a non-Jew is unable to purchase this state land. Under these conditions—given the particular circumstances—under which the state decides to allocate land to the agency, is the state's decision illegal due to the discriminatory outcomes vs a vs the Arabs?[34]

The Association for Civil Rights in Israel representing the Kaadan's argued that the ILA—by allocating land to discriminatory agencies—contradicts its commitment to act as a trustee for the entire citizen body and the residents of the state, and to act towards them equally. While the appeal to the court was entrenched in the supremacy of the principle of equality, the appellants were careful to note two central constraints to their argument:

1. They do not deny the Jewish character of the state, but argue that this is entrenched in laws such as the Law of Return—not property rights laws.
2. They do not deny the potential rights of groups to group rights. Hence they do not deny the right of a community to establish exclusive neighborhoods. These should apply in neighborhoods where the community has a high degree of solidarity and a high degree of collective characteristics to the community or settlement itself. This does not apply in Katzir.

In its ruling, the Supreme Court focused much of its argument on the supremacy of the principle of equality. The state is seen as obliged to adhere to the principle of equality in all its policies, even those implemented indirectly through intermediary institutions such as the national institutions.[35] Hence, discrimination is ruled illegal both directly and indirectly.

Furthermore, the ruling relies on the principle that the state, its institutions and workers are public trustees. The ruling assumes that the land of the state is public, and should therefore be distributed honestly and in accordance with the principle of equal opportunity. The court relied heavily on the Declaration of Independence, which obliges the state to establish "equal social and political rights towards all its citizens, with no difference of religion, race and sex." This ruling strengthens the status of the Declaration:

> Equality is one of the basic values of the state of Israel. Every authority in Israel including the state, its institutions and workers, must operate with equality towards the different individuals in the state . . . this is extrapolated from the Jewish and democratic nature of the state; this is derived from the principle of the rule of law in the state. Expression of this is to be found, among other places, in the Declaration of Independence: the state of Israel will maintain equal social and civic rights for all its citizens disregarding differences of religion, race and sex. . . .[36]

As was to be expected, the ruling created a tremendous uproar. From the right, politicians immediately initiated legislation which would prohibit the settlement of non-Jews on so-called "homeland lands," "property of the Jewish People," or simply Jewish land.[37] A vociferous, though short-lived public debate emerged in the media and in the parliament concerning the implications of the ruling, in which the imminent demise of Zionism was either applauded or bemoaned. As was the case with the Law of Return, the daily newspaper *Haaretz* printed an editorial on the day immediately following the ruling, in which it applauded the decision, and supported the declaration that discriminatory land distribution on the basis of nationality is illegal. The editorial emphasized that this welcomed emphasis on equality should not be taken as undermining Israel's Jewish identity.[38]

In response to the right wing attacks on the decision, Justice Barak, leading author of the ruling, defied accusations of being a "post-Zionist," and stated that by instituting equality as a principle which should guide Jewish-Arab relations in Israel he was implementing the spirit of Zionism: "the demand for equality in land distribution is a Zionist determination par excellence."[39]

Clearly, the significance of the ruling would depend on the extent to which its implications were seized and exploited by the Palestinians. The legal ground was prepared for demands for equal land allocation. One month after the decision, the Israeli press reported that the government and the Jewish Agency were laying down plans to allocate additional land for the expansion of existing Arab towns, and were seriously considering the establishment of the first Arab city in Israel. The proposal, initiated by MK Ahmed Tibi, had been planned for months, but with the Supreme Court ruling, seemed to garner legitimacy.

The response to this plan was indicative of the impact of converging factors. Then Minister of Housing Yitzhak Levi from the National Religious Party argued that the allocation of additional lands for Arab settlement was aimed at preventing the infiltration of Israeli Palestinians into existing Jewish settlements (which was the specific issue at hand in the Kaadan ruling).[40] Thus, as was the case with the Law of Return, conflicting political interests, from both the right and the left, brought about a convergent outcome: the allocation of additional land for Palestinians, and the inadvertent recognition of Israeli Palestinian interests as a legitimate part of the national interests.

Earlier, on March 27, Minister of Interior Natan Sharansky (from the Russian immigrant party Yisrael Bealiyah) declared his intention to transfer six hundred dunams from the municipal jurisdiction of Rosh Haayin (an Israeli Jewish city), to the jurisdiction of the neighboring Israeli Palestinian village of Kfar Kassem. This was the second unprecedented event of the same month: the transfer of lands from Jewish to Arab hands. The background to the case was the expropriation during the 1950s of land owned by residents of the village for military or security reasons. An investigative committee was established in 1995 at the request of the villagers, who demanded the return of these lands. They argued that the said lands were currently under jurisdiction of the neighboring Rosh Haayin, and were earmarked for the establishment of a new industrial park. Hence, the security reason was no longer valid. Explaining his decision Sharansky noted that:

> We are implementing social justice for the residents of Kfar Kassem. These are actually lands that were taken from the village, and now I decided to return them. Rosh Haayin has enough land for expansion, but Kfar Kassem doesn't.[41]

Hence, Sharansky's decision was motivated, as he himself testified, by the same motivation as the Kaadan decision, as were the plans for the Arab city—a desire to fortify the principle of equality, and promote "social justice."

POLITICAL RIGHTS:
THE RIGHT TO POLITICAL ASSOCIATION

According to Israeli political scientist Yoav Peled, Jews and Palestinians in Israel enjoy two different types of citizenship. The Jews, who are joined by a common goal, and who are able, within the context of the state, to promote the values of their own community, enjoy republican citizenship. Palestinians, on the other hand, who benefit from individually distributed civil and political rights, can partake in liberal citizenship, which precludes their ability to partake in any collective or community-defined good.[42] One of the test-cases for this distinction between types of citizenship is the right to political participation which, he argues, is severely limited in Israel for its Palestinian citizens.

In studies that are not devoted exclusively to the study of Israel, Israel is generally classified as a democracy. In Arendt Lijphart's classic study of democracy in divided societies, Israel is employed as a case, and hence categorized as a democracy that employs both majoritarian and consociational mechanisms.[43] The parameters which define democratic regimes are usually, as is the case with Lijphart, taken from Robert Dahl's classic study of polyarchy, and are focused on the different institutions established to maintain free and periodic elections, which serve as a mechanism of accountability. Hence, it is presumed, governments are accountable and will therefore preserve and protect individual rights.

Israel is able to enter into the category of democracies despite the fundamental inequalities elaborated upon above. This is the case because formally all Israeli citizens, Jews and non-Jews alike, enjoy full political rights, secured through the maintenance of a secret ballot, universal suffrage (over the age of eighteen), the right to political association, and the right to campaign freely.[44] Closer examination of the rules regulating political participation reveals an inherent and structural bias which results in discriminatory conditions for Palestinian citizens; a bias which, as was the case in the previous two discussions, was also subject to a revised assessment at the end of the 1990s.

The Fall and Rise of Palestinian Political Participation

The first attempt to organize politically by an independent Arab list was the case of el Ard. The group, officially called Usrat el Ard (family of the earth) was founded by two members of a local group called the Popular Front, which was banned by Ben-Gurion at the end of 1959. It started out by publishing weekly reports, aimed at Israeli Arabs, highly critical of Israeli policies, and encouraging Arabs to take their own issues in hand. They were identified as sympathetic to Arab Nationalism and to the Nasserite movement. Their publications were confiscated, and any attempt to locally organize lecture and study groups was met with severe objection from the Israeli authorities.[45] Finally, in 1964, the two founders announced the official establishment of the el-Ard movement, hoping to be able to organize Arab nationalists into a list which would run for the next Knesset elections. The District Commissioner refused to register their association on the grounds that it was unlawful in its aims.[46] They appealed to the Supreme Court which dismissed their petition. The basis for the ruling was that they intended, albeit implicitly, to convince people of their cause through "subversive and hostile activity" and that it was in line with "Arab nationalistic propaganda . . . urging the destruction of Israel . . ." el-Ard was subsequently declared an unlawful association.[47] This was also, it should be recalled, the heyday of military rule, during which all activity, and especially political activity, was severely regulated, supervised and curtailed.

The second case concerned the Socialist List, which was composed of many former el-Ard members, and which hoped to run for the elections to the Sixth Knesset in 1965. The chairman of the Central Elections Committee disqualified it. The grounds for the disqualification were that it was "an unlawful association, because its promoters deny the integrity of the State of Israel and its very existence."[48]

The list appealed the ruling, and the Supreme Court, in what came to be known as the *Yardor Decision*, denied the appeal. The substance of the leading opinion, that of Chief Justice Agranat, is significant. Essentially, he voiced the opinion that Israel was established not merely as a sovereign state, but as a Jewish state in Eretz Yisrael. And that:

> A list of candidates who reject the above fundamental principle, does not have the right, as a list, to participate in the elections for the House of Representatives . . .[49]

The underlying rationale was that no regime could authorize the existence of a group or movement which was intent on undermining the existence and raison d'etre of the regime. As such, the interpretation given to the opinion, that denying the Jewish existence and nature of the state was illegal, was but one way of comprehending a more general statement. The conclusive opinion on this matter would come twenty years later, with the Neiman case.

The Neiman case arose when the Central Elections Committee for the eleventh Knesset in 1984 decided to disqualify two lists—the Kach list, and the Progressive List for Peace (PLP). The first was banned on the basis of racial arguments promoted by its founder Rabbi Meir Kahane, and the rationale for banning the latter was that the list "believes in principles that endanger the . . . preservation of [Israel's] distinctiveness as a Jewish state . . ." The decision of the Committee was appealed by both lists. The PLP won its appeal, while the Kach list lost. In accepting the appeal, the judges implied that only lists dedicated to the *physical* destruction of the state would be deemed illegal. However, as a direct result of the Neiman case, the law governing political parties was altered in the form of an Amendment to the Basic Law: the Knesset (1985):

> A list of candidates shall not participate in the elections for the Knesset if its aims or actions, expressly or by implication, point to one of the following:
> 1. denial of the existence of the State of Israel as the state of the Jewish people.
> 2. denial of the democratic nature of the state.
> 3. incitement to racism.[50]

Undoubtedly, the implications of this amendment are more far-reaching than any previous court ruling, or, for that matter, legal statute. In essence, this amendment granted legal status not merely to Israel's existence as a Jewish state, but placed a legal boundary on the limits to free association and free speech. For the first time the Knesset put limits on political association which transcended the more acceptable "security" issues—i.e., the need to safeguard Israel's democracy from those who want to destroy it. Thus, the amendment implied that *redefining* Israel as a state which belongs to its citizens, is tantamount to attacking Israel's right to exist. Similarly, any list which put forward a bi-national arrangement to Arab-Jewish relations within Israel would be disqualified. The majority opinion of the Supreme Court was that the definition of Israel as a state of the Jewish people was dependent upon three characteristics: "a majority of Jews in the country; priority for Jews over other groups to return to their land; and a reciprocal relationship between the state and the Jews of the Diaspora."[51] Rejection of these characteristics automatically disqualified a political association from running for election.

Consequently, this definition of the basic norms which underlie the state of Israel goes against a most fundamental, even "sacred" tenet of democracy which posits the sovereignty of the citizens of the state. The notion of a state as a mechanism which exists to further the interests of its citizens is redefined, *legally*, so as to read that the state exists to further the interests of the member nation. Non-Jewish citizens of Israel do not qualify in this membership, and hence the inference is that Israel is not *their state*.

The first test case for the amendment came during the 1996 elections. Two lists registered to compete during these elections which should have been rejected on the basis of the first clause. These lists included Ahmed Tibi's list (later withdrawn), and Balad, headed by Azmi Bisharah. Then, in 1999, Balad registered once again, including Tibi as the number two choice after Bisharah. Moreover, Bisharah also competed as an independent candidate for the prime ministerial election. In all three cases, but particularly in the case of Bisharah, the ideological guidelines of the three respective platforms called for recognizing Israel as a state of all its citizens (hence rejecting or denying the definition of Israel as a Jewish state). Moreover, in all three cases requests were put forward to the formal parliament office to disqualify these lists on the basis of the said amendment. In the case of Bisharah's candidacy, the request was based on newspaper interviews in which Bisharah was quoted as stating his preference for an Israeli "state of all its citizens."[52]

All three lists were allowed to compete, and were not asked to redefine their ideological goals. This is particularly surprising because of the saliency of Bisharah's views, and the openness with which he presented them. It is common knowledge that Bisharah believes in the definition of Israel as a state of all its citizens, and indeed Bisharah is commonly cited as having coined the phrase. In addition, an acknowledged part of Bisharah's platform consists of granting autonomy to Israel's Palestinian citizens. Curiously, defense of Bisharah's candidacy was based on an argument which stated that his opinions were well known, and were included in the platforms of Balad which was never disqualified by the Knesset office. This argument was accepted.[53]

In general, the three electoral campaigns which took place during the 1990s were characterized by a plethora of Palestinian political parties, which spanned the entire political spectrum: Islamic, nationalist, secular, communist, and traditional. The dearth of Arab lists which characterized the first three decades of independence is long gone, as is the relatively submissive pattern of political participation. The increase in both the number and diversity of Palestinian political lists, although not matched by a comparative increase in the number of Palestinian MKs (the number of Palestinian members of parliament has remained at a steady 9–12 for the past twenty years) has resulted in an increasingly active pattern of legislative participation. During the fifteenth parliament in particular, leaders of both the Communist Party and of Balad have been particularly active in proposing legislation aimed at improving the condition of the Palestinian citizens, as well as weakening the Jewish bias of the state. In 1999 alone Palestinian MKs proposed legislation aimed at, for example, abolishing the Jewish National Fund and the Jewish Agency, abolishing the Law of Return, equalizing citizenship laws, recognizing the Palestinian citizens as a national minority and recognizing Israel as a multicultural state.

Hence, the reluctance of the government to enforce the Amendment to the Basic Law along with a dramatic change in the pattern of political participation seems to have initiated a slightly new reality. In this emergent reality Palestinians are increasingly acting towards the attainment of their own collective goals, and their own definition of the public good. Possibly, a reassessment of Peled's aforementioned argument will be required.

NOTES

1. For an encompassing discussion see, Kretzmer, *The Legal Status of the Arabs in Israel* (Boulder, Colo.: Westview Press, 1990). See also, Lustick, *Arabs in the Jewish State* (Austin, Texas: University of Texas Press, 1980), chap. 2, and Elia Zureik, *Palestinians in Israel: A Study of Internal Colonialism* (London: Routledge and Kegan Paul, 1979); Alouf Hareven, *Retrospect and Prospects: Full and Equal Citizenship?"* (Jerusalem: Sikkuy, 1998); *Legal Violations of Arab Minority Rights in Israel, A Report on Israel's Implementation of the International Convention on the Elimination of all Forms of Racial Discrimination* (Shfaram: Adalah the Legal Center for Arab Minority Rights in Israel, March 1998).

2. The discrimination against Palestinians is also manifested in a series of indirect mechanisms. One of the main indirect mechanisms of discrimination is the military. The Defense Service Law does not discriminate against non-Jews. However, recruitment is left to the discretion of the recruiting officers. Hence, since the establishment of the state, Palestinians have not been recruited. The implications of this are widespread. For example, many of the financial benefits in the country—ranging from real estate mortgages to university fellowships are often limited to veterans. In addition, most government jobs require security clearance which is unavailable to Palestinian citizens.

3. For background concerning the disbanding of the Constituent Assembly, and the debate concerning the writing of a constitution see, *Knesset Protocol*, 1949–1950; Amnon Rubenstein, *The Constitutional Law of Israel*, 3d. ed. (Tel Aviv: Schocken, 1980) [Hebrew]; Ze'ev Segal, *Israeli Democracy: Constitutional Law* (Tel Aviv: Ministry of Defense, 1988) [Hebrew].

4. Kretzmer, *The Legal Status*, p. 8.

5. Kretzmer, *The Legal Status*, p. 8.

6. Thus, according to Kretzmer, "Equality before the law is a basic principle of Israel's legal system . . . [This principle] has grown to become a well-rooted, binding legal rule." *The Legal Status*, 9. For the centrality of equality in the legal system, see also Amnon Rubenstein, *The Constitutional Law of Israel*.

7. See Gideon Doron and Michael Harris, *Public Policy and Electoral Reform* (Lanham, Md.: Lexington Books, 1999).

8. See Ruth Gavison, *Israel's Electoral Revolution* (Jerusalem: Israel Democracy Institute, 1998).

9. Basic Law: Human Dignity, prolegomena.

10. Over the past few years, a number of scholars have addressed the tension between Israel's democratic and Jewish self ascribed identities. For two opposing views see, Oren Yiftachel, "'Ethnocracy': The Politics of Judaizing Israel/Palestine," *Constellations* 6, no. 3 (September 1999): 364–91; Ruth Gavison, *A Jewish Democratic State* (Jerusalem: Israel Democracy Institute, 1999).

11. Law of Return, 1950, Section 4. "Oleh" literally translates into "ascender". In Zionist rhetoric, the concept Oleh was used (and in Israel is still used today) to describe the process of Jewish immigration to Israel. Hence, while a Jewish immigrant to Israel will be called an Oleh, a non-Jewish immigrant is "merely" an immigrant.

12. The different ways in which individuals gained citizenship included naturalization, residency, and birth. Over the years the distinctions have been significantly diminished. For details concerning the history of the transformation, see, Kretzmer, *The Legal Status*, chap. 3.

13. 5710 Hatzaot Hok, 194.

14. See *Rufheisen v. Minister of Interior*, High Court of Justice 62/72, decision 2428.

15. See *Shalit vs. Minister of Interior*, High Court of Justice 68/58, decision XXIII (2) 477; and *Shalit v. Minister of Interior* 72/18, decision XXVI (1) 334.

16. The percent of non-Jews amongst the immigrants rose from 16.7 in 1994, to 19.5 in 1995, to 22.7 in 1996, to 27.2 in 1997 and 32.1 in January 1998. See *Haaretz* 27/10/98, page 3b. See also Ian S. Lustick, "Israel as a Non-Arab State: The Political Implications of Mass Immigration of Non-Jews," *Middle East Journal* 53, no. 3 (summer 1999): 417–33.

17. The proposed bill ignited a sharp controversy when it was placed on the Knesset floor. (Proposed legislation #2290, by MK Muhammad Baraka.)The controversy resulted mainly from the introductory clause of the bill which defined Israel as a "democratic and multicultural state," and not as "democratic and Jewish." It was on these grounds that the parliament's legal advisors advised canceling any discussion concerning the bill, on the grounds that the bill proposes to deny Israel's existence as a Jewish state (a declaration which, based on the aforementioned amendment to the Basic Law: The Knesset, is deemed illegal). On January 4, however, the presidency of the parliament decided to authorize debate on the bill, reflecting the recommendation of the speaker of the parliament MK Burg (*Haaretz*, 4/1/00). Ultimately, the bill which was presented to the parliament was rewritten, omitting the controversial statement.

18. Whether or not it is an indication of a weakening of the resolve—is up to debate. Special mention of this issue was given in a report by Deborah Sontag, "Debate in Israel: Jewish state or Now a Multicultural state?" *New York Times* (December 6, 1999).

19. See Oren Yiftachel, "'Ethnocracy': The Politics of Judaizing Israel/Palestine," *Constellations* 6, no. 3 (September 1999): 390. (364–91).

20. Yiftachel, "'Ethnocracy.'"

21. See amongst other sources, Kretzmer, chap. 4 and Jiryis, 75–102.

22. On the general circumstances during the War of Independence, and directly following it, see Benny Morris, *The Birth of the Palestinian Refugee Problem, 1947–1949* (Cambridge: Cambridge University Press, 1987). On the events of 1949

see, Tom Segev, *1949: The First Israelis* (Jerusalem: Domino Press, 1984), chap. 1. [Hebrew].

23. For surveys of these laws see, Eli Rekhess, *Israeli Arabs and the Expropriation of Lands in the Galilee* (Tel Aviv: Shiloah Institute, 1977) [Hebrew]; Don Peretz, *Israel and the Palestinian Arabs* (Washington, D.C.: The Middle East Institute, 1956); Sabari, "The Legal Status of Israel's Arabs," *Iyunei Mishpat* 2, no. 568 (1972) [Hebrew].

24. See Tom Segev, "Independence is el-Nakba," *Haaretz* 27 March 1998.

25. Deborah Sontag, "Israeli Arabs and the Police Clash in North on Land Plan," *The New York Times* (September 28, 1998), section A, page 6.

26. See A. Granott, *The Land Issue in Palestine* (Jerusalem: 1936); E. Orni, *Land in Israel: History, Policy; Administration, Development* (Jerusalem: Jewish National Fund, 1981).

27. Orni, *Land in Israel*, 22.

28. Orni, *Land in Israel*, 22.

29. See "After the Crisis: New Directions for Government Policy towards the Arab Minority in Israel," p. 17.

30. Meron Benvenisti, "The Last Zionists," *Haaretz* (1 October 1998): page B1.

31. See Alouf Hareven, 1995.

32. Biram and Ikrit were awarded the right to return by the Israeli Supreme Court as early as 1951. Nonetheless, the Israeli governments have refused to acknowledge this right. See Sarah Ozacky-Lazar, *Ikrit and Biram*, Survey no. 10, (Givat Haviva: The Institute for Arab Studies, February 1993).

33. See coverage in the Israeli press, *Haaretz*, April 20–21, 2000.

34. *Haaretz*, 9 March 2000, p. b3.

35. The Jewish Agency, The Jewish National Fund, The World Zionist Agency.

36. *Haaretz*, 9 March 2000, section b, p. 3.

37. *Haaretz*, 9 March 2000, section b, p. 3; and *Maariv*, 9 March 2000, p. 4.

38. "Discrimination is Prohibited in Land," *Haaretz*, 9 March 2000: section b, p. 1.

39. "Justice Barak . . ." *Haaretz*, 22 May 2000: internet edition.

40. "For the First Time: Considering a New Arab City," *Haaretz*, 10 April 2000, internet edition.

41. "600 Dunams from the lands of Rosh Haayin . . .", *Haaretz*, 29 March 2000, internet edition.

42. Yoav Peled, "Ethnic Democracy and the Legal Construction of Citizenship," *American Political Science Review* 86, no. 2, pp. 432–42.

43. See Arendt Lijphart, *Democracies; Patterns of Majoritarian and Consensual Government in Twenty-One Countries* (New Haven, Conn.: Yale University Press, 1984).

44. Compare with the requirements of polyarchy as noted by Robert Dahl, *Polyarchy, Participation and Opposition* (New Haven, Conn.: Yale University Press, 1977).

45. See details in Jiryis, *The Arabs in Israel*, pp. 187–90.

46. A District Commissioner in Israel is an officer employed by the Interior Ministry. He is a legal heir of the Mandatory Commissioner, although much of the essence of his responsibilities have been altered by the state of Israel.

47. See Jiryis, *The Arabs in Israel*, p. 190. For the history of El-Ard see also, Benziman and Mansour, *Subtenants*, chap. 8; Zureik, *Palestinians in Israel*.

48. *Yardor v. Central Elections Committee for the Sixth Knesset* (1965) 19 P.D. III 365.

49. The opinion of Judge Agranat in *Yardor v. Central Elections Committee for the Sixth Knesset* (1965) 19 P.D. III, 387.

50. Section 7a of Basic Law: The Knesset.

51. This interpretation is taken from Kretzmer, *The Legal Status*, p. 30.

52. According to Lawyer Hasan Jabarin, head of the Adalah Organization, the moment Bisharah's views were recorded in Hebrew language newspapers, they gained legitimacy. The reproduction of radical political positions in accepted Hebrew newspapers throws them into the mainstream. (Lecture at Ben Gurion University, Be'er Sheva, Israel, December 6, 2000).

53. Hassan Jabarin, ed., *Adalah Notebooks*, issue 1, (winter 1999), p.45

Part Three

The Symbolic Contours of Identity

Collective national identity can be mapped legislatively and symbolically. As part two argued, the status of minorities is first and foremost reflected in the distribution of fundamental rights, including property rights, the right to political participation and rights of belonging. Any analysis of membership in national identities must however, include a review of the symbolic representations of the identity as well.

The cultural and social impact of symbolic representation is significant both for those excluded and for those included. Often the contours of national membership are visible to those included only through what I have called the symbolic matrix: the monuments, the stamps, the songs, and the texts serve as perpetual reminders of the boundaries of the group to which we belong. Taken together, these symbols constitute the landscape of identity. For the state, this type of nomenclature is of extreme significance: reinforcing legitimacy through culture is a primary political act, and the symbolic representations of culture are a central vehicle.

Finally, the national struggles of minorities often focus a seemingly inordinate amount of energy on symbols, the reason being the tremendous emotional potency symbolic representation carries for the generation and strengthening of identity. In this part the national symbolic matrixes of the two cases, Israel and the United States are reviewed. To what extent was the legal and national exclusion reflected in these symbols? Was the shift in membership illustrated in the symbolic matrix, and in what ways? These questions are explored through a systematic analysis of both written and commemorative symbols.

Chapter Six

Reinventing the Invisible Man: African Americans and the American Symbolic Indexes of Identity

By the end of the twentieth century, symbols of African American heritage had been incorporated by most, if not all, aspects and avenues of American public culture. From literature and schoolbooks, through stamps, monuments, and holidays, the American national symbolic matrix had acknowledged the African American as an integral, if not central, part of the American national heritage.

This, however, was not always the case. For the first one hundred years following Reconstruction, American heritage, as it was symbolically represented in American public culture, incorporated no mention or illustration of African Americans, save from periodic, and usually degrading, representations of slavery. In social studies and history texts, Africans Americans were avoided, and the few monuments and stamps dedicated to them were either a product of private initiative, or were so sparse as to be unnoticeable. In this chapter I examine two main categories of symbolic representation, and compare the extent of African American representation prior to and following the Civil Rights decade.

NATIONAL IDENTITY AND NATIONAL SYMBOLS

The fundamental essence of national identity, or of any group identity for that matter, implies a sense of *sameness* (i.e., identity) which transcends both time and space. This *sameness* is achieved through the elaboration of a shared, or collective, memory. It is the collective memory that serves as the vehicle of the national imagination that Anderson identified as the essence of nationhood. National identities, however, as Gillis has noted, are not something we think about, but rather something we think with.[1] To achieve this something, collective national memories are projected upon reality through an elaborate system of physical representations, which are known as symbols.

Symbols have long been acknowledged as playing a very important role in the construction of national identity. Indeed, taken together, the form and content of national symbols can be treated as indexes of national membership.[2] Two primary categories of national symbols can be identified: written symbols that present a narrative of the official history of the nation through a variety of written texts, and commemorative symbols that commemorate the central figures of that history.[3] National narratives tell the official version of the nation's story. This story involves a time-line, beginning with the birth of the nation, and plowing through the tragic and glorious events in the nation's history. The narrative also provides a mapping of the story's central characters—heroes, leaders, and mythic figures. The backdrop of the story is the community and its fundamental characteristics—religion, race, language, and so on.

The images triggered by the symbols cumulatively make for the memories of the national past. Commonly, one will encounter monuments, or other commemorative events that stand for, or symbolize, some event of heroism, or contrarily—tragedies—that are presented as central to the nation's history. The Battle of Kosovo in 1389 in which the Ottomans defeated the Serbs, was one of the main symbols around which Serbs garnered nationalist sentiment in their involvement in the war against Bosnia-Herzegovina—despite the fact that it commemorated a humiliating defeat rather than a glorious victory.

Echoing Renan's famous observation concerning the centrality of national amnesia to national memory, what is *not* symbolized is as significant as what is. The existence of a stamp in memory of Lou Gehrig—an American baseball player—is significant to the construction of the American national past (and to the American national identity). Similarly, as the fact that representations of both African Americans in the American case and Palestinians in the Israeli case were absent from their respective national stamps for so long was a very significant statement about their membership in the national identity.

As discussed above, national identities are constructed and often reconstructed entities. As such, their commemorative representations frequently undergo processes of reconstruction so as to conform to the dominant interests and rationale of the time. Reconstruction is most likely to occur during times of crisis. During such times, one can witness heightened commemorative activity and even, to cite Pierre Nora, the establishment of new cites of memory.[4] In this chapter, I argue that the events of the 1960s transformed this decade into such a period. The crisis which erupted impacted perhaps most obviously on the organization of interests that in turn dictated a reconstruction in the contours of the national identity. Evidence of this is particularly apparent in the main arenas of memory construction.

AMERICAN NATIONAL IDENTITY: THE WRITTEN TEXTS

The process of writing the past, in the formal framework of history books, is perhaps the most direct way of constructing a national memory. The textbook offers the quintessential means of transmitting the national narrative without the need to symbolize or codify meanings. Thus, the writing and rewriting of history, through conventional history books, and more significantly, textbooks, is a classic symbolic vehicle. The history book can be seen as the biography of the nation. The vivid images that people retain of a nation's past are drawn from its pages. Much has been written about the theoretical and practical objectivity of the historian, and the process involved in the selection of which facts to include or exclude in the writing of any kind of history.[5] Public furors will occasionally occur around new textbooks. This happened in Israel during the post-Oslo period when new history textbooks were introduced into the high school curriculum. The historical narrative presented by these books seemed, to their critics, to assign too little attention to the military arena, and to be too "even-sided" on the Palestinian refugee question. Thus, emphasizing certain aspects of a nation's history determines the portrait and identity of that nation. An additional simple yet fundamental aspect of this vast debate is who is included in the nation's history, and who is excluded. In other words, when one speaks of a nation's history, whose history is one referring to? About whom is one reading in the books?

Textbooks

Many changes occurred in American society in the aftermath of the 1960s. In textbooks published up until this time, American collective identity was treated with a large degree of complacency and passive disregard. Discussions of American identity, when they came up, revolved around ideological questions of the day, rather then self-conscious discussions of identity. The 1960s ushered in a new era of skepticism and challenge, in which discussions of identity became a central, and very conscious sphere of intellectual activity. The fundamental pluralist vision of a society composed of assimilating minority groups was questioned and criticized. All at once the traditional Rockwellian self portrait that Americans likened themselves to was shattered, and a less idyllic, more realistic image began to emerge.

The changes introduced during that time are multi-faceted, yet they center around one theme: the ethnic/national context of American society. The very way in which Americans perceived how they were incorporated together as Americans, and how they contemplated the relationship between the whole and its constituent parts was subject to a fundamental rethinking. The change in the relationship between African Americans and American society constituted one of the most dramatic of these changes.

Early textbooks, from the first decades of the century, rarely mention African Americans, and when they do, the references are imbued with racist implications and commentary. While by the 1950s the blatant racism gradually disappeared, African Americans were still, at that time, portrayed as part of American history only in their capacity as slaves. Hence, it is actually slavery, as an institution, which is discussed and not the group itself. They were neither perceived as, nor did they constitute, an integral part of the American collective identity. Classic texts of the 1950s, such as, David Saville Muzzey's, *A History of our Country* would begin their discussion of American society by saying, "leaving aside the Negro and Indian population," and would proceed to do just that.[6] Ralph Ellison's *Invisible Man* was an apt metaphor: African Americans—along with their excluded partners—were quite literally invisible.[7] In general, while racism is not explicitly condoned, it is explained:

> And since northerners saw so few of them they began to think of the Negroes as persons like themselves . . . the Southerners, who were so used to seeing thousands of them, grew to think that Negroes had been created to work for the white men.[8]

The yearbooks of the National Council for Social Studies tell a very revealing story (NCSS).[9] Published periodically by the National Education Association (NEA) in Washington, D.C., these yearbooks serve as pedagogical guides for high school educators. They provide extensive bibliographies, and summaries of the new developments in the various sub-fields of American history. As guides published by the NEA, they are read by thousands of educators, and are of great influence in the determination of school curriculum. The yearbook published in 1961, for example, is structured chronologically. It has seventeen chapters, starting with colonial history, and ending with contemporary issues such as the cold war. Its self declared aim was "to encourage critical thinking through the interpretive approach."[10]

As is expected, it states in its general introduction, that "the slavery dispute, the Civil War and Reconstruction constituted a three decade long crisis, the sharpest and gravest through which the nation has gone."[11] Out of a three hundred page volume, only three pages are devoted to this "gravest" crisis. Two additional pages are devoted to a discussion of "local politics and the

Negro." The history of the African Americans, their role in the development of American history, African American cultural and political figures—none of these, or similar issues, are even remotely related to. The NEA guide is typical in this aspect of most pre-1960s textbooks.[12] Classic textbooks that were reprinted in numerous editions, and used in classrooms across the country, such as Todd and Curti's *America's History*, and West and West's *The American People*, are cases in point.

On the other hand, take the 1973 publication of the NCSS. The volume, written by the authors of the 1961 yearbook, is divided into four parts, with the second part entitled "Race and Nationality in American History." Within this part an entire chapter is devoted to African Americans which explores African American history, economics, and sociology. In addition, other chapters—on slavery, Reconstruction, the Depression and domestic politics—refer frequently to African Americans. Thus, in this volume, published barely one decade later, African Americans have become both an integral part of American society, as well as a distinct part worthy of extensive discussion.[13]

While the change proved to be a gradual one, it is fair to say that all textbooks published from the mid-1960s begin to incorporate and reflect this change. The change is reflected in three central dimensions—quantitative, qualitative, and contextual. I shall discuss each in turn.

The first dimension, the quantitative one, is the most blatant and obvious and is manifested in two ways: first, in the sheer number of so-called African American "exemplars" discussed and portrayed in textbooks, and second, in the length of the narrative devoted to African Americans. Up till and throughout the fifties, the only African American exemplars were Booker T. Washington and Dred Scott (always pictorially presented with his cross-eyed gaze). Clearly the reason that portrayals were limited to these did not reflect a lack of African American personages worthy of representation, but rather that these two constituted two legitimate token Negroes whose representation did not threaten the White hegemony portrayed in the books. Washington's representation strengthened the notion of the "good Blacks"—similar in connotation to the idea of the "good Arab" prevalent in the pre-Oslo Israeli discourse. Good Blacks—much like good Arabs, were those who sought to live up to the White (or Jewish) notion of Black-White relations, and to the values and ideals set up by White society for Blacks (and Jewish society for Arabs). Beginning in the late sixties, more and more African American personalities are discussed, from sports figures, through artists and musicians, and ending with political personalities.[14] Gradually, the entire notion of legitimate Blacks is abandoned, and contemporary textbooks that cater specifically to minority audiences represent as diverse a spectrum of African Americans as of any other member of American society.

Similarly, the examination of the concept of ethnicity plays a far larger role in textbooks of the 1970s and 80s than in earlier ones. Employing content-analysis, numerous qualitative studies reveal that the number of pages devoted to discussions of ethnic groups and issues of ethnicity have grown substantially since the 1960s, and that amongst the ethnic groups included in typical discussions of ethnicity, African Americans receive the most attention. For example, Garcia and Goebel in their study comparing textbooks between 1956–1976 find a dramatic increase in the space devoted to the African American experience.[15] A study conducted by Sleeter and Grant, who analyzed forty-seven textbooks copyrighted from 1980–1988, found that after Whites, African Americans are the next most included racial group, in both pictorial representation, and sheer text.[16] This is reconfirmed by a similar study carried out by Ueda and Glazer.[17]

The second dimension concerns the way in which African Americans are portrayed, and involves an increasing emphasis on positive qualities, personalities and contributions. The images associated with African Americans, their personality traits and their contribution to the development of American society are vastly more positive than before. Prior to the 1960s, African Americans, when portrayed, were done so according to the prejudiced stereotype, which served to legitimate and perpetuate slavery; i.e., they were depicted as submissive, carefree, contented, lazy, and irresponsible. From the end of the 1960s this changes dramatically. In the context of the exemplar, as was noted above, not merely does the African American appear more often, but he appears increasingly as a positive role model. The range of pictorial illustrations increases, representing African American doctors, scientists, and artists, who reflect traits such as intelligence, talent, ambition, and success.[18] Most significantly, then, the image of a positive exemplar emerges, reflecting the same qualities associated with the American character and with the good citizen: ambition, energy, self improvement through education, training, and hard work. Finally, the African American soldier emerges as a dominant model, exemplifying the American qualities of patriotism, loyalty, courage, and selflessness.[19] As one scholar has noted, "the underlying textbook message calls for Blacks to draw upon traditional qualities of "good" citizenship and Americanism, such as restraint, moderation, patience, perseverance, optimism, faith, compassion, strength, and intelligence."[20] The African American becomes an American.

Finally, one cannot ignore the fact that both the quantitative and qualitative differences in the depiction of African Americans come embedded within a wider contextual change. The metaphor of the melting pot gradually lost its appeal, and a debate emerged surrounding the proper relationship between the separate ethnic/racial/cultural identities, and the American collective identity.

New concepts and categories were introduced to describe and examine the fabric of American society: ethnicity, minorities, and eventually multiculturalism. The changing context was both a cause and a result of the particular change undergone by African Americans. The sudden inclusion of a variety of groups required a reappraisal of the entire narrative of American history and identity: "There was the problem of internal consistency: either the blacks belonged to American history or they did not, and if they did they belonged to all of it. To include a section on the civil rights movement meant that the whole of American history had to be rewritten to include blacks and their perspective on events."[21]

Born of the civil rights and feminist movements, the notion that individual cultural identities should naturally be subsumed within a larger, shared American identity, was rapidly losing currency. Thus, the increased attention granted to African Americans should be seen within this proper context of a more general change in the conception of minorities. The experiences of the minorities, as minorities, were now being viewed as legitimate subjects of history—in and of themselves—and not merely as an additional constituent part of the American whole. In other words, the late 1960s witnessed the beginning of the deconstruction of the narrative of American history; the hegemony of the single narrative is challenged with a multiplicity of stories, as numerous as the groups themselves.

U.S. NATIONAL IDENTITY: COMMEMORATIVE SYMBOLS

Postal Stamps

From 1847 (with the initial issuing of postal stamps series) until 1967 a total of four stamps were issued that commemorated African American persons or events (all four were printed in or after 1940). The first stamp to honor an African American appeared as part of the Famous Americans set, in 1940. This stamp honored Booker T. Washington. Two of the remaining three commemorated Washington as well (one picturing his house) and one Dr. George Washington Carver. Thus those stamps issued prior to the passing of the 1964–65 civil rights legislation which do pertain to Blacks portray either symbols which are relatively neutral—proclamations of equality and portrayals of national symbols such as Lincoln, or the well known "token" black figures such as Carver and Washington.

From 1967–2000, a total of eighty-four stamps were issued which commemorated African Americans.[22] In 1981 the Black Heritage series was initiated which issues a new stamp annually. Moreover, we witness the gradual inclusion of African Americans in all-American series such as the American Arts series; the American Revolutionary Bicentennial series; Great Americans Regular series; Performing Arts series.

Clearly a radical change took place in the frequency and type of African American stamps issued following the passing of the 1965 civil rights legislation. The change is exhibited in two ways. First, there is a marked increase in the number and variety of African American personalities that are considered worthy of national symbol status. Second, a marked increase in the number of African Americans integrated into all-American symbolic categories.

In the American context, postal stamps curiously emerge as a major symbolic indicator. This might be explained by the fact that given the highly decentralized nature of American symbolic production, the United States Postal Service emerges as one of the few national-level institutions that are involved in official commemorative activity. This fact grants additional significance to the shift in representation.

Months and Holidays

An additional commemorative category includes holidays and special extended-commemorative periods. Prior to the passing of the civil rights legislation in 1964, no national holidays, or commemorative weeks or months, had ever been established to celebrate either an African American person, or event of significance to African Americans. Since the 1960s two such holidays have been established.

In February 1976 President Ford proclaimed February as National Black History Month.[23] Black History Month is the heir to Negro History Week, later to become Black History Week, established in 1926 by Dr. Carter G. Woodson. Woodson, historian and founder of The Association for the Study of Negro Life and History, established this week to mark the development of Blacks in the United States. As a result of an initiative started by the Association for the Study of African American Life and History, President Ford granted official recognition to the commemorative month, and declared it a national event.

The second event is the establishment of the federal holiday to commemorate Martin Luther King Jr. On November 2, 1983 President Reagan signed the bill establishing a federal holiday in honor of Martin Luther King Jr. The holiday was to take place on the third Monday in January, starting in 1986. On January 20, 1986, the first national Martin Luther King Jr. Day was celebrated across the nation.[24] Martin Luther King Jr. is the first African American ever to be commemorated through a national holiday.[25]

In sum, as was shown, federal commemorative days and national holidays celebrating African Americans were instituted in the United States only following the passing of the 1964 Civil Rights Act.

Museums

The museum has emerged in the twentieth century as one of the main institutions through which the state comes to imagine its dominion. This imagination includes the nature and scope of the people under its jurisdiction, the geography of its domain, and the legitimacy of its ancestry. Both within and through the museum, societies reproduce themselves, presenting something similar to a social genetic mapping.[26]

The 1970s ushered in a period of progressive inclusion of African American cultural representations into the mainstream of American culture in general, with the museum being one of the primary avenues. The riots of the civil rights movement had, in this context, two primary implications. First, they served as a catalyst for raising the awareness of the Black community itself. Within this process of consciousness raising, history, and the recognition of history, emerged as a primary tool of community empowerment. For African-American public historians, the riots were stark evidence that a new and volatile audience existed—the Black underclass—which, unlike the Black working and middle-class public, had probably never attended a Negro History Week celebration. The need to reach out to these poorer African American communities prompted new ways of thinking about culture. Hence, the new museums which were established in the 1970s were designed to reach out to different types of communities, and to provide a link between leaders and masses.

Viewing culture as a source of empowerment went against the traditional orientation of culture as improvement and a means of integration—an orientation characteristic of Woodson's generation. In contrast to the historical institutions that emerged in the 1950s—Margaret Burrough's Ebony Museum of Negro Culture in Chicago, Elma Lewis' School for the Arts in Boston (1950), and the San Francisco Negro Historical and Cultural Association (1956)—which were explicitly integrationist, those that emerged in the 1970s reflected new interpretations of African American history, emphasizing African roots, origins, and traditions.[27] They sought to reconstruct and reproduce the identity of African Americans in the context of American society. The portrayals of African Americans within these new museums transcended their traditional image as victims, and carved out their identity as a people with a distinctive culture.

The second implication of the riots of the civil rights movement was to raise the awareness of White America to the existence of an African American culture and heritage. The 1970s were witness to the construction of a mass White audience to African American public history. This in turn stimulated corporate and government funding of diverse African American public history projects.[28] Hence, African American public history efforts that had previously been unsupported, enjoyed unprecedented amounts of both government and corporate funding. This government funding reflected the concerns and anxieties of the White national leadership that the unrest would lead to more permanent instability, and that funds and efforts towards integration were necessary. For example, while the Smithsonian foundation had been considering an African American wing or museum, the words turned into action immediately following the worst summer rioting in September 1967.[29] The Anacostia Museum and Center for African American History and Culture was founded as a community-based and constituency-focused museum that increases public awareness of the Black experience through research, programs, and exhibitions.

By the late 1970s African American culture became a part of most American public and academic institutions. The most prestigious arts institutions—the Brooklyn Museum, the Field Museum in Chicago, the Los Angeles County Museum of Arts, the National Portrait Gallery, and the National Museum of History and Technology all sponsored exhibits that focused on African American culture. At the same time, separate museums were established, including most notably Chicago's DuSable Museum of African American History; The National Afro-American Museum and Cultural Center in Wilberforce, Ohio; and of course the Anacostia Museum in Washington D.C. All in all, more than one hundred museums around the country have been established over the past thirty years, most of which are members of the Association of African American Museums which was established in 1978. Recently, numerous websites have been established that bring this information together and make it easily accessible to both the African American and White publics.[30]

National Landmarks and Monuments

As is the case with other symbolic categories, representations of African Americans on war memorials was also slow in coming. Despite the fact that African Americans have participated on all the American war fronts, their contribution and indeed their participation has only been recognized and honored since the 1970s.[31] Clearly, the efforts of African Americans have played a critical role in achieving this goal, an effort which dates back to Frederick Douglass' tireless efforts to commemorate Black military participation in the Civil War.[32]

Since the 1960s a number of memorials have come to commemorate African Americans in particular. Some U.S. Army museums now recognize the contribution of the nineteenth century Black cavalrymen that the Indians called "the buffalo soldiers." In 1983 the National Air and Space Museum included a temporary exhibit of the Black Eagles, a fighter squadron which was a pioneer in demonstrating Blacks' ability and courage in battle. A memorial erected in Baltimore Maryland is particularly interesting as it both commemorates and attests to the previous lack of commemoration. In the memorial an African American soldier is depicted reading a scroll inscribed with the dates of the wars fought by African Americans. The symbolic reading of the dates can be taken as a public condemnation of the historic exclusion of African American soldiers from American war memory. Finally, the Vietnam Memorial in many ways represents the major shift in orientation, including a Black man as one of the three soldiers in the highly contested and acclaimed main official national monument to the war established on the mall in Washington, D.C.[33]

Similarly, up till the 1970s, virtually no landmarks or parks existed which honored African Americans. The designation of landmarks is accepted as an additional central avenue of official commemoration controlled by the National Parks Service, and is an indication of official historical recognition. In 1970, the Parks Service initiated a landmark program for "relevance" which sought to address this lacunae.[34] The service contracted an outside association, the Afro-American Bicentennial Corporation (ABC) to undertake a study of potential African American sites, and the program received substantial congressional funding.[35]

The survey designated three relevant themes: development of the English colonies, 1700–1775; major American wars, and society and social conscience. Thirty sites were nominated. In July 1974, thirteen sites were chosen and designated as landmarks including, among others, Martin Luther King's church during the bus boycott, the Ida B. Wells-Barnett House in Chicago, the Harriet Tubman Home for the Aged in Auburn New York. Continued surveys resulted in sixty-one African American landmarks by 1977.[36]

By the beginning of the 1990s the repertoire of African American commemorative programs initiated by the National Parks Service was rich and diverse. These include the designation of African American "sites" as national historic landmark parks and sites, as well as constructing a narrative of African American heritage and history through the designation of national travel itineraries composed of the different historical national sites. The main itineraries include the "story" of the underground railroad, and the narrative of the civil rights movement, entitled "We shall overcome: historic places of the civil rights movement."[37] The civil rights movement itinerary includes a list of forty-one sites, spanning twenty-one states.[38]

CONCLUSION

Two important conclusions can be drawn from this analysis. The first is that membership changes impact directly upon the symbolic representations in major national symbolic vehicles, both written and commemorative. The major impact of symbols is to influence the way in which members of society think of themselves. Including African Americans in these representations was an extremely significant step in the incorporation of African Americans into the American self-portrait.

The second conclusion is a more general one. As the discussion of textbooks illustrated, incorporating a new group into the general narrative of history necessitated not merely making room for that specific group. History is not a zero-sum tale which has a finite number of pages allocated for each story. Incorporating a new group necessitates a rethinking of the general narrative of American history. American history with African Americans was not the same history as it was without them. Hence, the act of incorporation impacted upon the entire self-imagination of American society, not only upon African Americans themselves.

NOTES

1. John R. Gillis, ed. *Commemorations: The Politics of National Identity*, (Princeton, N.J.: Princeton University Press, 1994).

2. See for example Michael Billig, *Banal Nationalism* (London: Sage, 1995); Murray Edelman, *The Symbolic Uses of Politics* (1967; reprint, Chicago: University of Illinois Press, 1985); and John Gillis, *Commemorations: The Politics of National Identity*; Lynn Spillman, *Nation and Commemoration; Creating national identities in the United States and Australia* (Cambridge: Cambridge University Press, 1997).

3. On the different uses of the concept of narrative see Hayden White, *The Content of the Form* (Baltimore: Johns Hopkins University Press, 1987).The concept of narrative in the context of national identity was utilized in an insightful and interesting paper by Nadim Rouhana, "The Palestinian Dimension in the National Identity of the Arabs in Israel," Presented at the conference, "The Arab Minority in Israel: Dilemmas of Political Orientation and Social Change," organized by the Moshe Dayan Center for Middle Eastern and African Studies at Tel Aviv University, June 3–4, 1991.

4. Pierre Nora, *Constructing the Past* (Cambridge: Cambridge University Press, 1985).

5. See, E. H. Carr, *What is History?* for the counter argument, see, K. Popper, *The Poverty of Historicism* (1957; reprint, London: ARK Paperbacks, 1961).

6. David Saville Muzzey, *A History of our Country: A Textbook for High School Students* (Boston: Ginn, 1949, 1950, 1955), p. 5.

7. Ralph Ellison, *The Invisible Man*, (1952; reprint, Harmondsworth: Penguin, 1965).

8. Mary G. Kelty, *Teaching American History in the Middle Grades of the Elementary School* (Boston and New York: Ginn and Company, 1928), p. 442.

9. William H. Cartwright, and Richard L. Watson Jr., eds., *Interpreting and Teaching American History*, 31st Yearbook of the National Council for the Social Sciences, (Washington, D.C.: National Educational Association, 1961).

10. Cartwright and Watson, *Interpreting*, p. xxi.

11. Cartwright and Watson, p. xx.

12. For example, Lewis Paul Todd, and Merle Curti, *America's History* (New York: Harcourt Brace, 1950); Willis Mason West and Ruth West, *The American People: A New History for High Schools* (1928; reprint, Boston: Ginn, 1934), and *The Story of our Country* (Boston: Allyn and Bacon, 1948).

13. William Cartwright and Richard L. Watson, Jr., *The Reinterpretation of American History and Culture* (Washington, D.C.: National Council for the Social Studies, 1973).

14. Micheline Fedyck, "Conceptions of Citizenship and Nationality in High School American History Textbooks, 1913–1977" (unpublished Ph.D. dissertation, Columbia University, 1980), pp. 135–43.

15. "A Comparative Study of the Portrayal of Black Americans in Selected U.S. History Textbooks," Jesus Garcia and Julie Goebel, *The Negro Educational Review*, Vol. 36, Nos. 3–4 (July–October 1985): 124–125.

16. Christine E. Sleeter and Carl A. Grant, "Race, Class' Gender and Disability in Current Textbooks," in *The Politics of the Textbooks*, ed. Michael W. Apple and Lina K. Christian-Smith, (New York and London: Routledge, 1991), p. 97.

17. Nathan Glazer and Reed Ueda, *Ethnic Groups in History Textbooks* (Public Policy Center: Washington, D.C., 1976), p. 17. Glazer and Ueda, who employ a quantitative research method to assess the place and role played by ethnicity in history textbooks following the sixties and seventies, compare six major textbooks published in the late seventies.

18. Fedyck, "Conceptions of Citizenship," p. 139.

19. Fedyck, "Conceptions of Citizenship," p. 145.

20. Fedyck "Conceptions of Citizenship," p. 148. Garcia and Goebel, who also identify the change as an increasing identification of African Americans with national characteristics identified as "American," strengthen this conclusion. They conclude that following the 1960s, there is "a willingness among authors to illustrate Black Americans often and in varied settings and roles . . . in settings and roles similar to other Americans." Garcia and Goebel, p. 127.

21. Fitzgerald, *America Revised*, p. 84.

22. See "An African American Philatelic Experience," www.slsabyrd.com.

23. *New York Post*, 10 February 1976.

24. Alton Hornsby, Jr., ed., *Chronology of African-American History* (Detroit: Gale Research, Inc., 1991). See also, Harry A. Ploski, ed., *The Negro Almanac: A Reference Work on the African American*, 5th ed. (Detroit: Gale Research, Inc., 1989).

25. On January 20, 1976 the U.S. House of Representatives votes to authorize $25,000 to create a bust of Martin Luther King to be installed in the Capitol. He is the first African American so honored. On January 16, 1986 the bust was erected. See *Chronology of African-American History*.

26. Benedict Anderson, *Imagined Communities*, chapter 10.

27. Stewart, Jeffery C. and Fath Davis Ruffins, "A Faithful Witness: Afro-American Public History in Historical perspective, 1828–1984," in *Presenting the Past; Essays on History and the Public*, ed. Susan Porter Benson, Stephen Brier and Roy Rosenzweig, (Philadelphia: Temple University Press, 1986).

28. Jeffery C. Stewart and Fath Davis Ruffins, "A Faithful Witness: Afro-American Public History in Historical Perspective, 1828–1984," p. 328.

29. Stewart and Ruffins, 331.

30. "Black Museums: Keeping the Legacy Alive," *Ebony* 1994 (reprinted on http://usinfor.state.gove/usa/blackhis/blkmus.htm).

31. "Remembrance as Political Critique," in *War Memorials as Political Landscape; The American Experience and Beyond*, James M. Mayo, (New York: Praeger, 1988), p. 256.

32. David W. Blight, "For Something beyond the Battlefield: Frederick Douglass and the Struggle for the memory of the Civil War," in *Memory and American History*, ed. David Thelen (Bloomington: Indiana University Press), pp. 27–50.

33. James Mayo, "Remembrance as Political Critique," pp. 256–57.

34. On the general meaning and purpose: "The national survey of historic sites and buildings . . . is the principle means by which the United States government, through the national park service, has identified properties of national historical significance . . . it has served to qualify and disqualify sites for the national park system, to appease politicians and interest groups" Barry Mackintosh, *The Historic Sites Survey and National Landmarks Program: A History* (Washington, D.C.: History Division, National Park Service, Department of the Interior, 1985), p. vi.

35. Mackintosh, *The Historic Sites*, p. 73. Very shortly, $180,000 was given by the house subcommittee on interior appropriations. The contract would be renewed through mid-1976 for a total of $540,000.

36. Ironically, what resulted was a bias in favor of African American sites, or in essence the selection of landmarks on racial grounds. Because of guilt resulting from the past inaction, many Whites felt intimidated and forced to designate most of the sites recommended. See Mackintosh, *The Historic Sites*, p. 75.

37. Note that part of the itinerary is designated as an "All American Road" (the Selma Montgomery March Route) and as a National Historic trail—indicating the incorporation of African American history as American history. See the National Parks Service website: http://www.cr.nps.gov/cultural.htm

38. National Parks Service website: http://www.cr.nps.gov/cultural.htm.

Chapter Seven

Nationalizing Religion: the Israeli National Symbolic Matrix

Typical of many post-colonial states, symbolic production has been a central part of the political process of nation-building in Israel, and as such tremendous amounts of resources have been invested in developing and maintaining an official national symbolic matrix. From the outset the creation and development of national rituals, celebrations, and commemorations was a central activity of the state. Indeed, a special government ministry, the Ministry of Symbols and Rituals, is dedicated exclusively to the planning of state celebrations and symbols.[1]

Hence, in the case of Israel, as opposed to that of the United States, the production of national symbols is a highly official activity. As such, analysis of the development of both the symbolic content and form reflects very clearly the official intentions of the Israeli state. In this chapter I review the historical development of Israeli written and commemorative national symbols, focusing on the particular way in which the Palestinian citizens of the state have been portrayed in this matrix. Roughly three phases can be detected. During the first period, that of military rule from 1949 to 1966, Palestinians are non-existent in the matrix of symbols and rituals. Neither written nor commemorative narratives discuss the Israeli Palestinians as an entity distinct from the general Arab society that features prominently in the national narrative as the enemy. This is the period which marks the formation of the Israeli symbolic complex, and the peak of state centralized control. It is an era of memory-construction in its most self-conscious phase.

The second period, from the end of military rule through the 1980s, emerges as a period of transition. Following the abolishment of military rule the Palestinians are acknowledged as citizens of the state, and a piecemeal and cautious process of incorporation begins. References to Palestinian citizens of the state start appearing, primarily in the written narratives and texts.

In terms of the general symbolic complex, this period witnesses a certain re-
laxation of centralized control, and the beginnings of decentralized symbolic
production. In addition, especially towards the end of this period, gradual
recognition of the extent of state domination is acknowledged. Literature concerned with the Palestinian citizens of the state, which starts to appear in the
late 70s and throughout the 80s, is increasingly aware of the impact of their
national exclusion on their civic status.

The third period begins roughly with the signing of the Oslo accords. The
political and ideological context dictated an intellectual and political agenda
that acknowledged the contradictions inherent in the definition of the Israeli
state as both Jewish and democratic, and the implications of this contradiction for the civic status of its Palestinian citizens. Issues of exclusion and
membership are openly debated. Hence, this third period is characterized by
what might appear to be contradictory processes: on the one hand, increased
recognition of the exclusionary capacity of the Israeli corporate identity, and
on the other, the beginnings of both symbolic (commemorative and written)
and legislative incorporation.

1949–1966: MILITARY RULE

The period of military rule, from 1949–1966, coincided with the period of intense and centralized nation building, identified with the ideologically driven
state-building policies of Israel's first Prime Minister David Ben Gurion.
During this period Jewish-Israeli society is mobilized towards the fulfillment
of national goals: absorbing immigration, developing the land and securing
the foundations of sovereign Jewish existence. In this agenda, non-Jewish,
Palestinian citizens play no role.

Virtually all texts on Israeli society during this period were dominated by
the nation-building paradigm.[2] This paradigm, rooted in the modernization
and development approach fashionable at the time in American political science and sociology, defined the process of nation building as a uni-directional
process of development from traditional forms of cultural, political, and economic activity, to modern ones. The creation of a shared national identity
formed a very important stage in this process, as this shared identity served
as the basis of political legitimacy for state policies, and as a basis for mobilizing the members towards the attainment of national goals. The Palestinian
citizens of the state were not part of this modernization project, they were exogenous to it, and as such had absolutely no role to play in the modernization
texts. If referred to at all, they were defined and treated as passive recipients
of the benefits of modernity.[3] Textbooks and sociological texts on Israel dur-

ing this period are exclusively dedicated to a discussion of the Jewish society of Israel. Diversity, when dealt with, concerns diversity within the context of the Jewish community.[4]

1967–1992: A SYMBOLIC AWAKENING

Written Texts

The termination of military rule in 1966 followed by the Six Day War less than one year later introduced, in a very short period of time, vast new arenas of interaction between Jews and Palestinians. Until this period, very limited avenues of joint activity existed. The lifting of mobility restrictions from the Israeli Palestinians, and the large-scale incorporation of the cheap Palestinian labor force into the Israeli economy, brought these two societies face to face with each other. No longer able to relegate the Palestinian into the fuzzy abstract identity of the "Arab," the enemy and the other, the growing inter-dependency between the Palestinian and the Israeli Jewish society grew, and was eventually reflected in the way in which the written texts about Israel portrayed Israeli society.

Later, the deep psychological and political crisis brought about by the 1973 war, and finally the dramatic 1977 change of regime which ended the thirty year hegemonic rule of Mapai (Israel Labor Party), brought about intense soul searching and self criticism in much of the writing on Israeli society. This change incorporated a re-evaluation of the nature of Israeli society, its goals, and its membership. Israeli critical sociologist, Uri Ram refers to this period as one of general disillusionment in Israeli society.[5]

It is also during this period that Israeli sociology constructs the contours of the discourse on ethnicity in Israel, defining the range of ethnic groups in Israel as encompassing only Jewish groups. Hence, the emerging critical discussion on ethnicity and identity in Israel engages only the power relations between Ashkenazi and Sepharadi Jews.[6] The emergent discussions of the Palestinian citizens of Israel are incorporated in general studies of Israel (not in studies about ethnicity in Israel), but they are attached as a separate chapter, under the category "minorities."[7] Thus Israeli pluralism is constructed so as to include two distinct "types" of groups: ethnic groups which include the different Jewish groups—classified according to their country (or culture) of origin, and minority-quasi-national groups, which include the Palestinians.

At the same time, writing about the minority Palestinians emerges as a separate intellectual preoccupation, and the 1980s ushers in the beginning of scholarship devoted to separate studies of this population. Classic studies of the Palestinians in Israel, such as Ian Lustick's *Arabs in the Jewish State*, which presents a critical exposition of the Israeli mechanisms of power and control, provided both Israeli and non-Israeli readers with what was in many cases a first acquaintance with the particular dilemmas and realities of the Palestinian citizens. Lustick's emphasis on the Israeli structure of control is atypical; the focus of most of these studies is on questions of identity and integration. Moreover, the mainstay of Israeli scholars who began to write about Palestinians in Israel were part of the Orientalist tradition of Middle East scholars, who for the most part were also closely affiliated with the military intelligence establishment.[8] Their intellectual and scholarly interest in this population thus served a dual purpose, and on a basic level reflected the system of control they wrote about. True to the Orientalist tradition, Palestinian society was analyzed in the context of its own culture and religion. It was portrayed as straddling an identity spectrum. The question the Orientalists addressed and actually codified was *Israelization vs Palestinianization*: are the Palestinians in Israel becoming more Israeli, or are they attaching themselves to the Palestinians? Focusing on the question of identity enabled the scholars to confront the challenge posed by Israel's treatment of this group while bypassing the responsibility of the state for discrimination and neglect. The self identification of the Palestinians is posited as a matter of *choice*, they are seen as having the potential to determine their reality. The construction of the alternatives is presented as hinging on the autonomous choice of the Palestinians themselves, to the neglect of the economic, political, and psychological constraints which serve to determine this process of identification. Ultimately, therefore, Palestinian citizens are not really written into the Israeli narrative; they are either written up outside of the narrative, or are relegated to the status of an appendage.[9]

Commemorative Texts

During the first four decades there were no representations of Palestinians in the primary symbols, i.e., in the flag, anthem, and national holidays. The Israeli symbolic matrix commemorated and manifested only Jewish events and persons. There were virtually no monuments which symbolized Arab heroes, or historic events which Palestinians may take pride in.[10] There are no Arab faces on any of Israel's stamps. The only street names which bear Arab names are either in Arab cities or in Arab populated neighborhoods in mixed cities like Jaffa or Lod.[11]

POST-OSLO: TOWARDS A NEW SYMBOLIC MATRIX?

Written Texts

From the late 1980s onward, discussions of Palestinians in Israel change both quantitatively and qualitatively. For the first time, texts appear that discuss the Palestinians in Israel as an integral part of Israeli society. During this period, the cumulative impact of the Lebanon War and the Palestinian uprising (Intifada) made it impossible for Israelis to ignore the impact of the Israeli Palestinian conflict upon the nature of Israeli society itself any longer. The Lebanon War was the first war in the history of Israel that encountered severe criticism on the home front, perceived as it was by many as fundamentally illegitimate. The existence of political draft dodgers emerged as a significant issue in Israeli society, and the debate concerning the war threatened the almost legendary consensus which characterized Israeli society until that period. The Intifada had a similar impact, evoking protest and criticism which focused on the changing nature of the role of the military. The type of face to face involvement of the military with a civilian population, characteristic of both the Lebanon War and the Intifada, raised serious ethical questions and brought about what many people saw as a declining sense of morality. The same types of observations concerning the impact of Israel's relationship with its "own" Palestinian civic population was soon to come. The same dilemmas, it was realized, were unfolding within Israeli society itself.

The changing orientation of Israeli intellectuals towards the relationship between Israeli Jews and Israeli Palestinians, from a relationship which is exogenous to an understanding of Israeli society and Israeli identity, to one which is endogenous, or even defining of Israeli society, is best described by sociologist Shafir in his description of this perception of the meaning and significance of the relationship between Israelis and Palestinians:

> I came eventually to the conclusion that, during most of its history, Israeli society is best understood not through the existing, inward-looking, interpretations, but rather in terms of the broader context of Israeli-Palestinian relations.[12]

Curiously, yet not insignificantly, the precise context of "Israeli-Palestinian" is left undefined. Does this context include the relationship between Israelis and the Palestinian citizens? It would appear that increasingly that is the case. The two relationships, in the perception of both Jews and Palestinians in Israel, are inextricably linked: not identical, but closely related.[13] Indeed, most of the studies of Israeli society in this period incorporate discussions of Palestinian citizens as an integral part of the study, and by extension, of Israeli society.

If previously Palestinian citizens were studied as a separate social unit, understood only by examination of their internal cultural traits, the basic assumption underlying many of the recent approaches is that they should be conceptualized as an integral component of the Israeli political and social formation. Accordingly, the studies concentrate on the power relationship between Palestinians and the Jewish population and state institutions, defining these relationships as the central factor shaping the position of Palestinians in the political, economic, and cultural arenas.[14]

The different approaches emphasize different aspects of Israeli society. Some have emphasized the differentiated categories of citizenship;[15] the conflicts emerging in the labor market,[16] and finally those who focus on mechanisms of control employed by the state and the force of state ideology.[17] Hence, the study of the Palestinians in Israel serves as a vehicle for the examination and study of Israeli society as a whole, attributing to the structural situation of the Palestinians explanatory value in terms of Israeli society in general.

Civics and Education

The status of the Palestinian citizens is perhaps nowhere more blatantly manifested and reflected than in the educational system, and its core curriculum. From the early years of statehood, the Palestinian citizens are educated in a separate educational system, which promotes a different curriculum, receives different government funding, and is conducted entirely in the Arabic language. The establishment of this parallel educational track has always been seen as reflective of Israel's recognition of the Palestinian's right to a certain degree of linguistic and cultural autonomy. The chronic lack of funds, most apparent in the extent of run-down facilities, lack of infrastructure, and crowded classrooms, would attest perhaps to the contrary. In addition, both the curricula and the teachers themselves are subject to tight control and supervision by the Ministry of Education, which is careful not to allow the penetration of materials or educators which would enhance or promote nationalist tendencies. The irony of this, of course, is that the official premise for the maintenance of a separate educational track is the national and cultural integrity of the local Palestinian population.[18] Palestinian students are in fact taught little if any Palestinian history, and Palestinian cultural studies are by and large limited to religious studies. Ironically, religious studies, being a source of contention and potential politicization, are also limited. Palestinian students thus graduate with a more extensive knowledge of Jewish and Israeli culture and history than of their own.

To see how Palestinians are represented in the Jewish curriculum, one has to look at the study of civics.[19] Close examination of civics textbooks offers a fascinating window into the official articulation of the status of Palestinian citizens. These textbooks teach Israelis how to think of their Palestinian co-citizens by highlighting those issues that should be paramount in the discussion of the minority (the emphasis is on equality for example as opposed to nationalism).

Civics has been an obligatory course since the establishment of the central curriculum. High school students study civics for the duration of one school year (either during the eleventh or twelfth year), for a total of three hours a week. All students must take civics, and all must take a matriculation examination in civics. A major reform introduced in 1974 instituted a structural change in the civics course. The course is now divided into two parts, the first—Israeli government—is obligatory, and the second is optional. Within the second part there are three options: "religion, society and the state," "the Arab Citizens of Israel" and "the Welfare State." The choice is made by the school. According to the Ministry of Education the section on the "Arab Citizens of Israel" is the most popular. In the obligatory part of the course, that dealing with the government of Israel, the students study about the Palestinian minority in Israel in the context of a general discussion of minorities and minority rights in democratic regimes.

The way in which the official discourse surrounding the Palestinian minority has developed can be seen in a review of the development of the civics textbooks. One of the most blatant changes in the realm of textbooks concerns the growing number and diversity of texts available to students. By the year 2000 there were three authorized textbooks for the study option 'Arab Citizens of Israel.' The texts deal directly with the issues of rights, social structure, and organization, identity and what is called the "general relationship to the state."[20]

In the 1984 version of the basic textbook, the introduction poses the following question, and dilemma:

Is the relationship between the Jewish majority and the Arab minority a topic which should concern us? If so, from which vantage point should we deal with these issues?

There will be some who say that this question doesn't interest us, and that there are others, more important to deal with . . .[21]

The answer provided by the textbook suggests that this particular relationship should interest Jewish-Israeli students insofar as the nature of their democratic system should interest them. In other words, the civil rights abuses and the discriminatory treatment suffered by the Palestinian citizens of the state (all discussed in this textbook) pose a threat to the robustness of Israel's democracy. It is the system, and not the people or the society, which define the context of the discussion.

The defining event for Israeli society during the early 1980s was the appearance of Kahane's Kach party on the political landscape.[22] Kahane articulated in no uncertain terms what most Zionist ideologists knew, but were reluctant to admit: that taken to their logical conclusions, the tenets of Zionism lead to an intractable dilemma—full democracy and total equality of rights is impossible in a state whose entire institutional network is defined in terms of the Jewish people. Very quickly, the political, legislative, and educational agenda was set: the goal was to salvage the Jewish state from the threat of its own contradictions. The agenda of the civics textbooks is clear: remove the threat by resolving the contradiction.

Very much in tune with the nation-building perspective explained above, the text focuses upon the internal dynamics of Palestinian society at the expense of dealing with the role of the Israeli state or political system. An example is offered by the chapter concerned with education:

> During the 50s the educational system was lacking classrooms, curricula programs, books and other equipment. There was also a shortage of teachers. All of this required enormous sums of money and infrastructure within a short period of time. The ministry of education did not wait for these problems to be solved. It immediately started to absorb the Arab students. . . .[23]

The rest of this chapter describes the efforts of the Israeli Ministry to "develop" the school system in the Arab sector, phrasing it in such a way to suggest that the initial underdevelopment resulted from inherent tendencies within Palestinian society. During this period schools and teachers existed throughout the country, and the ministry's responsibility was to develop this infrastructure. The lack of development, the shortage of classrooms up till today is a direct result of the unequal allocation system in all Israeli ministries, education notwithstanding. The textbook does not acknowledge the responsibility of the state for the conditions of underdevelopment. The way in which the text confronts discrimination and inequality is in its treatment of the feelings and perceptions of inequality and discrimination, on both sides.

The 1990s textbooks begin to introduce a slightly different vantage point, and a critical one at that. In the 1990s the role and hence responsibility of the state for the inequality is introduced for the first time. Accordingly, there is a copy of a newspaper article which explains the Supreme Court case which dealt with the inequality of the two pre-school systems. Furthermore, many of the questions which the student is supposed to contend with concern the role of the state in perpetuating the inequality. Finally, this is the only book which adds extra sources at the end of each chapter, and amongst these sources are new scholarly books which incorporate critical vantage points concerning Jewish-Arab relations, some even written by Palestinian authors.

The 200-page textbook marks a dramatic change. The book is divided into thirteen separate chapters. The first four deal with the structural conditions governing the existence of the minority—their status as a national minority—who they are, demographic statistics, and civic juridical elements which define their status. The following four chapters deal again with "changes" within Arab society and deal respectively with the economy, education system, social structure, and the village—but in a more integrated manner, incorporating to a slightly larger extent the role of the state in these changes. The following chapter deals with the "struggle over lands between Jews and Arabs." This is an entirely new chapter, and is the first time the issue of land is dealt with explicitly. This can be interpreted as recognition and acknowledgement of the significance and centrality of the issue of land to the Palestinians themselves. The last four chapters deal with politics—also a novel approach. One deals with the question of identity, two others with municipal government and the last chapter with the national political activity. All in all the books present a more detailed, and less patronizing approach to the population. It should be noted, however, that in terms of substance, not much has changed.

The chapter on the relationship between Israeli Arabs, Palestinians, and the Arab world is complicated. It presents the Israeli Arabs as a separate political and social unit, and deals with the "relationship" with the Palestinians as one between two separate ethnic or social units. It presents the Right of Return as a primarily ideological issue, manipulated by the Palestinian leadership to make political gains, and not as one which is grounded in any moral or political reality. It presents the identity predicament of the Palestinians as an almost intractable dilemma:

> The struggle of the Israeli Arabs takes place on two polar and contradictory levels: A struggle as citizens of the state of Israel who are committed to loyalty towards her and her goals: a struggle for equality and equal rights. . . . On the other hand a struggle as members of the Arab nation for the Palestinians and the Arab nation: identity with the PLO and with the Palestinian identity, joining the struggle alongside the Palestinians: publications, flag raising, participation in demonstrations etc. . . . From here emerges the difficulty of the Israeli Arabs to define their identity.[24]

Again, no mention of the role of the state in defining, articulating, and perpetuating this difficulty.

Literature Curriculum

Since the establishment of the Education Ministry, the main mention of Palestinian citizens was in the context of civics education. In all other subjects the Palestinians were invisible. The first significant challenge to this orientation occurred with the advent of the Labor led government in 1999.

On March 2, 2000, then Education Minister Yossi Sarid (from the left wing Meretz party) shocked the Israeli parliament and public by the inclusion of

Palestinian poets—mainly Mahmoud Darweish the renowned nationalist Palestinian poet—into the main curricula, alongside such national poets as Bialik and Agnon. Amending the curricula occurs very infrequently. It had been twenty-one years since the educational curricula had been formally changed. The changes are determined by a professional committee laboring for months, if not years, on the program. The intervention of the presiding minister, however, is an unusual occurrence. Sarid, in response to a claim pointing this out, announced: "this is the way of democracy, and this is the meaning of regime change in the Educational Ministry. I am the Minister, and I determine policy." His proposal was part and parcel of a new orientation in the teaching of literature, and an attempt to contextualize literature; many of the books and poems were chosen on the basis of their relevance to some social or political issue. Hence, new items were introduced that reflected gender identities, multiculturalism and Palestinian authors. Sarid proposed including the poems of two Palestinian poets, Mahmoud Darweish and Siham Daud, alongside other Palestinian authors such as Anton Shammas. The two Palestinian poets are best known for their evocation of the loss of their homeland, and their longings for a land and society which were destroyed. The proposed curricula was intended only for the national public schools (this did not include the religious, nor, ironically, the Arab school systems).

The new additions were praised by some, and slandered by most. So, writes columnist Gideon Levi:

> High school students will now read Darweish and Daud . . . smell the smell of the coffee his mother used to prepare for him in his lost village in the Galilee, and feel the taste of longing for a homeland . . . perhaps they will understand the dimensions of the tragedy befallen upon the Palestinian people.[25]

Commemorative Texts

As yet, the main official state holidays remain entirely defined by the Jewish narrative. These include Rosh Hashanah (the Jewish new year), Yom Kippur (the religious day of atonement), two days of Succhot, one day of Hannukkah, two days of Pesach, and Shavuot. Independence Day is the only secular holiday in the pantheon. However, subtle changes have appeared in the ritualized observance of these holidays.

In the fall of 1999, then Minister of Education Yossi Sarid ordered high schools to observe and commemorate what has come to be known as the massacre of Kfar Kassem. On October 29, 1957 a unit of the border patrol received an order to enforce a curfew from 5:00 P.M. and to shoot anyone breaking the curfew. Shortly after 5:00 P.M. a group of forty-nine villagers, including women and children, returned from work in the fields having been detained briefly by soldiers at the barrier at the entrance to the village. They were duly shot at short range by the border patrol soldiers in the village. The soldiers' defense was that they were merely obeying orders. The presiding judge did not accept their defense and sentenced them to seven to seventeen years in prison (the sentences were commuted three years later).

Kfar Kassem has become a symbol of the aggression of the Zionist occupation ever since, and a symbol of the evolving Palestinian nationalism. In 1999, Sarid recommended that the massacre be commemorated for the first time in the public national educational system, that is, in the classroom. Sarid made the request in an open letter to civics teachers across the country. While the letter does not imply Israel's responsibility for the massacre, it is indicative of a more critical examination of Israeli history, as well as an acknowledgment of the membership of Palestinian citizens in Israeli society, and the importance of incorporating "their memories" into the collective memory.[26] As Israeli journalist Joseph Elgazi noted, it is difficult to attack Israel for condemning a massacre of innocent women and children, citizens of Israel, which received condemnation by the highest moral institution of the state— the Supreme Court.[27] Nonetheless, for the best part of fifty-one years, even such a politically neutral acknowledgment was not forthcoming; its final acknowledgment signifies some shift in recognition.[28]

Independence Day Ceremonies

Independence Day ceremonies are traditionally problematic ceremonials for discriminated minorities. Indeed, for many years July 4 celebrations were perceived by African Americans as the "other nation's" celebration. Israel is clearly no exception. Increasingly, in recent years, Palestinians in Israel tend to identify Independence Day with the Nakbah, which means tragedy in Arabic and denotes the fact that what signified independence and a cause for celebration for the Jewish people, marked a foundational tragedy for the Palestinian people.[29]

During the late 1980s, in the same type of dialectical process characteristic of most developments during this decade, the state initiated a process of incorporation of Palestinian citizens into the official state ceremonies. The official ceremony for Independence Day is conducted on Mt. Herzl, the official national memorial site.[30] The celebration opens with a ceremony known as the Lighting of the Torches, whereby twelve torches are lit by twelve representatives of different groups or sectors within Israeli society.[31] Up till 1984 the torch bearers represented different groups or ideals within Jewish Israeli society. Since 1984 one torch bearer represents one of the non-Jewish groups.

In most years, a Druze or Bedouin was selected, and not a Moslem Palestinian. This is clearly an "easier" decision, since Druze and Bedouin are considered by the state to be non-Palestinian Arabs.[32] Moreover, those selected are always chosen as representatives of activities that promote co-existence between Jews and Arabs.

Monuments

No official, i.e., state, monuments have been erected to commemorate either events or persons of the Palestinian community in Israel. Nonetheless, as of the winter of 2000, a number of municipal projects were in the process of development. These included a proposal to establish a monument to commemorate the victims of the Nakbah (the catastrophe of 1948); in Kfar Kassem, the municipality has submitted a proposal to erect a memorial for the victims of the massacre; finally, in Saknin there is a monument for those killed during the events of the first Land Day in 1974 and in Shfaram there is a monument to those killed in 1948.[34]

Stamps

As the following list indicates, representations of Palestinian motifs in stamps began in the 1980s (one stamp was printed earlier, in 1972). It should be noted that the motifs are all cultural and politically neutral.[35]

1972—April 17, "Tomb of Nebi Shuaib." Motif : Jethro's Tomb
1984—April 26, "Memorial to Fallen Druze Soldiers."

1986—May 4, "The Al-Jazzar Mosque, Akko." ('Id Al-Fitr—Feast of Breaking the Ramaddan fast). Motif: The Al-Jazzar Mosque, Akko.

1986—July 22, "The Nabi Sabalan Tomb, Hurfeish." ('Id Al-Nabi Sabalan— Druze feast of Nabi Sabalan). Motif: the Nabi Sabalan tomb, Hurfeish.

1990—February 13, "The Museum of Bedouin Culture." (Motif: A musical instrument used by the Bedouin, framed by a Bedouin carpet).

1990—February 13, "The Circassians in Israel." (Motif: a couple, in traditional costume, performing a Circassian dance).

CONCLUSION

This analysis of some of the main written and commemorative texts in Israel's national symbolic matrix supports the conclusions arrived at in the previous discussion of rights and legislation. The base line is a lack of representation and of exclusion: as discussed above, the Palestinian minority in Israel was non-existent up until the 1980s. Only after that time did symbols begin to reflect the existence of Palestinians within Israeli society. Two main observations can be made:

The first is that the focus in both the written texts, and to a lesser extent in the commemorative texts, is on the impact of the status of the minority on Jewish Israeli society. This is seen most clearly in civics textbooks, where discussions of the Palestinians are contextualized within discussions of Israeli democracy. Absent from most written and commemorative texts is an examination of Palestinian society, history, or culture as an object of study in its own right, and as a potential source of enrichment for Israeli society and culture.

This is inherently connected to the second observation. The treatment of the Right of Return is a good example. In the most recent textbook, as well as in recent books on Israeli society, the Right of Return is discussed. The context, however, is almost always set by the implications of the Right of Return on the nature of Israeli society. The refugees themselves, their stories, their tragedy and their despair do not play a role in the discussions.

The case of the Independence Day ceremonies is a good example. Recognition, even if it is severely constrained, marks recognition of the Palestinian's potentially legitimate claim to incorporation. At the same time, one must keep in mind that those chosen are deemed worthy of symbolic representation as part of Israeli society only in their capacity as "good Arabs," implying those whose existence is dedicated to co-existence. The mere fact of their incorporation in a ceremony whose entire symbolic representation is geared towards the construction of a Jewish national identity begs the question whether they are deemed, momentarily at least, to be honorary Jews. Or is their incorporation indicative of a potential liberalization of the ethno-religious national identity, one which would enable the integration of non-Jews in a common, public identity? It is this question, that of interpretation, that I address in the following chapters.

NOTES

1. Research on Israeli memory and identity has flourished over the past decade. See for example Maoz Azaryahu, *State Cults; Independence Day Ceremonies and Commemoration, 1948–1956* (Sde-Boker: Ben Gurion University Press, 1995); Yael Zerubavel, *Recovered Roots: Collective Memory and the Making of Israeli National Tradition* (Chicago: Chicago University Press, 1995); Michael Keren, *The Pen and the Sword; Israeli Intellectuals and the Making of the Nation-State* (Boulder, Colo.: Westview Press, 1989).

2. On the history of Israeli sociology see the excellent account by Israeli sociologist Uri Ram, *The Changing Agenda of Israeli Sociology: Theory, Ideology, and Identity* (Albany: State University of New York Press, 1995).

3. For a classic text see S. N. Eisenstadt, *Israeli Society* (London: Weidenfeld and Nicolson, 1967).

4. History books of the state of Israel are a relatively difficult category to identify. Most of the books catalogued as historical discussions are devoted to specific events, most particularly, the wars of Israel. Thus, many of the books are primarily defense and military histories. These include discussions of the Arab population as they relate to the issue of land, or of terrorist activities.

5. Uri Ram, *The Changing Agenda*, chapter 4.

6. On the nation-building approach see S. N. Eisenstadt and Stein Rokkan, *Building States and Nations* (Beverly Hills: Sage Publications, 1973). On the pluralism approach see Sami Smooha, *Israel; Pluralism and Conflict* (Berkeley: University of California Press, 1978); for the directed discrimination approach see Amos Swirski, *Not Failing, but Failed*, (Haifa: Research Notebooks, 1981) [Hebrew]. For a similar comment see Majid al-Haj, "Ethnic relations in an Arab Town in Israel," in Alex Weingrod ed., *Studies in Israeli Ethnicity; After the Ingathering* (London: Gordon and Breach, 1985).

7. Examples of this tendency abound. I cite only the most prominent and popular books. For example, Eliezer Ben-Rafael, *The Emergence of Ethnicity: Cultural Groups and Social Conflict in Israel* (London: Greenwood Press, 1982); Michael Inbar and Chaim Adler, *Ethnic Integration in Israel* (New Jersey: transaction Books, 1977); S. N. Eisenstadt, *The Development of the Ethnic Problem in Israeli Society* (Jerusalem: Jerusalem Institute for Israeli Studies, 1989); Yochanan Peres, *Ethnic Relations in Israel* (Tel Aviv: Sifriyat Hapoalim, 1976); Rivka Rahat, *Social Patterns in Israel: Unity and Disruption* (Ramat Aviv: Everyman's University, 1983). A popular reader in the University on ethnicity follows this same pattern: Ze'ev Ben-Sira, *Identity, Alienation in Israeli Society: Inter-Ethnic Relations* (Jerusalem: Magnes, 1978).

8. See Tania Forte, "Archives and Documents in a Democracy," presented at the conference *Peripheral Challenges to Democracy*, Ben Gurion University, May 22–24 2000.

9. See S. N. Eisenstadt, *Israeli Society*. In this classic volume, which deals with such issues as social structure, stratification, history, and culture, and totals 450 pages, the penultimate chapter, of 10 pages, is devoted to the Arab population. In such books as Leonard Weller, *Sociology in Israel* (Connecticut: Greenwood Press, 1974), and Aviva Aviv, *Israeli Society; Formative Processes* (Tel Aviv: Ministry of Defense, 1990), there is no discussion of the Arabs. Another classic reader, extensively used in university courses, Moshe Lissak ed., *Sect, Nationality and Class in Israeli Society* (Tel Aviv: Everyman's University, 1989), includes close to thirty separate chapters on such diverse issues such as employment, poverty, economy, stratification etc, in which the discussion is exclusively of the Jewish population. There is one chapter on the Arabs. Another popular reader, Dr. Reuven Kahane and Simcha Kopshtein, eds. *Israeli Society 1967–73* (Jerusalem: Academon, March 1974). This reader includes thirty articles, is 450 pages long. One article is devoted to the Arabs, and is entitled, "Change, Barriers to Change and Contradictions in the Arab Village Family," by H. Rosenfeld. Typically indeed articles on the Arabs are anthropological in nature.

10. See Charles Liebman and Eliezer Don Yehiya, *Civil Religion in Israel* (Berkeley: University of California Press, 1983).

11. See, Maoz Azaryahu, "Street Names in Haifa," *Zionism* 10, no. 1, (fall 1991).

12. Shafir in Ram, *The Changing Agenda*, p. 176.

13. Interestingly, Ram avoids these types of questions. In his discussion of the colonialism perspective, he has one quite laconic paragraph on the perspective on Palestinians in Israel: "In addition, there is scarce research on Arabs by Arabs in Israel" (p. 177).

14. Zeev Rosenhek, "New Developments in the Sociology of Palestinian Citizens of Israel: an Analytical Review," *Ethnic and Racial Studies* 21, no. 3 (May 1998): 559.

15. Yoav Peled, "Ethnic Democracy and the Legal Construction of Citizenship," *American Political Science Review* 86, no 2, pp. 432–42.

16. Stanley Greenberg, *Race and State in Capitalist Development*, (New Haven, Conn.: Yale University Press, 1980); Michael Shalev, *Labor and the Political Economic in Israel* (Oxford: Oxford University Press, 1992); Gershon Shafir, *Land, Labor and the Origins of the Israeli Palestinian Conflict, 1882–1914* (Cambridge: Cambridge University Press, 1989.)

17. Baruch Kimmerling, *Zionism and Territory: The Socio-Territorial Dimensions of Zionist Politics* (Berkeley: Institute of International Studies, University of California Press, Research Series No. 51, 1983); Baruch Kimmerling, "State Building, State Autonomy and the Identity of Society—the Case of Israel," *Journal of Historical Sociology* 6, no. 4, 1993; Rebecca Kook, "Dilemmas of Ethnic Minorities in Democracies: The Effect of peace on the Palestinians in Israel," *Politics and Society* 23, no. 3 (September 1995): 309–36; Ian Lutick, *Arabs in the Jewish State* (Austin, Tex.: University of Texas Press, 1980).

18. For a good historical and sociological discussion of education in the Palestinian sector see Majid Al Haj, *Empowerment and Control: The Case of the Arabs in Israel* (Albany: State University of New York Press, 1995).

19. See Amy Gutmann, "Civic Education and Social Diversity," *Ethics* 105 (April 1995): 557–79; Stephen Macedo, "Community, Diversity, and Civic Education: Toward a Liberal Political Science of Group Life," *Social Philosophy and Policy*, 241–69; Joe Coleman, "Civic Pedagogies and Liberal-Democratic Curricula," *Ethics* 108 (July 1998): 746–61.

20. *The Arab Citizens of Israel; Cooperation in Israel between Jews and Arabs* (Jerusalem: Van Leer Institute, 1984); Yoram Peri, *The Minorities in Israel: The Arab Citizens of Israel and the Druze Citizens of Israel* (Petah-Tikvah: Lilackh, 1998); Rachel Groman, *The Arab Minority in Israel* (Petah-Tikvah: Lilackh, 1995); Oded Liphshitz, *The Arab citizens of Israel and the State of Israel: Processes of Equality and Integration* (Tel Aviv, 1995).

21. *The Arab Citizens of Israel: Cooperation in Israel between Jews and Arabs*, p. 5.

22. The Kach party established by the Rabbi Meir Kahane aspired to establish a purely Jewish state, and argued for the physical transfer of all Arabs to Jordan.

23. *The Arab Citizens of Israel: Cooperation in Israel between Jews and Arabs*, p. 74.

24. Yoram Peri, *The Minorities in Israel*, p. 63.

25. Gideon Levi, *Haaretz* March 4, 2000, p. 1a.

26. Criticism of Sarid came mainly from the left. They argued that the way in which Sarid recommended the commemoration detaches it from its political and

historical context. By defining it merely as a lesson in civics—the implications of following an illegal or immoral order—its meaning is neutralized. Without discussing it in the context of the land expropriation, the real issues masked by the Kfar Kassem massacre remain hidden and unexplored.

27. *Haaretz*, October 27, 1999.

28. Kfar Kassem (*Haaretz*, October 27, 1999, October 31, 1999; *New York Times*, October 7, 1999; *Jerusalem Post*, October 30, 1997).

29. Tom Segev, "Independence is el-Nakba," *Haaretz*, March 27, 1998, p. 6b.

30. Maoz Azaryahu, *State Cults*, Sde-Boker: Ben Gurion University Press, 1995.

31. See Don Handelman, *Models and Mirrors; Towards an Anthropology of Public Events* (Cambridge: Cambridge University Press, 1990).

32. This reflects the general attitude in Israel which differentiates between Moslem (and Christian) Palestinians, and the Druze and Bedouin who serve in the armed forces, and are more integrated in, and accepted by, Israeli society.

33. *Maariv*, April 25, 1986.

34. According to Muchamad Taha (one of the initiators of the Nakbah activities), these projects reflect a growing self confidence, a growing consciousness of Arab Palestinian identity, and a mature critical faculty. Tom Segev, "Independence is el-Nakba," *Haaretz*, March 27, 1998, p. 6b.

35. Israel Postage Stamps 1948–1998, Catalogue no. 13, Israel Postal Authority, Philatelic Service, (Jerusalem: Keter Publishing House, 1998).

Part Four

Explaining Inclusion:
The Search for Stability

Both the legislative and symbolic indicators reveal a shift—to differing degrees—in the membership status of both minorities. In the American case it is clear that during the 1960s African Americans were incorporated into the definition of American collective national identity. In the 1990s, in Israel, it would appear that some kind of inclusionary trend is emerging.

Different approaches can explain these shifts. Most theories of national identity tend to place the onus of explanation on cultural and ideological variables. In this final part, I argue that the shifts in membership boundaries are best understood in terms of shifting political—or material—contexts. What incentives do governments, or regimes, have to set in motion a process of change which involves costs—often high costs—for both the society and the government? Why alter a status-quo which appeared to serve their interests so well?

In each case I raise what would appear to be the dominant relevant political and economic contexts that bear upon the boundaries of the collective national identity.

Chapter Eight

Re-writing National Identity—From Blacks to African Americans

The end of Reconstruction conveyed one message. This message was that racial equality, and hence racial inclusion, was neither the concern nor the responsibility of the United States government. In the 1960s, however, it resumed this discarded role, and, in the words of both Kennedy and Johnson, set out to make racial equality not only the rule of the heart, but the rule of law. What prompted this action? Why were African Americans included when they were? What were the issues at stake, and who served to gain from this act of inclusion?

The civil rights movement fulfilled the necessary condition for inclusion: it made racial segregation, and the reality of the exclusion of African Americans from the mainstream of American society, a reality that Americans— White Americans—could no longer ignore. The civil rights movement forced Americans to reckon with the American dilemma. The televised coverage of brutality and violence facilitated the process of identification by constructing a clear image of victim and victimizer. The issue of exclusion was seen in graphic and simple terms. Racial equality was no longer an abstract moral issue, but a concrete one, which every American could do something to change.

Whilst inclusion was a necessary condition of racial equality, the American power brokers, in whose hands that inclusion lay, had to be convinced that it was in their interest to permit this act. In short, the U.S. government needed political incentive.

According to Derrick Bell's principle of interest-convergence, "The interests of Blacks in achieving racial equality will be accommodated only when it converges with the interests of Whites."[1] This recommendation tells us to look at the different sets of interests involved in the highly politicized process of civic and national inclusion. I argue that the convergence of four fundamental incentives prompted action towards the inclusion of African Americans in the

American collective national identity. The first is the gradual social and economic integration of the United States which increasingly dictated that domestic stability hinge upon racial integration. The second was the growing importance of the African American vote which contributed towards a radical change in party political alignment resulting in the evolution of race as a defining political issue. Third, Washington, D.C., was also influenced by the intensity and impassioned nature of the civil rights campaign, from the freedom marches in Birmingham to the freedom summers in Mississippi, an intensity which lent itself to the media and which the latter, especially television, exploited to shape public opinion.

These three domestic concerns were supplemented by a final fourth concern of a more international nature. The cold war with the Soviet Union, the de-colonization of Africa, and growing U.S. involvement in Vietnam made racial segregation impossible if America wanted to uphold its freedom-fighting and liberty-loving image. The international and ideological milieu which existed in the United States at the time made such ideological considerations part of the decision-making context, and greatly enhanced the inclusion of African Americans into the American national identity.

SOCIAL AND ECONOMIC INTEGRATION AND THE SEARCH FOR DOMESTIC STABILITY

More than any moral imperative, the desire for stability has been the single most important value governing the federal government's relationship with African Americans. Since the end of the Civil War the legal status of African Americans has entirely depended upon the particular way in which the federal government believed stability would be best advanced. Twice in the course of American history racial equality was pursued as a means of attaining stability. For most of its history, however, the abandonment of equality and freedom were the price that the federal state paid—and along with it American society as a whole—for maintaining stability and order.

The first time racial equality was seen as a means to attain stability was during the Reconstruction period following the end of the Civil War. The reconstruction of racial relations in the South was fundamentally motivated by the expansion of the power and sovereignty of the American government, and the Republican desire to exercise this power and impose it on the South. No less important was the fact that many Blacks had joined the Union army and had consequently won significant political leverage.[2] With the passing of the 14th amendment, which added Southern Black votes to the rostrum, civil rights was a winning ticket for the governing Republicans. This period, beginning at the end of the war in 1865 and ending in 1877 with the withdrawal of federal troops from the South, began with the writing of the thirteenth, fourteenth, and fifteenth Amendments, which basically entailed redrafting the Constitution. The abolishment of slavery and the establishment of a universal racial franchise empowered Southern blacks for the first time. In this brief time, close to 70 percent of the one million newly eligible Blacks registered, and Black voter turnout was between 70 and 90 percent. Sixteen Black Representatives were elected into the Senate.[3]

Ultimately, reconciliation and compromise with the South involved the abandonment of the racial cause, and, as always, African Americans paid the price. Fear of alienating the Southern states, and the equating of stability with federal unity led the federal government to grant the South autonomy in conducting their relations with African Americans. Racial reconstruction was abandoned and, as anticipated, this led to the creation of alternative mechanisms of discrimination and domination.[4]

Racially dominated stability was maintained for nearly a century. From the post-Reconstruction era, when the Supreme Court reversed many of the breakthroughs attained by African Americans, until the depression and World War II, the aspirations of Black freedom were abandoned, and with them hopes of inclusion in the American identity. Jim Crow was based upon total disenfranchisement of African Americans, achieved through mechanisms such as the poll tax, literacy and property requirements, and even, early on, grandfather clauses. Residential segregation, though not enforced by law, was enforced popularly. Segregation in public accommodations was enforced through constitutional interpretation, and entrenched in state laws throughout the deep South.[5]

This status quo regarding race relations prevailed from the 1880s through the first two decades of the twentieth century. Jim Crow was allowed to flourish in the South, and informal segregation was the norm in the North. Neither Congress nor the Supreme Court acted to change the situation; racist and segregationist opinions were prevalent in both the South and North, and the issue of race was low on the agenda of White America.[6]

The great migration of African Americans from the South northward was the first sign of change to come. World War I dramatically reduced European immigration and with it the labor flow that the economy had come to depend on. When the United States joined the war in 1917, the recruitment of White males exacerbated the already acute labor shortage. These two facts forced factories to open their gates to Black workers, and Black migration from the South was quick to follow. By the end of the 1920s, over one million southern Blacks migrated north. From 1910 to 1930 the African American population of New York City alone rose from ninety-two thousand to two hundred fifty thousand.[7] While the second migration during World War II was of more consequence demographically, this first migration was significant in the sense that it constituted the first real change in southern Black mobility patterns, paving the way for future social and economic integration.

The Depression and Roosevelt's New Deal had a seriously detrimental effect on racially dominated stability. The New Deal was the first major development in economic and social integration following Reconstruction. Economic hardship during the Depression was so widespread that even the South, despite its vested interest in maintaining state autonomy, looked favorably on the intervention of the central government to ameliorate economic conditions.[8] The allocation of federal funds to the South through various projects, the Farm Subsidy Program, the Social Security Act, and the National Recovery Administration, was a strong integrating force despite impacting detrimentally on poor southern Blacks.[9] At the same time, the New Deal policies reoriented the Democratic Party away from its exclusive bond with the South and opened it up to new and expanding coalitions of support, ranging from labor unions and ethnic minorities to northern farmers. The Democratic Party was no longer an exclusively southern party, but a national one. Diversifying the basis of support of the party enabled them, for the first time, to place the racial issue on the agenda.[10] Northern Blacks benefited from many of the projects, and consequently gave increasing support to the democratic president. This initiated the shift in loyalty to the Democratic Party. If in 1932 two-thirds of African Americans voted for Republican nominee Herbert Hoover, in 1936 76 percent of African American voters voted for F.D.R.[11]

The New Deal impacted on the status of Blacks in the stability formula in two ways. First, it provided an inroad for federal intervention in the South, a step towards eroding the bastion of federal opposition and paving the way for federal demands for inclusion. Second, by nationalizing the Democratic Party, it allowed for race to become a politically negotiable issue. On the eve of World War II, the African American vote, and hence race, started to emerge as a significant political issue. It is to this issue that I now turn.

THE EMERGENCE OF THE AFRICAN AMERICAN VOTE

Up until World War II the Black vote played no significant role in American party politics. Briefly, during Reconstruction, African Americans gained and exercised political power in the South and played a significant role in the radical Republican state governments. They were embraced by the Republican Party and gave it their loyalty[12]. Their empowerment, however, was short-lived, and with the end of Reconstruction and the entrenchment of Jim Crow in the South, any political power they had enjoyed, disappeared. Disenfranchised in the South, and of inconsequential number in the North, the African American vote failed to constitute a significant political issue. Neither party thus had sufficient incentive to push ahead on civil rights.

Social and economic integration provided the necessary backdrop for the second great migration of southern Blacks. The labor shortages created by World War II, along with a war-fed economy, hastened the migration of Blacks in search of work. Many industries faced acute labor shortages, and once again drew their labor from the sector of the American economy that had a labor surplus: agriculture. The steel mills in Cleveland, the aircraft factories of southern California, and the auto plants of Detroit attracted hundreds of southern Black agricultural workers. The African American population of Michigan, for example, rose by 113 percent in the 1940s.[13] The pull of the booming northern economy, combined with the push of agricultural unemployment and segregation, created an unprecedented migration flow which began in 1940 and continued for the following three decades. During each of these there was a net migration of close to one and a half million southern Blacks. In 1940, 77 percent of the African American population lived in the South. This had dropped to 60 percent by 1960, and to 53 percent by 1970. In 1940 35 percent of African Americans were still living on southern farms. By 1960 this figure had dropped to 8 percent.[14] The percentage of African Americans in central cities of twelve large SMSAs grew from 7.6 in 1930, to 9.0 in 1940, to 13.7 in 1950, to 21.4 in 1960 and finally to 30.8 in 1970.[15] This was accompanied by a tremendous increase in the percentage of African Americans concentrated in major industrial centers. Over 85 percent of African American migrants settled in industrial centers in New York, New Jersey, Pennsylvania, Ohio, Michigan, Illinois, and California. These seven states alone controlled nearly 80 percent of the electoral votes necessary to elect a president. As a result of these changing demographics, and following the electoral realignment made by Roosevelt's presidential victories, these states became electorally competitive, with the racial issue one of the loci of the competition.[16]

Migration and realignment had a concrete and immediate impact: it gave African Americans political leverage for the first time in American history. So long as African Americans stayed in the South, a Black vote was inconsequential; their immigration to the north transformed Blacks from an invisible to a visible electorate.

The impact of World War II was not limited to its influence on migration. It was the first war in which Black soldiers played a significant role. The number of Black recruits was close to a million. While conditions for African Americans in the military had improved since the First World War, when Blacks were employed exclusively in service positions, the military was still a segregated institution. Limitations were placed on the number of Blacks allowed to enlist, and those that did enlist were allocated to particular job categories, segregated from White units. Although no longer the rule, Blacks, along with other minorities, still tended to occupy the more traditional service posts such as cooks and stewards. Although some Blacks made it to officer level, the percentages were minimal.[17] The affront of a segregated military was overwhelming not merely because of the equal sacrifice demanded of Whites and Blacks, but because of the cause for which they were fighting. Few Blacks could distinguish between the Nazi racism they were fighting abroad, and the White racism they encountered at home.

As a result, African Americans returned from service empowered and motivated: having successfully overcome racism abroad, they felt better able to fight racism at home.[18] The budding civil rights movement, encouraged by the creation in 1941 of a Fair Employment Practices Committee,[19] was fueled by the discontent of the veterans, and gained much needed momentum. This was not a new phenomenon. Speaking after the Civil War, Frederick Douglass declared: "If he knows enough to shoulder a musket and to fight for the flag, fight for the government, he knows enough to vote. Shall we be citizens in war, and aliens in peace?"[20] The fact that most African American veterans who returned to the South encountered heightened racial discrimination served to motivate activism even further. Veteran Percy Sutton recalls: "I was thrown off a train in my captain's uniform. It was a castration I remembered for a long time. I fought a war to stop that."[21] During the war and in its immediate aftermath, membership in the National Association for the Advancement of Colored People (NAACP) increased tenfold.

By the end of the 1940s, two necessary conditions for Black inclusion had been met: migration north had provided the numbers necessary to translate demographics into political leverage, and the sense of empowerment following World War II had motivated Blacks to act. What was necessary was for these two conditions to be translated into partisan action.

THE CHANGING PARTY REALIGNMENT
AND THE EVOLUTION OF THE RACIAL ISSUE

Starting during the war, and continuing afterwards, Black unemployment rates began to fall. African Americans employed by the government tripled during the war, and employment gains were qualitative as well as quantitative. The number of Blacks employed in skilled positions grew, and average income increased substantially, contributing to the emergence of a Black middle class. This had important implications. First, a growing number of African

Americans were financially independent of Whites, increasing their ability to participate in protest actions without fear of recrimination. Increasingly the leaders of the movement were coming from sectors independent of White employers: Black churches and Black colleges as well as the NAACP. Second, enhanced financial status increased the motivation to protest. Frustration at segregation rose as the opportunities denied them expanded. In addition, segregating a middle class is more difficult than segregating the poor, disenfranchised illiterate classes. Finally, including middle-class Blacks in the American identity was a more inviting prospect than their working-class counterpart.

The impact of the post World War II growth was immediate. If previously Democrats had been satisfied to rely on their traditional power base in the south, they now increasingly sought solid bases in the north. As Black migration rose, bases of support in the north meant catering to the Black vote. Hence, the demographic and political dynamics inspired by World War II led to the increased empowerment and political significance of the Black American electorate.

The immediate implication of this growing empowerment was that racial segregation was no longer easily ignored. Civil rights activism, which increased dramatically following World War II, translated anger and frustration over segregation into concrete political demands: the equal right to vote, and the end of legal segregation in public facilities and accommodations. On the eve of the cold war, race was about to become a reference point in American political ideology and electoral politics.

Harry Truman, Roosevelt's successor, was the first Democratic president since Reconstruction who opted for northern liberal and Black support, at the expense of alienating the south. Promoting a relatively strong civil rights platform, Truman established a President's Committee on Civil Rights which published a report called *To Secure These Rights*. The practical impact of the report was minimal, but symbolically it was significant. Condemning segregation as immoral, the publication of the report secured Black loyalty to the Democratic Party.[22] The Democratic Convention in 1948 reinforced this shift. Deciding to gamble on liberal support, Truman gave a strong civil rights speech at the convention, which ultimately split the party. Delegates from Mississippi and Alabama, the two most radical Jim Crow states, left and established the States Rights Democratic Party (Dixiecrats). The gamble paid off and Truman won the election by a slim margin, gaining 70 percent of the Black vote. The southern states of Alabama, Mississippi, South Carolina, and Louisiana voted for the Dixiecrat Party abandoning the Democrats for the first time since reconstruction. In 1948 Truman signed an executive order banning segregation in federal employment and in the armed services.

During the 1950s the race issue was less prominent. The most important Supreme Court decision of the century, the 1954 *Brown vs Topeka Board of Education*, rendered the separate but equal clause unconstitutional and demanded the desegregation of the public school system. At the time however, *Brown* had little save symbolic impact, and on the other hand served to trigger a growing violent resistance to desegregation in the south. Republican and Democratic platforms in 1952 and 1956 were similar, and moderate on civil rights. The Democrats were clearly withdrawing from the more radical 1948 position for fear of losing further southern support. The Republicans, on the other hand, with liberals and Blacks opting for the Democrats, had less and less incentive to promote a progressive position on race. The 1950s were thus a time when the Republicans and Democrats were converging on race in preparation for the great racial races of the 1960s.

Civil rights emerged fully on the national scene in the 1960 presidential campaign, when both Kennedy and Nixon adopted more progressive positions than they had before. The strategic location of Blacks in the north had convinced national lawmakers to provide legislative assistance to Black southerners; although since 1936 most Blacks had aligned with the Democrats, new trends hinted that the Grand Old Party might lure enough of them away to swing a close election. In six vital cities, Blacks gave less support to Stevenson in 1956 than to Truman eight years earlier. Unless the 1960 democratic candidate received a larger proportion of the Black ballot, he had little hope of winning Illinois, Ohio, Missouri, and the election.[23] According to then political analyst Oscar Glanz,

Neither party can afford to ignore the numerical weight of the Negro vote. In the next campaign the democratic candidate will have the responsibility of reversing the changing image of the democratic party, while the republican candidate will have the responsibility of enlarging . . . the appeal of the republican party.[24]

The civil rights movement was in full swing, having just succeeded in its campaign to desegregate buses in Montgomery. It continued to garner more and more support—active and passive—to its cause. Martin Luther King had established himself as a leader of national stature. Moreover, it was clear that Kennedy's victory had depended on a very fragile coalition of northeastern and southern states. 70 percent of Black voters voted for Kennedy, as opposed to 61 percent for the democratic candidate in 1956.[25] While this was a substantial increase, the margin of victory was so slim that every vote was crucial.

The role played by the Black vote is not clear-cut. While the democratic platform adopted a much stronger position on civil rights than ever before, Kennedy was far from a full-fledged civil rights proponent. One of his first judicial appointments after taking office was William Harold Cox, a southern racist known for his hostility towards African Americans. During the first two years of his administration it appeared that the support of the southern states was politically much more important to Kennedy than preserving the Black support that had helped him to office.[26]

The full force of the racial issue descended on the Kennedy administration two years into his term of office. It now had an additional context that was to determine the future of civil rights for the rest of the decade: state rights versus federal authority. Since World War II, the federal government had been undergoing a relatively consistent process of growth and centralization. With continued economic prosperity increasingly dependent on federal and northern support, the southern states were reluctant to oppose the federal government. The intensification of the civil rights movement and its growing support in Washington might have been a bitter pill, but it was one the south might have had no choice but to swallow, were it not for two events: Little Rock in 1957 and Mississippi in 1962.

Both cases centered on desegregating educational facilities based on Federal Court orders. In Little Rock, the authorities had agreed to accept nine Black students at Central High School for the 1957–1958 school year. The governor of the state, Orval Faubus, employed the Arkansas national guard to prevent the Black students from entering the school, claiming that his intention was to protect them from violence. When a federal order was delivered demanding that he withdraw the troops, violence did indeed break out. Eisenhower had no option but to send in federal troops. The ensuing struggle received extremely wide media coverage at home and abroad.[27] While neither side started out wanting to make too much out of the desegregation, the situation had escalated and determined the steps each player would take. Faubus, though actually moderate on civil rights, felt that the local political scene left him no option but to take a strong position on what had become not merely an issue of segregation, but of state rights. Similarly, Eisenhower, who two weeks prior to the bloody battle declared that he would never send federal troops into a state, had no option when faced with Faubus' defiance of federal authority. The short-range political horizon of southern politicians like Faubus forced the issue, and strengthened the wider, political context of racial rights.[28]

A similar scenario unfolded five years later in Oxford Mississippi. In September 1962 a federal district court ordered the University of Mississippi to admit its first Black student, James Meredith. Governor Ross Barnett, following Faubus' path, chose to employ the national guard to prevent Meredith from registering. Back and forth negotiations with President Kennedy, who wanted to avoid the Little Rock violence, proved futile. The ensuing battle was bloodier than at Little Rock. 166 federal marshals were wounded, and two civilians were killed. Twenty-three thousand U.S. Army troops were called in and Meredith finally registered.[29] The events at Oxford were the first to be televised live on national television, and the impact was immense. State troopers fighting the national guard added an extra dimension to the racial issue and struck deep in the national collective memory.[30] As one civil rights historian has noted: "The protection of the federal government, not the protection of civil rights, was the issue for Eisenhower at Little Rock, and it was also the issue for Kennedy at the University of Mississippi. Both presidents viewed the abrogation of Black rights as a sideline to the main issue at hand: federal government rights."[31] As conditions ripened for full federal intervention, this dimension constituted a significant incentive. The upcoming events at Birmingham signaled that the time had come.

The events of spring 1963 in Birmingham, Alabama, occurred in the shadow of Oxford, and the growing tension surrounding civil rights, state rights, and federal rights. The question was basically whose capacity to impose stability on the public was greater. King and the civil rights protestors had made a strategic decision before Birmingham. Giving up on the courts, they sought out the president, and placed the burden of proof directly on the chief executive in Washington. Calling on Washington to face "its moral commitment and with it, its political fortunes,"[32] the burden of inclusion was now placed squarely on the shoulders of the federal government.

The Birmingham campaign was dubbed Project C, and its success hinged on the ability of the non-violent protestors to provoke a violent confrontation with local law enforcement officials. After a slow start, the campaign achieved its objectives. Fire hoses, clubs, and dogs were used against the thousands of young Black protestors, many of whom were jailed, and the scenes were televised nightly on the national news. Birmingham applied the final blow to White public opinion. By July 1963, 49 percent of the total population (including southern Whites) were convinced federal legal intervention was necessary to secure equal rights; by September 1963 it was 54 percent, and by February 1964, it reached 61 percent (among the northern White population support reached 71 percent).

The events in Birmingham capped a process that involved transforming the issue of race from a sectarian and local issue, confined to the interests of southern Blacks, into a national issue with direct bearing on the interests of Americans at large. In May the executive council of the AFL-CIO called for legislation, and warned of the ramifications of continued segregation for American society. Later that month the president, speaking at Vanderbilt University, contextualized the demonstrations in the "highest tradition of American freedom." Walter Lippman talked about transforming the civil rights movement into a "national movement to enforce national laws, led and directed by the national government." [33] Finally, in a televised speech to the nation, Kennedy spoke in the language of identity and belonging:

Are we to say to the world, and much m
is a land of the free except for Negroes; t
except Negroes; that we have no class or c
race except with respect to Negroes?[34]

The federal government had the capacity t
tions, and a majority of the American public b
that. On August 28, 1963, one quarter of a milli
cans marched on Washington to demand equal
speech offered a dramatic and unequivocal reminde   ...ntity
of Black Americans:

> The Negro is still sadly crippled by the manacles of segregation and the chains
> of discrimination, and finds himself *in exile in his own land* . . . I still have a
> dream. It is a dream rooted in the American dream that one day this nation will
> rise up and live out the true meaning *of its creed* . . .[35] (italics mine, R. K.)

At that moment a comprehensive civil rights bill was well on its way to ap-
proval in Congress, but would ultimately be pushed through by Johnson, following Kennedy's assassination.

Johnson did not enter the presidency as a racial liberal. While instrumental
in passing the 1957 and 1960 civil rights legislation as senate majority leader,
his position was moderate. As a staunch Texan politician he was neither particularly liked, nor trusted by the northern liberals and the Black leadership.
To demonstrate his commitment to the Kennedy legacy, and to warm up the
liberal democrats, Johnson on taking office adopted his predecessor's civil
rights proposal. His fervent commitment to passing the 1964 legislation was
as much a reflection of the achievements of the civil rights movement as it
was of his need to establish legitimacy amongst the democratic constituency:
"I knew that if I didn't get out in front on this issue, [the liberals] would get
me . . . I had to produce a civil rights bill that was even stronger than the one
they'd have gotten if Kennedy had lived. Without this, I'd be dead before I
could even begin."[36]

Johnson brought about the speedy passage of the act. His desire to gain legitimacy in the party was coupled with his desire to see the act passed as soon
as possible to avoid further violent confrontation. His fear of unrest was later
recalled by his aide Doris Kearns: "The biggest danger to American stability
is the politics of principle which brings out the masses in irrational fights for
unlimited goals . . ."[37]

The 1964 Civil Rights Act marked the first stage of the formal inclusion
of African Americans into the American national identity. As a result of its
strong federal enforcement clauses, and its overwhelming emphasis on

, it ended, for all intents and purposes, the segregation s from the mainstay of American society. In addition, the d two major developments in American politics. Firstly, it ated the capacity of the federal government to get its way, and the t to which federal power was now consolidated. Secondly, it demonstrated the intensity of the Democratic Party's commitment to civil rights. Henceforth, reliance on liberal and Black votes was a done deal.

The thrust of the 1964 civil rights legislation was its immediate impact on public accommodations. In failing to secure Black voting rights, however, it denied the Democratic Party the much needed votes.[38] Further legislation was thus a pressing issue. The electoral interests of the Democratic Party, and the civil rights interest of the movement converged perfectly.

The Goldwater-Johnson campaign of 1964 brought race to the forefront of the political agenda, putting an end to the democratic dilemma of choosing between the traditional allegiance to southern conservative states, and the growing commitment to a newly emergent and empowered Black electorate.

Goldwater, probably more of a staunch conservative than pure racial bigot, adopted racial conservatism as his running ticket. Racial conservatism was based less on open support for segregation, and more on opposition to federal intervention in civil rights issues. At least on the face of it, racism was not the issue. Well aware that the Republicans could not compete for the Black vote given their conservative position, and the fact that they were losing whatever Black support they had, Goldwater adopted the racial issue as a defining one, hoping to shatter the very fragile democratic coalition. The Democratic Party continued to straddle an increasingly unstable and fragile coalition: torn between its traditional southern loyalty and its newly growing liberal and Black constituency in the north. Playing down the issue of race was thus in the interests of the Democrats. It was precisely this dilemma that Goldwater sought to exploit. He forced the race issue to the forefront of the electoral campaign. While in the short run his gamble did not pay off, it did put the final touches on the positioning of race as a defining issue. From 1964 until today, liberalism means racial liberalism, and voting Democrat means voting in favor of civil rights.[39]

Johnson had been in office only sixteen months when a peaceful civil rights march in Selma, Alabama was brutally quashed. Johnson's response was swift and extreme: he called for the "goddamnedest toughest voting rights bill" possible.[40] Within a week a comprehensive voting rights bill was submitted to Congress, and approved in record speed on August 4, 1965. The bill gave the Attorney General the power to appoint federal examiners to supervise voter registration in states where a literacy test was in force, and where fewer than 50 percent of voting age residents were registered in the 1964 elections. The seven states in question were precisely those where Blacks were prohibited from voting: Alabama, Georgia, Louisiana, Mississippi, North Carolina, South Carolina and Virginia. The effect was immediate. In Mississippi, Black registered voters increased from 6.7 percent in 1964, to 66.5 percent in 1969; in Alabama the percentage rose from 23 to 61.3; in Georgia from 44 to 60.4.[41] By securing the right of Blacks to register and vote, and thus participate fully in the democratic politics of American society, Black Americans were finally included into the American national identity. The values of the Creed now applied equally—at least in potential—to both Whites and Blacks. The fact that the interests of the Blacks had converged so fortuitously with those of the federal administration had provided the necessary conditions for this act of inclusion.

THE IMPACT OF THE MEDIA
ON PERCEPTIONS OF STABILITY

No less important than the African American vote was the impact of the media on White public opinion. The response of the media, in turn, was in direct relation to the level and intensity of violence. To a large extent, as I demonstrate below, the leaders of the civil rights movement were aware of this correlation and orchestrated their strategy accordingly. The relationship between media, violence, and government response underscores the significance of stability and perceptions of it to the success of the civil rights campaign.

Hence, the second period in American history during which stability and order depended upon the pursuit of civil rights occurred during the 'Second Reconstruction' in the early 1960s. The responsiveness of the federal government to the demands of the civil rights movement was conditioned by the increasingly violent response of southern states to the growing Black protest. Domestic stability was now increasingly dependent upon resolving the civil rights issue.

Overshadowing each legislative act was the threat of violence and instability. As early as 1962, the first major federal civil rights project assumed by the Kennedy administration, the Voter Education Project, instituted in March 1962, was a direct response to the administration's fear of the unpredictable nature of the freedom marches in the previous months.[42] As the demonstrations continued, and as White violence escalated, legislation became an increasingly appealing option.

From the mid-1950s until the passage of the civil rights legislation in the mid-1960s, the south experienced unprecedented violence. The wave of violence represented what has come to be known as the "massive resistance" of the segregationist forces in the deep south states. To a large extent this violence was facilitated by the election to public office of staunch segregationist leaders during this period. The growing salience of the civil rights issue, and the expansion of protest activities, propelled southern politics into one of the most racist and violent spirals it had witnessed.[43] Each side appeared to manipulate the extent of the violence for its own interests. The segregationists and racists for their part were holding on to the remaining vestiges of the old order.[44] The protestors were only too aware of the political value of White violence on the national news, and their actions aimed to provoke as extreme a response as possible to gain maximum coverage and visibility.

The percentage of American homes with television sets rose from 9 percent in 1950 to 87 percent in 1960. This fact had a tremendous impact. The logic of television ratings emerged overnight and worked to bolster the civil rights cause—the more brutal the encounter, the more media coverage it received. The link between public support for civil rights and the impact of White violence on the evening news is supported by both journalists and politicians. This elevated an abstract notion of justice to the palpable realm of empathy and sympathy. The effect was exploited by the leaders of the civil rights movement, who frequently used the impact of White violence to their advantage.[45]

The political value of White violence was an integral part of the strategy developed by King in 1963, when he shifted the tactics of the movement from "nonviolent persuasion" to "nonviolent provocation," aiming to convince Whites of the necessity for legislation through the extreme violent reactions of law enforcement in the south.[46] This strategy depended upon the perceived legitimacy of the protestors. This legitimacy rested on two things. First, that they present a nonviolent front, demonstrating that the violent response was unprovoked by violence on their part, and second, that their demands be limited to equal access to the ballot and to public accommodations. This legitimacy was critical. Any expansion of their demands into the social and economic dimension would threaten the thin line they were straddling. When the civil rights demands did in fact expand and venture into political territory, White support and empathy dropped dramatically.[47]

The introduction of the 1964 and 1965 civil rights bills was preceded by the intensification of protest action by the civil rights movement, which in turn was met by unprecedented violence. This violence was broadcast directly into the homes of northern, White Americans (and non-Americans). This provoked the first significant shift in public opinion, and of course, it was this substantial shift in White public opinion on the issue of racial desegregation that finally forced Kennedy to take action.[48] It took vivid images of Bull Connor and his police dogs lashing out at peaceful children to give the necessary jolt to White public opinion. The *New York Times* coverage of the civil rights issue more than doubled between 1962 and 1963, and polls taken before and after Birmingham showed a 1,200 percent increase in the number of Americans regarding civil rights as the most important issue facing America.[49] Following Kennedy's dramatic civil rights speech in June 1963, there were close to eight hundred protests and demonstrations in 186 different communities. More than fifteen thousand Blacks were arrested. The fear of a violent Black protest was growing.[50] Fearful of the consequences for domestic stability, Kennedy deemed legislation a better solution than struggle.

The immediate impetus behind the 1965 voting bill was no different. The summer of 1964 witnessed some of the most brutal southern expressions of racism the nation had known. The 1964 Freedom Summer in Mississippi was intentionally designed, by the leaders of SNCC, to provoke reaction, and thus force the hand of American opinion. Thousands of White student volunteers from the north came down to Mississippi to register voters. That summer saw the death of four civil rights activists, the injuring of eighty and the jailing of three hundred. The murder of White volunteers elicited an immediate response. The pressure put on Washington resulted in the quick passage of the 1965 Voting Rights bill. Once again, fear of violence and instability had given the final push to the end of segregation. Johnson and his advisors knew that the violence that had spread to northern cities that summer, if left unheeded, would spread like wildfire. At that time, legislation ending formal segregation was enough to hold the peace.[51]

THE COLD WAR IMPERATIVE AND
THE GROWING INVOLVEMENT IN VIETNAM

During the post–World War II period, continued racial segregation became a growing source of embarrassment for the United States. It blatantly contradicted the image put forward by the United States as the defender of equality in its fight against Nazi Germany, and as the main representative of the free world in its growing ideological confrontation with the Soviet Union. In the words of the Justice Department:

> The United States is trying to prove to the people of the world, of every nationality, race and color, that a free democracy is the most civilized and most secure form of government yet devised by man.[52]

International coverage of racial segregation in the United States was increasingly embarrassing to the State Department. Soviet propaganda played on it, and the newly-established United Nations discussed it. From the early 1950s through the civil rights struggle in the early 1960s, the cold war

imperative was an important impetus for civil rights reform and was "a critical motivating factor in the development of federal government policy."[53]

The anti-communist culture which developed in the United States during the
cold war played race relations in two ways. On the one hand, civil rights activists
were often labeled communists by dissenters, and the FBI under Hoover staged
elaborate investigations of major civil rights activists including Martin Luther
King. The struggle for civil rights was portrayed as a communist plot, aimed at
subverting the autonomy and dignity of the individual states. The fear of communist infiltration of Black organizations peaked again in the early and mid
1960s with the flourishing of diplomatic contacts between the newly-established
African states and African American leaders. Demonstrations of support for
African causes were often a source of concern and allegation that communist
sources were behind the political activities.[54] At the same time, pro-civil rights
activists, the NAACP included, presented the struggle for equality as the best
weapon to fight the communist ideological and political threat.

On the other hand, the cold war spurred on civil rights activity. Each major
demonstration, event and decision surrounding segregation was given extensive
coverage in the foreign press. Of particular relevance was the coverage in the
newly-emergent third world countries and in the Soviet Bloc. In third world
countries such as India and in Africa, continued racial segregation was narrated
as the continuation of colonialism, thus categorizing the United States as one
more power of domination to contend with. As a major Indian paper noted: "if
the United States wants to 'lead' [as opposed to dominate] the world, it must
have a kind of moral superiority in addition to military superiority."[55] In an act
of particular symbolic significance, the Indian Ambassador to the United States
in 1959 addressed cadets at the Maxwell Air Force Base in Montgomery Alabama, expressing admiration for Martin Luther King, and comparing Indian efforts to eradicate caste to federal efforts to end segregation. With serious U.S. involvement in Vietnam just around the corner, the international perception of the
United States as the last bastion of White domination was an image neither the
Kennedy nor the Johnson administrations could afford. Martin Luther King himself made the connection at the funeral of a young Black killed by law enforcement violence in Jackson, Mississippi. In his eulogy King noted "the timidity of
a federal government that is willing to spend millions of dollars a day to defend
freedom in Vietnam, but cannot protect the rights of its own citizens at home."
Indeed, Black leaders, from King to Malcolm X, made explicit references to the
relationship between domestic and foreign affairs pretty consistently during the
1960s. Asked to comment in May 1961 on the Bay of Pigs, King responded:

> There is a revolt all over the world against colonialism, reactionary dictatorship,
> and systems of exploitation. Unless we as a nation join the revolution and go
> back to the revolutionary spirit that characterized the birth of our nation, I am

afraid that we will be relegated to a second class power in the world with no real moral voice to speak to the conscience of humanity . . . I am as concerned about international affairs as I am about the civil rights struggle in the United States.[56]

The irony of the fact that by 1963 thirty-four new African nation states had gained independence after national liberation struggles, while African Americans were still struggling for integrated lunch counters was not lost on the leaders of the civil rights movement. This served to further intensify their struggle and commitment. In addition, it galvanized the Black community to try and exercise their impact on the direction of American foreign policy vs a vs the new African states. Indeed, one of the primary arenas of American foreign policy during the 1960s was Africa. The link between future U.S. relations with these new states, and the domestic racial issue, was clear and unavoidable. Early on Kennedy made an effort to connect Africa policy and domestic civil rights goals in the hope of rallying Black support. In assessing his low-key position on civil rights during the campaign and especially in the first three years of his administration, some observers have noted that "Kennedy offered little in the way of concrete programs to Black Americans during the campaign. Instead, he made constant references to relations with Africa."[57]

Later on, however, the significance of civil rights to the advancement of international relations with the new African states became an unavoidable reality. At the time, rivalry with the Soviet Union made domestic politics a real obstacle to obtaining a serious foothold in Africa. The shift in Kennedy's civil rights policy must be understood in the context of the international arena.[58] Even symbolic gestures aimed at tempering desegregation were seen as facilitating the development of good relations with African and some Middle Eastern states. For example, in 1963 the ambassadors of the United Arab Republic, Morocco, Nigeria, and Somalia voiced complaints against racist rhetoric used by southern senators. White House disavowals and apologies were accepted by the diplomats, and the complaints withdrawn.[59] The passing of the 1964 and 1965 Civil Rights Acts helped the United States considerably, at least in avoiding further international embarrassment.

Black leaders began a variety of initiatives aimed at influencing foreign policy. In 1962, the American Negro Leadership Conference on Africa (ANLC) was established which sought to take a lead in serving as an intermediary between the United States and the African countries and in promoting civil rights in the United States through a variety of initiatives. Amongst other things, the ANLC sought to promote Black foreign service appointments and Black ambassadorships to African countries.[60]

In terms of the Soviet press, according to memos written in the State Department, "the Negro question was one of the principal Soviet propaganda themes regarding the United States."[61] Soviet coverage of the dramatic manifestations of segregation (the Montgomery bus boycott of 1955–1956, the race riots in Little Rock in 1957–1958, the violent reaction to the freedom rides in the summer of 1961, the marches in Birmingham and Selma in 1963 and 1965), as well as of the violent repercussions of the civil rights movement, was extensive throughout the 1950s and 1960s. Indeed, both Eisenhower and Kennedy tended to legitimize their positions on civil rights by the bad press segregation was giving the United States.[62] In his speech to the 1960 Democratic Convention, Kennedy linked the civil rights issue to the American image abroad: "Can we honestly say that it doesn't affect our security and our fight for peace when Negroes are denied their full constitutional rights?" He repeatedly commented on how the racial issue was "making our country look ridiculous before the world."[63]

An added source of embarrassment and hence incentive to act quickly on civil rights were the repeated incidents involving foreign dignitaries from the newly-independent African states. Some of the more embarrassing incidents involved segregated housing areas in the capital itself. These incidents finally forced the State Department to intervene with real estate agents who refused to show new ambassadors housing in the more prestigious White areas. On one occasion the secretary of the Nigerian Embassy received his meal in a take-out bag at a Virginia restaurant, implying that he would not be served sitting down.[64] Secretary of State Dean Rusk would later recollect that "the biggest single burden that we carry on our backs in our foreign relations in the 1960s is the problem of racial discrimination here at home."[65]

The high profile of the cold war imperative, and the growing involvement with Vietnam made racial segregation just that much harder to justify. These issues informed the developing social and cultural milieu of most of the political elites in Washington. Cleaning up the image of Americans abroad undoubtedly provided both administrations with additional incentives to push ahead with civil rights legislation and do away with undue causes of embarrassment.

The sensitivity of the United States to international opinion, and the impact of this sensitivity on government which provided an incentive to push towards desegregation is "axiomatic."[66] From the end of World War II, cold war rivalry implicated continued segregation on the home front as an essential element of the American image abroad. In the 1960s, the unfolding of the politics of decolonization—from the developing relations with the African community to the growing involvement of the United States in Vietnam—added a new context to the fight for desegregation. Clearly, the incentive to pass serious civil rights legislation, and bring an end to this source of embarrassment, was part and parcel of the United States need to maintain internal order and external credibility. Seen in this context, the international arena constituted a serious incentive.

CONCLUSION

In the mid-1960s, civil rights activist and noted social scientist Kenneth B. Clark gave a speech at the State Department. He stated:

> The degree of change which is permitted in the status of the Negro is determined not primarily in terms of the need of the Negro, but in terms of the needs of others. And this remains the fundamental dilemma.[67]

This speech gives credence to the interest-convergence hypothesis of Bell cited earlier in the chapter. Indeed, as the discussion here has illustrated, the change "permitted in the status of the Negro" was clearly brought about not merely by the African American agency—although without the determination of the civil rights movement none else would have followed—but because of the convergence of a number of critical interests. As I have demonstrated, four interests emerge as prominent: the first is the growing integration of the American state, and the increasing power of the federal government. Second was the growing significance of the Black vote, and third the consequent realignment of partisan politics. The fourth is the emerging international context of the cold war, and later, decolonization. Taken together, these four developments made it clear that desegregation and the inclusion of Black Americans into a redefined American corporate national identity was in the interests of stability and domestic order. Inclusion was ultimately defined as a less costly, and more efficient solution than continued segregation, and exclusion. Then, and only then, could African Americans be acknowledged as full-fledged members of the American nation.

NOTES

1. Derrick Bell, "*Brown* and the Interest-Convergence Dilemma," in *Shades of Brown: New Perspectives on School Desegregation*, ed. Derrick Bell (New York: The Teachers College Press, 1980), p. 95.

2. Eric Foner, "The Blacks and the Constitution" *New Left Review* 183 (1990): p. 70.

3. Anthony W. Marx, *Making Race and Nation: A Comparison of the United States, South Africa, and Brazil* (New York: Cambridge University Press, 1998), p. 129.

4. Marx, *Making Race*, pp. 135–36.

5. On the mechanisms of Jim Crow see C. Van Woodward, *The Strange Career of Jim Crow* (New York: Oxford University Press, 1966).

6. Reliable opinion survey data is available only from 1940 on. Data from 1940, which is relatively late, indicates the prevalence of segregationist opinions throughout

the country. For example, in 1940 82 percent of White northerners were opposed to mixed residential areas, with that percentage reaching 97 percent in the south. See Gerald David Jaynes, and Robin M. Williams, eds., *A Common Destiny: Blacks and American Society* (Washington, D.C.: National Academy Press, 1989), p. 138. In 1942 53 percent of northern Whites believed that Whites were more intelligent than Blacks; in the south that figure was 79 percent. See Stephan Thernstrom and Abigail Thernstorm, *America in Black and White: One Nation, Indivisible* (New York: Simon and Schuster, 1997), p. 104.

7. Thernstrom and Thernstrom, *America in Black and White*, p. 54.

8. Anthony Marx, *Making Race and Nation*, p. 145.

9. These projects often had a detrimental impact on poor Blacks in the south. They were excluded from the Social Security Act since it excluded agricultural workers, were denied farm subsidies since they did not own land, and were often below the minimum wage that was dictated by the NRP. Indeed, during Roosevelt's first term of office, day to day management of the New Deal remained in the hands of the hierarchy which repressed them. Blacks as a result never shared equitably in the benefits of such programs as the AAA, the Resettlement Administration, and the Farm Credit Administration. In Atlanta, relief checks for Whites were $32.66 and $19.29 for Blacks. See Harvard Sitkoff, *A New Deal for Blacks: The Emergence of Civil Rights as a National Issue, Vol. 1: The Depression Decade* (New York: Oxford University Press, 1978), pp. 49–67. Blacks began to benefit from New Deal projects during Roosevelt's second administration after 1936. This was to no small extent because of Roosevelt's liberal wife Eleanor, and her tremendous impact on Congressmen and Senators. See Thernstrom, *America in Black and White*, pp. 60–62, and Anthony Marx, *Making Race and Nation*, pp. 35–37.

10. As Klarman notes: "As the federal government came increasingly to pay the fiddler, it began to exercise its prerogative to call the tune." Michael Klarman, "How *Brown* Changed Race Relations," p. 35.

11. Thernstrom and Thernstrom, *America in Black and White*, p. 65.

12. Indeed, from Reconstruction until the New Deal, African Americans largely remained Republican loyalists. See Edward G. Carmines, and James A. Stimpson, *Race and the Transformation of American Politics* (Princeton, N.J.: Princeton University Press, 1989).

13. Thernstrom and Thernstrom, *America in Black and White*, p. 80.

14. Thernstrom and Thernstrom, *America in Black* 80, and Jaynes and Williams *A Common Destiny: Blacks and American Society*, p. 60.

15. Cited in Edward G. Carmines and James A. Stimpson, *Race and the Transformation of American Politics*, p. 33.

16. Michael Klarman, "How *Brown* Changed Race Relations," p. 22 and E. E. Schattschneider, *Politics, Pressures and Tariffs* (New York: Prentice-Hall, 1935), pp. 89–90.

17. See Mary L. Dudziak, "Desegregation as Cold War Imperative." *Stanford Law Review* 41, 61; (November 1988), pp. 15, 24, and Thernstrom and Thernstrom, *America in Black and White*, p. 74.

18. This, interestingly, has always been the impact of war, and is true of the Civil War, and to a lesser extent, of World War I. The effect of joint combat, and a sense of shared sacrifice, clearly highlights the injustice of inequality on the home front. This point was made by Klarman, "How *Brown* Changed Race Relations," p. 8, and is echoed by others. See for example Harold R. Issacs, *The World of Negro Americans*, 1963, pp. 43–44 and Richard Polenberg, *One Nation Divisible* (New York: Penguin Books, 1980).

19. Thernstrom and Thernstrom, *America in Black and White*, p. 72.

20. Cited in Judith Shklar, *American Citizenship: The Quest for Inclusion*, p. 52.

21. Marx, *Making Race and Nation*, p. 227.

22. Edward G. Carmines and James A. Stimpson, *Race and the Transformation of American Politics* (Princeton, N.J.: Princeton University Press, 1989).

23. Steven F. Lawson, *Black Ballots: Voting Rights in the South 1944–1969* (New York: Columbia University Press, 1976), pp. 250–55.

24. Lawson, *Black Ballots*, p.251.

25. Thernstrom and Thernstrom, *America in Black and White*, p. 124.

26. On Kennedy's civil rights record see Michael Stern, *Calculating Visions*, and Carmines and Stimpson, *Race and the Transformation of American Politics*.

27. Mary Dudziak, "The Little Rock Crisis and Foreign Affairs: Race, Resistance, and the Image of American Democracy." *Southern California Law Review* vol. 70 (September 1997).

28. Thernstrom and Thernstrom, *America in Black and White*, pp. 129–31.

29. Thernstrom and Thernstrom, *America in Black and White*, p. 130.

30. See Michael Kammen, *The Machine that Would Go of Itself: The Constitution in American Culture* (New York: Knopf, 1986).

31. Michael Stern, *Calculating Visions*, p. 73.

32. Stern, *Calculating Visions*, p. 80.

33. Stern, *Calculating Visions*, pp. 83–90.

34. See Carmine and Stimpson, *Race and the Transformation of American Politics*, page 40.

35. Thernstrom and Thernstrom, *America in Black and White*, p. 145.

36. See Robert A. Divine, ed., *The Johnson Years Part 2: The Great Society*. (Lawrence: University Press of Kansas, 1987), p. 100.

37. Michael Stern, *Calculating Visions*, p. 163.

38. It has been argued that the Black vote became critical to presidential victory as early as 1948. While clearly Blacks began the process of empowerment from the end of World War II, the evidence is sketchy. See Mary Dudziak, "Desegregation as Cold War Imperative," p. 22.

39. Klarman offers a somewhat similar argument concerning the impact of the *Brown* decision. He argues that while the impact of *Brown* on school segregation was minimal, its significant impact was in its effect on southern racial positions. It served, according to Klarman, to crystallize southern resistance to civil rights, eliminate any vestiges of southern racial moderates, and thus posit the southern stance on civil rights on the far right side of the political spectrum. See Klarman, "How *Brown* Changed Race Relations," p. 76.

40. Thernstrom and Thernstrom, *America in Black and White*, p. 156.

41. Thernstrom and Thernstrom, *America in Black and White*, p. 157.

42. Stern, *Calculating Visions*, pp. 65–66.

43. See David J. Garrow. "Hopelessly Hollow History: Revisionist Devaluing of *Brown v. Board of Education*," *Virginia Law Review* 80 (February): p. 9.

44. Klarman, "How *Brown* Changed Race relations," p. 85.

45. On the media see Garrow, "Hopelessly Hollow History," p. 156, and on the civil rights movement see Stern, *Calculating Visions*.

46. David J. Garrow, "Hopelessly Hollow History," p. 602.

47. Garrow and Macadam.

48. Cited in Klarman, "How *Brown* Changed Race Relations," note 601.

49. See the discussion in Gerald N. Rosenberg, *The Hollow Hope: Can Courts Bring about Social Change?* (Chicago: University of Chicago Press, 1991).

50. Stern, *Calculating Visions*, p. 90.

51. In *Black Violence* James Button argues that Washington's response to Black protest and ensuing violence fluctuated. From 1963 to 1965 the response was positive, further pushing the administration to work towards ending the core of the protest i.e. segregation. From 1967 to 1968, however, Black violence in the northern ghettoes was met with hostility and retrenchment, reflecting the more diffuse goals of the demonstrations, and the more radical nature of the organizers. James Button, *Black Violence*, (Princeton, N.J.: Princeton University Press, 1978), pp. 174–76.

52. Button, *Black Violence*, p. 5.

53. This argument has gained much credence as a result of recent research. See in particular Dudziak, "Desegregation as Cold War Imperative," and "The Little Rock Crisis and Foreign Affairs: Race, Resistance, and the Image of American Democracy," *Southern California Law Review* 70 (September 1997). See also Brenda Gayle Plummer, *Rising Wind: Black Americans and U.S. Foreign Affairs, 1935–1960* (Chapel Hill: The University of North Carolina Press, 1996), p. 302.

54. See Brenda G. Plummer, *Rising Wind*, pp. 301–15.

55. Dudziak, "Desegregation as a Cold War Imperative," p. 28. Also, see Klarman, "How *Brown* Changed Race Relations," p. 15.

56. Cited in Plummer, *Rising Wind*, p. 305.

57. Plummer, *Rising Wind*, p. 302.

58. Given the drastically different course of events that developed in Africa it is important to keep in mind that at the time that arena was seen as potentially critical, and that appeasing African leaders was a substantial political incentive.

59. Plummer, *Rising Wind*, p. 321–322.

60. Plummer, *Rising Wind*, p. 308.

61. Dudziak, "Desegregation as a Cold War Imperative," p. 36.

62. Klarman, "How *Brown* Changed Race Relations," p. 21; also, Taylor Branch, *Parting the Waters* (New York: Simon and Schuster, 1988).

63. Harris L. Wofford, *Of Kennedys and Kings* (New York: Farrar, Straus and Giroux, 1980), p. 21.

64. Plummer, *Rising Wind*, p. 270.

65. In Klarman, "How *Brown* Changed Race Relations," p. 21, taken from Harold Issacs, p. 18–19.

66. Cited in Plummer, *Rising Wind*, p. 326.

67. Plummer, *Rising Wind*, p. 327.

Chapter Nine

The Crisis of Israeli Collective National Identity

On June 11, 2000, Omri Padan, the CEO of McDonald's Co. in Israel printed a full page advertisement in the Israeli liberal daily newpaper *Haaretz*. The advertisement was an open plea to the liberal political parties Meretz and Shinui not to cooperate with the plans of then-Prime Minister Barak to include SHAS, an ultra-orthodox party, in the reestablished ruling coalition. The ad read—"Stop Giving in to SHAS, or Israel will turn into Iran." The ad focuses on the NIS 80,000 in fines his company was forced to pay the government for employing Jewish youth on the Sabbath in his restaurants. SHAS and other orthodox political parties are key forces in promulgating this type of religious legislation. Padan linked his plight with that of what he called "the secular public" in his call for a secular Israel.[1]

There have been no ruling coalitions, since the establishment of Israel's parliamentary system in 1949, that have not relied on orthodox and religious parties. Hence the dependency of relatively secular ruling parties on religious ones is a permanent facet of Israeli political life. The close linkage between religion and politics was upheld by the left as well as the right, and formed one of the building blocks of what was seen as the Zionist consensus. Demands to separate religion and state, therefore, have also been a relatively permanent fixture in the Israeli political and public arena. However, and this is the important point, the voices demanding separation have always been either marginal (and hence lacking in fundamental legitimacy), or apologetic, halfhearted, and never long lived.

Padan's full page ad can be seen, in this context, as representing a shift in the patterns of secular protest. Indeed, both the form and content is indicative of a new type of political force and a new type of political interest. This interest is based in liberal economic incentives and worldviews, and is detached from the traditional political values inherent in the political discourse in

Israeli society since its inception. Padan's ad represents an almost classic liberal convergence of economics and politics.

A close content analysis of the ad reveals absolutely no direct mention of political principles. It is all about labor and earning power. After noting the heavy fines, Padan goes on to state that over fifteen hundred Jewish youth are employed on the Sabbath by McDonald's, and that by doing so they are supporting themselves, and their families. (A classic liberal value of self-help). Finally, the large McDonald's Golden Arches insignia on the bottom of the ad makes its message ambiguous: is this an ad for McDonald's, or is it an ad for political freedom? Is this yet another clever advertising trick, or is it a sincere appeal to the principles of liberalism?

This and more. Omri Padan is not a marginal character in Israel, on the contrary: he is Israel's "salt of the earth." A "Sabra," and a former army officer, Padan was a co-founder of Israel's mainstream peace movement, Peace Now. In his mid-40s Padan is an Israeli financial success story, CEO of one of the major symbols of economic globalization. The indicators of Padan's success however, are representative of the new Israel, and the new economy. McDonald's serves non-kosher meals; is open on the Sabbath and is the quintessential symbol of Americanization and consumerism. Hence, the new Israeli success story is young, secular, status oriented, and non-ideological. For the new Israeli, economic freedom reigns supreme, and the desire for political change is a derivative interest. He represents what commentators have referred to as the new "Sabra":

> If the old Zionist ideal envisioned gritty farmers turning the deserts green . . . the last decade brought about the image of the savior as a latte drinking, twentysomething computer whiz.[2]

The ad, therefore, can be seen as indicative of a new emerging paradigm governing state society relations, and as offering a vista into the new way of thinking about national identity. This paradigm posits the individual rather then the community as central, and places the values of individualism, i.e., liberty and equality, before those of community, i.e., belonging, idealism, and virtue. Israel at the turn of the century, was at a crossroads: the old paradigm, that governed by the dominance of collectivist values and the maintenance of a strict and exclusionary corporate identity, was starting to be challenged by this newly emergent one. In this chapter I suggest that the growing dominance of this paradigm signifies a potential for inclusion of Palestinian citizens into the boundaries of the Israeli collective identity. I explore the amalgam of political, economic, and social interests pursued by Israeli leaders and officials that underlie and converge with the liberal paradigm. Since the liberal paradigm is posited on equal rights, and civic equality as a primary value, the gradual adoption of these underlying paradigmatic values will impact upon perceptions of and practices concerning the construction of collective national identity.

The first two sets of interests are systemic and structural. The first, illustrated by the above anecdote, is the development, during the 1990s, of a new financial class in Israel that translates politics through economic perspectives, and defines political interests according to economic values. The second is directly related to the large wave of immigration from the former Soviet Union—again, during that same decade—whose large non-Jewish population has generated demands, within both the state and society, for increased secularization and the gradual elimination of the Law of Return. These two interests signify a structural shift in the Israeli political and ideological systems, whereby the ability of collective ideology to define the parameters of membership in society is giving way to secular and individualist interests.

The final element concerns the evolution of Palestinian political participation and the way in which the changing patterns of their political behavior is impacting upon the partisan positions of the mainstream Israeli political parties, and the positions of the policy makers. In this section I argue that increasingly Palestinians in Israel are taking advantage of the democratic system to advance political and legal interests. This is evident in the growing autonomy of Palestinian political behavior, the prominance of national identity, the radicalization of Palestinian leadership, and the growing use of the legal system, particularly the Supreme Court. By threatening the political status-quo with a far more radical alternative, namely the bi-national paradigm, I argue that the radicalization of Israeli-Palestinian politics has served to render the liberal, nationalist-inclusive option a far more acceptable one.

THE NEW ISRAELI LIBERALISM

The relationship between civil society and democratization is well documented and has been the focus of scholarly attention in studies of societies as diverse as Italy, India, and Russia.[3] If we define civil society as that dimension of public activity that is independent of state control, then typically activity within civil society is both social and economic. The class most often identified with this activity is the middle class. Indeed, the classic democratic revolutions, in the United States, France, and England had strong middle class interests at heart. Modern waves of democratization involve a more complex multitude of social forces, but undoubtedly the advent of a free civil society is seen as both a precondition and a characteristic of democratization.[4]

Israeli society, since its pre-independence days in the so-called Yishuv, until the 1980s was characterized by the existence of a centralized economy and society, a pervasive and strong state structure, and a relative absence of civil society activity. As an ideologically driven society, all interests were subordinated to those of the state. This was true of all social activity: intellectual, economic, and political.[5] Economically, business and financial interests were, up until the 1970s, weak, unorganized, and lacked political backing and legitimacy.[6] Comparatively, the labor unions, collected under the state-controlled umbrella of the Histadrut, epitomized the collectivist, labor-led interests of the state. Within this general context, little space was available for the development of a civil society. Indeed, democratization in Israel during this period was restricted and subordinated to ideological dictates. Rights were only minimally and reluctantly extended to non-Jews, and even to Jews. Israel was a classic example of a non-liberal democracy that focused on political rights at the expense of securing civic rights and liberties.[7]

The general decline in the power of ideology and its main political carriers—the traditional mobilizing political parties—from the late 1970s, has been accompanied by the expansion of the autonomy of civil society. Hence, two inter-related processes are at play. The first is the gradual decentralization of state control, and with it the gradual disintegration of many of its supportive institutions. The second is the emergence of independent economic interests, and the growing dominance of market and consumer forces.

Policies aimed at economic liberalization were initiated by the joint labor and likud government in 1984 which began the first effective set of policies aimed at decentralization. This process was accelerated in the government policies of the late 1980s known as privatization. Since the 1980s major companies owned and run by the state have been gradually privatized or semi-privatized. This runs the full gamut of social and economic activity: in the media this was manifested in the establishment of a quasi private television and radio conglomerate known as the Second Channel. In addition, many of the large agricultural concerns owned by the state-run labor union have been transferred to private ownership; and finally, the labor union itself, the Histadrut, has been largely dismantled.[8] In the area of health the passing of the Health Bill has weakened the strength of the party-affiliated health care organizations and has given rise to a growing range of private medical facilities. This is also the case in education with the emergence of large so-called "grey areas" which allow for the introduction of private entrepreneurs and financial concerns. Finally, the military industries underwent serious economic difficulty and have been all but dismantled.[9]

The 1990s have witnessed very impressive economic growth in Israel. Recognition of this growth was expressed by the addition of Israel to the list of developed countries by the IMF in April 1997.[10] High levels of employment, impressive growth of GDP and a burgeoning high tech market have all contributed to this economic development. Over three thousand start-up companies were established in Israel between 1998 and 2000, with over one billion dollars invested in private Israeli companies in 1999 alone. The Israeli high tech market has emerged as one of the world wide recognized technology leaders in fields as diverse as telecommunications, software, semiconducters, pharmaceuticals and biotechnology. Israel is second only to Canada in terms of foreign companies listed on the American Nasdaq high-tech exchange.[11] Coming in the wake of the economic liberalization of the 1980s, the newly generated growth and wealth has given rise to an expanding individualism which far from subordinating individual interests to those of the collective, glorifies and sets as paramount the interests of the individual.

The articulation of these new interests has been perhaps most obvious in the development of Israel's foreign policy. According to many observers, the peace process would not have gained such a momentum were it not for the mobilization of the business community whose interest in peace is inherent in its need for stability.[12] Seen in this context, a move towards the inclusion of the Palestinians within the boundaries of the corporate identity converges with a number of these interests. First, the growing radicalization of the Palestinians threatens the stability of the country which is a necessary precondition for economic growth. The extent of the reality of this threat has been once again demonstrated in the severe economic setback incurred in Israel as a result of the "El Aksa Intifiada" during the fall of 2000. Second, the emergence of this liberal-impulse cannot, by definition, be selective in its targets. Thus in Israel, demands for less regulation and state intervention have a two pronged effect: the first is a systematic attack on the network of social services provided by the state, and the second is an attack on structural disciminatory institutions. Thus demands for equality should be understood as emanating less from concerns for social justice, and more from economic and market rationality. As demonstrated above, the *Katzir* decision of the Supreme Court is part and parcel of a gradual predominance of the liberal-individualist paradigm over the republican-collective paradigm. Hence, while perhaps advancing the interests of the as yet under-class Palestinian population is not necessarily an inherent interest of the growing business community in Israel, advancing the liberal paradigm is.

IMMIGRATION FROM THE FORMER SOVIET-UNION: THE GREAT WHITE HOPE

With the advent of glasnost and perestroika, and the renewed relations between the Soviet Union and Israel in 1989, the restrictions upon Soviet Jewish emigration to Israel were removed. As a result, from 1990 to 2000 close to one million former Soviet Jews emigrated to Israel. As Jews, they qualified for immediate citizenship under the Law of the Return. Thus, membership in the collective identity was immediately granted to the hundreds of thousands of Russians along with the material benefits and political rights attached to membership in the Israeli collective national identity. Moreover, as "returning Jews" the new immigrants qualified for large sums of aid—in the form of grants, loans, and other financial benefits—transferred to them by the Jewish Agency and the Israeli government.

The direct impact of the immigration was a sharp rise in unemployment, which, by 1992 reached approximately one quarter of a million people (10 percent of the labor force). In addition, lack of appropriate housing translated into drastic rent hikes, and a dramatic rise in the real estate market. By the end of the decade, however, the economy bounced back, and Israel began to reap the benefits of this new wave of immigration. Highly educated, oriented towards the sciences, and hard working, the former-Soviet immigration has fulfilled many of the hopes placed on them by the veteran Ashkenazi political leadership of Israel.[13] They were seen as a potential charge for the then-stagnant economy. According to recent data, the Israeli high-tech extravaganza would have been unimaginable without the know-how of the thousands of Russian educated engineers which virtually flooded the Israeli high tech market.

At the same time, the Russian immigration was perceived as the last chance to set back the so-called demographic demon by raising the relative percentage of Jews in Israel. Indeed, if in 1990, Palestinian citizens of the state constituted close to 20 percent of the population, by the year 2000 their percentage dropped to approximately 18 percent.[14] In this context, it is clear that the impact of this immigration upon the Palestinians in Israel has been direct and far reaching. Two main points should be made.

Initially, the advent of the immigration illustrated, like no other event previously, the reality of their exclusion from the collective identity, and the concrete implications of this exclusion. The pressures placed upon the employment and real estate market were felt most direly by the Palestinians and entailed both large-scale layoffs, as well as renewed land expropriation activity. The automatic preference revealed by the state and society for Jewish workers, Jewish tenants, and Jewish welfare was a lesson re-learned by the Palestinians fifty years after the establishment of the state. The quick appearance of Russian speaking clerks in government offices, of Russian-language subtitles on many of the Israeli television broadcasts, of immediate aid to Russian students are telling examples of the invisibility of Palestinians.

To illustrate the initial impact upon the Palestinians, a few examples concerning the enforcement of land expropriation plans, and massive layoffs will suffice. For example, in 1976 a law was passed which expropriated thousands of dunams of land in the eastern and western Galilee, much of the land concentrated in the outskirts of Nazareth, the largest Arab city in Israel, and in the Negev, for public purposes. The law however was not enforced, and the Arabs continued to grow crops on these lands. In 1990, when the immigration started, the law was enforced and the state immediately started building new settlements for the immigrants on the said lands.[15]

An additional case which received extensive coverage was that of the village Ramieh. The land of this village was expropriated by the state in 1976. At the time, the residents refused to leave and negotiate a settlement. They were left alone until May 1991, when they were sent eviction notices and requested to leave within three months. The reason for the urgency was cited as plans for constructing apartment buildings for new Russian immigrants.[16]

In the arena of employment, the impact was no less dramatic. One of the most dramatic transformations to have occurred to the Arab population with the establishment of the state of Israel was the transformation of their economy from an agricultural to a wage-labor basis. Since no industrial or other local economic base has been developed within Arab localities, the Arab wage-earner population is intensely dependent upon the Jewish centers for their livelihood. Hence, fluctuations in the Israeli-Jewish employment balance severely influence the entire economy of the Arab population.[17]

Unemployment rose very sharply in Israel with the influx of hundreds of thousands of immigrants within such a short period of time. The Arab sector, however, was hit the hardest. Three sectors were influenced most significantly—academics, doctors, and industrial workers. This occurred for the following reasons. The employment rate of academics amongst the Arab population has traditionally been one of the lowest—both compared to other professions amongst the Arabs, and compared to academic employment amongst Jews.[18] The Russian immigration embodies a very high percentage of academics (approximately 40 percent of all those arriving—or close, up till 1992, to 150,000 people.) Hence, according to current statistics, and predictive evaluations, it is this sector which is to be hit the hardest.

Unemployment in the Arab sector before 1990 was, on the average, 15 percent; by 1992 it grew to 25–30 percent. In Nazareth, the largest Arab city, unemployment grew by 10 percent in the same two years, from 20 to 30 percent. Numerous cases were cited in which Arab workers are fired and Russian immigrants are hired in their stead.[19] Petrol stations, supermarkets, sanitary workers, all sectors that typically employed mostly Palestinians, completely remanned their positions by Russians.[20] Statements of politicians reveal that the tendency to hire Russian workers at the expense of Arab workers (including the expressed firing of Arab workers so as to make room for Russian workers) is not merely the hidden hand of the market, but the expression of an ideological orientation: the return to Hebrew labor.[21]

The second way in which the immigration impacted upon the Palestinians is indirect. As opposed to previous waves of immigration to Israel from the Soviet Union in the 1970s, the bulk of the recent wave was non-ideological. Most arrived in Israel not because of Zionist sympathies, but because the Law of Return enables immediate naturalization of all Jews. Hence, entrance into Israel was perhaps not the most preferred option, but it presented itself as the most available.

As the years go by, the Russians have emerged as a unified and self-conscious ethnic group within Israel, with distinct political leadership, two political parties, and a vast network of written and electronic media in the Russian language. The political leadership is dominated by veteran immigrants from the 1970s, who underwent intense Zionist socialization and most of whom suffered political hardships in the Soviet Union on their passage to Israel. Russian political leadership is, on the whole, associated with right wing nationalist politics. In the 1999 elections, close to 50 percent of the Russian electorate voted for Russian parties, with the remainder divided pretty much equally between the Labor and the Likud.[22]

Despite this identification with right wing politics, by and large the Russian population implicitly supports a liberal and individualistic model of state-society relations. The support comes from two dimensions. First, the Russian immigration is a highly educated immigration with an extreme emphasis on scientific knowledge. During the 1990s, the percentage of skilled manpower as proportion of total workforce in Israel grew to 30 percent as a direct result of the high percentage of Russian trained engineers. (In the United States for example, the rate is closer to 15 percent). In addition, the number of engineers per ten thousand employees in the Israeli labor market, was 135, compared to 20 in Singapore, and 65 in the United States. According to research conducted by leading economic institutes, the high tech revolution in Israel is contingent upon the recruitment of Russian trained engineers.[23] The individualist-liberal model favors the strengthening of the secular, individualist principles. One of the main reasons behind the open preference of the Russians for the liberal model is the high percentage of secular, and non-Jewish immigrants.

The percentage of non-Jews amongst the immigrants rose consistently during the 1990s. Statistics gathered by researchers indicated a rise from 16.7 percent in 1994, to 19.5 percent in 1995, to 22.7 percent in 1996, to 27.2 percent in 1997 and 32.1 percent in January 1998.[24] The ability of non-Jews to immigrate into Israel results from the particularly liberal wording of the Law of Return (see Chapter 5) which enables children and grandchildren of Jews to enter Israel and receive automatic citizenship.

Having entered the state, however, the non-Jewish immigrants (all relatives of Jews) face innumerable difficulties in their dealings with both the Ministry of Interior and the Ministry of Religion concerning all personal affairs. Marriage and birth registrations are delayed, benefits are denied, and an increasing number of deportations have been reported. This predicament gave birth to the winning slogan of the main Russian political party during the 1999 elections: *MVD Nash Control*, (translated this means the Ministry of Interior is in our control). Indeed, the most important element of Russian political leader Sharansky's negotiation with then Prime Minister Barak was control of the Ministry of Interior. Having gained control of the desired post, Sharansky was quick to ease the conditions and treatments of his constituency.

The so called "penetration" of three hundred thousand non-Jews into an insularly Jewish immigration system evoked strong sentiments and reactions amongst the Israeli public. For the first time since its inception, a public debate of sorts took place over the efficacy, and also legitimacy, of the Law of Return. The liberal oriented daily *Haaretz* published an editorial in which it called for a reassessment of the law. The parliament conducted a long and vociferous session on the law. Articles were written in the press, and most political parties staked out a position on the issue. While debates surrounding the Law of Return have cropped up in the Israeli political discourse periodically, they have typically been limited to debates over the related question of who is a Jew. For the first time the debate centered around the question of who is an Israeli. It is this question which has, obviously, clear implications for the boundaries of the Israeli collective national identity and implicitly, for the status of the Palestinians.

To conclude, the advent of the Russian immigration created new structural conditions in Israel which brought the practical implications of membership to the forefront. First, the initial contact highlighted the adversarial nature of the relationship between any significant Jewish immigration and the indigenous Palestinians. Employment and land are zero-sum types of goods which, in the context of a Jewish state, are favorably distributed to Jews. Second, the secular (and non-Jewish) and non-ideological nature of the immigration, has conflicted with the religious and ideological character of Israeli society, and provided additional impetus for the forces of secularization. In other words, it has matched forces with the emergent liberal-individualist paradigm.

RADICALIZATION OF PALESTINIAN POLITICS

The final point to be addressed concerns the Palestinians themselves. During the first forty years of living under Israeli sovereignty, the civic Palestinian population was relatively passive and quiescent.[25] Even after the lifting of military rule, Palestinian protest and participation was limited and subdued.

As expanded above, in chapter 5, protest that expressed nationalist positions was defined as illegitimate, as in the case of el-Ard, and automatically repressed. Palestinian political participation was mainly channeled through the Communist Party, or through a series of Labor dominated satellite parties.[26] No authentic, independent Palestinian political party managed to survive until the 1980s and neither the Palestinians nor their leadership openly challenged the definition of collective identity in Israel, nor flushed out the inherent discriminatory elements of the leading ideology.

Beginning in the 1980s patterns of Palestinian political behavior and protest began to change, articulating and expressing the impact of long-term exclusion and discrimination. This change is reflected in two dimensions. The first concerns the gradual articulation of an independent Palestinian-Israeli national identity, and the second the means and intensity of political behavior and protest.[27]

The Prominance of National Identity

As I explained above, up until the 1980s, any expression of national identification was perceived by Israel as a threat to its security. Hence, Palestinian political behavior was characterized by a stark absence of open nationalism. The relative opening up of the political system characteristic of the mid-1980s gave way to a gradual change in the patterns of Palestinian protest and participation as well. This was expressed first and foremost in the nature of the Palestinian political parties.[28] Starting with the Progressive List for Peace, a joint Jewish-Arab party established in the early 1980s, through the establishment of Balad in 1995, the Democratic-Nationalist List headed by Azmi Bisharah, increasingly Palestinian political parties have come to reflect the growing diversity inherent in Palestinian society. Increased emphasis on nationalism, and national politics is reflected in this diversity.[29]

The second dominant characteristic of Palestinian politics during these two decades has been the growing strength and influence of the religious Islamic movement. The central arena of influence of the Islamic movement has been the municipal arena, where they have increased their influence during the 1990s manyfold. Contrary, however, to common perception, the spread and intensification of religious affiliation, has not challenged the extent of national identification, but rather reinforced and supported it.[30] Hence, the Islamic identity promulgated by the movement merely serves to underscore, and not diminish Palestinian national identity.

Reflected thus in the increasing general politicization of the Palestinian citizens of the state, the emergence of a distinct national identity is acknowledged by most Palestinian intellectuals and scholars.[31] Trapped between the exclusive Jewish identity in Israel, and the political identity emergent in the neighboring Palestinian Authority, Palestinians in Israel have been coming to terms with the development of a national identity of their own.

The response of the Palestinians in Israel to the two "Intifadas" conducted by the Palestinians in the West bank and the Gaza Strip—the first in 1987 and the second in 2000—can serve as two watersheds in the evolution of the Palestinian national identity. The initial Intifada, conducted by the Palestinians in the West Bank and Gaza Strip from 1987 until the initiation of the Madrid talks in 1991 served to mobilize national sentiments amongst Palestinians in Israel through a sense of identification and emulation. Most of the identification was expressed through material and political support, and less through active involvement. The second Intifada—known as the el-Aksa Intifada—had a much more direct impact by virtually spilling over into the Palestinian centers in Israel themselves. Indeed, during the first days of this uprising, spurred on by the violent conflict between Israeli police forces and West Bank Palestinians on the Temple Mount and resulting in dozens of Palestinians killed, the Palestinians in Israel began a two-day long series of radical protest during which thirteen Palestinians were killed by the Israeli police. The dramatic direct involvement of Palestinians in Israel in this protest is indicative of a change since the first Intifada, and is seen as reflecting a number of developments. First, it indicates an increase in the extent of identification with political events in the West Bank. In addition, however, the protests are also reflective of a growing sense of political frustration at the limitations for advancement within the Israeli political system. Ultimately, however, the scope and form of the protests indicate that despite feelings of frustration and alienation, there is also a growing sense of empowerment. Finally, Palestinian national identity in Israel has been bolstered by the legitimacy bestowed upon this identity by the Palestinian leadership. For years the Palestinians in Israel were treated with disdain and worse by their fellow Palestinian nationals. Excluded from the administration of the PLO and looked upon more often then not as traitors or collaborators, Oslo paved the way for their reintroduction into the world of Palestinian politics. Increasingly Palestinians in Israel are looked upon as interolocutors between the Palestinian Authority and the Israeli government and their role in any negotiations between Israel and the Palestinian Authority, while not dominant, is carved out. Indeed, this affiliation has redefined the nature of Palestinian demands from the Israeli government. Demands for equality are now accompanied by demands for further concessions in the negotiations with the Palestinians. Proximity to the Palestinian Authority impacted in a complex way upon the development of Palestinian identity. While clearly the growing political, cultural, and even economic cooperation has served to bolster a shared sense of destiny and identification, on other levels the renewed and open associations have served to entrench the interests of Palestinians in Israel as Israeli citizens. The inevitable economic and political comparisons of standards of living and of democratic freedoms elicit recognition of the benefits of living within the Israeli political system.

Political Participation and Behavior

In the electoral arena, norms governing political participation have undergone a significant change. First, Palestinians are increasingly voting for Palestinian parties, and less for mainstream Zionist parties. If in 1959 53 percent of the Palestinians voted for the Communist Party or other Arab lists, in 1977 this number rose to 66 percent, and in 1999 to 70 percent.[32] Moreover, Palestinian parties now reflect a growing diversity of ideological positions: from communist, to nationalist and to religious. Finally, during the 1990s, the Communist Party remained the only Palestinian-based party to include Jewish members.

In addition, the demands and behavior characteristic of the political leadership, both within and without the parliament have become increasingly radical. In the thirteenth Knesset for example, Palestinian parliament members presented legislative proposals, all pertaining to the status of the Palestinian citizens. In the fourteenth parliament all major bastions of Jewish hegemony were under attack: Baraka's proposal for a Basic Law; Arab citizens; Tibi's proposal for a redefinition of the Citizenship Law; Darawshe's proposal to cancel the Jewish National Fund. The Palestinian parliament members are amongst the most vocal.

Finally, during the 1999 elections for prime minister, the first Palestinian candidacy was presented, by Balad-leader, Dr. Azmi Bisharah. Despite the fact that Bisharah withdrew his candidacy at the last moment, ultimately leaving the race to the two mainstream Zionist candidates, his candidacy marked a watershed in Palestinian political behavior. Bisharah is known for his radical, nationalist views, and through widespread interviews in the Israeli press, alongside academic articles published in Arabic, English, and Hebrew, his views are well known. Aside from openly calling for the redefinition of Israel as a "state for all its citizens," Bisharah has demanded autonomy for the Palestinian minority in Israel, and has contributed towards the advancement of the bi-national framework within Israel.

A new characteristic of Palestinian political behavior is the fullfledged adoption of legal venues as a main arena of political struggle. Adalah, a civil rights organization dedicated to the defense of Palestinian civil rights in Israel, was founded in 1997.[33] Ever since, it has been one of the most active and vocal organizations promoting and defending civil and political rights abuses of Palestinians in Israel. Much like their African-American counterparts, Palestinians have transformed the legal venue into a primary political mechanism taking every opportunity to combat the deep rooted system of discrimination within the Israeli legal system. This was perhaps most evident in the full page ads Adalah published in Hebrew language newspapers in the aftermath of the killing of thirteen Palestinian citizens during the first days of the el-Aksa Intifada. The ads attacked the complacency of the Jewish left in Israel, bemoaning its silence in the face of such blatant abuses of fundamental human and civil rights of Israeli citizens. Adopting the mechanism of newspaper ads in Hebrew language newspapers is further evidence of the empowerment of these organizations, and their willingness to take on the system. The establishment of Adalah, along with dozens of other non-governmental Palestinian agencies is testimony to the vast change in the socio-political landscape of Palestinians in Israel.

CONCLUSION

The true significance of state-society models, or paradigms, lies less in any specific set of preferences or directives, and more in the types of solutions or frameworks which any model or paradigm is likely to come up with when faced with political, economic or social dilemmas. Under the traditional, Zionist paradigm, breaches of inequality—towards the Palestinians, towards the Mizrachi Jews, towards women—were more often then not perceived as a necessary political price to pay in order to achieve the ideological goals of establishing a Jewish state. In fact, it can be argued that the attainment of central Zionist goals, such as the redemption of the land, and the ingathering of the exiles were premised on a fundamental inequality between Jews and non-Jews, and even between different groups of Jews themselves. The values and norms of society were derivative from those identified and defined as belonging (or adhering) to the collective, and were a-priori superior to those attributed merely to the individual.

The growing superiority of individualist values over collectivist ones has been one of the factors contributing towards the general decline in the collectivist, and nationally-exclusive ethos of the Zionist, Israeli state. Increased emphasis on individualism, and individual achievement as legitimate *normative* indicators of success has contributed towards the creation of a social context in which the demand for individual equality has gained extra momentum, and increased legitimacy. In this context, the post-Zionist views, discussed above, have been becoming increasingly significant. Arguing that the Zionist revolution had achieved its primary political goals with the establishment of the state in 1948, and that inequality was therefore no longer an acceptable value, invoked a redirection of energies inward, towards the domestic, Israeli community: how best to constitute the relationship between the Jewish people and the Israeli community, as well, of course, as the relationship between the Jewish society in Israel, and its non-Jewish, Palestinian members.

The question of course which has surfaced is what type of redefinition should—or could—take place. The radicalization of Palestinian politics, and the various post-Zionist alternatives calling for a secular state, should be interpreted in this context: the context of an ideological state in decline, of a society in the midst of an existential identity crisis. Thus, the changes discussed above can be seen as indicative of new possibilities; possibilities made possible, inadvertently perhaps, by the change in the general model of state society relations. Maintaining exclusive membership criteria of the collective national identity no longer contributes to the stability, and smooth functioning of the Israeli state. This has risen most clearly in the case of the Law of Return, and in the case of territory. It is no coincidence that the two defining pillars of Zionist thinking have come, during this transitional period, under serious attack. In this context, perpetuating collectivist and ideological values of the Zionist ethos, appears anachronistic, and contrary to the emerging discourse and paradigm.

The issue, however, of inclusion of the Palestinian minority clearly embodies a dimension that is unrelated to the paradigmatic discussion. The peace process with the Palestinians in general, and the Arab world in particular, have an ever lasting, and deep impact on any change in the status of this minority. The reaction of Israel's political and security establishment to the involvement of the Palestinian minority in the so-called el-Aksa Intifada is testimony to this impact and link. The killing of thirteen citizens without any official response from the government, the use of snipers against these citizens, and the sweeping condemnation of legitimate political protest, is indicative of the extent to which the Palestinian minority is still perceived as the "other", and is still, fundamentally, excluded. Whether or not the liberal impulse will prevail, is yet to be determined.

NOTES

1. *Haaretz*, June 11, 2000, p. 10a.
2. Quoted in "Israel—The Silicon Wadi," Presentation by Ron Lubash, conference on "Domestic Politics in Israel," May 17, 2000 Washington, D.C., State Department.
3. See Robert D. Putnam, *Making Democracy Work: Civic Traditions in Modern Italy*, (Princeton, N.J.: University Press, 1993). Patrick Heller, "Degrees of Democracy: Some Comparative Lessons from India," *World Politics* 52 (July 2000),

484–519; Alexander J. Motyl, *Revolutions, Nations, Empires: Conceptual Limits and Theoretical Possibilities* (New York: Columbia University Press, 1999).

4. The literature on civil society has expanded over the past decade. On the status of civil society in Israel see Gideon Doron, "Civil Society in Israel," in *Civil Society in the Middle East*, ed., Richard Augustus Norton (Leiden: E.S. Brill, 1995). On the relationship between democracy and civil society see Jean Cohen and Andrew Arato, *Civil Society and Political Theory* (Cambridge, Mass.: MIT Press, 1992); Thomas Janoski, *Citizenship and Civil Society: A Framework of Rights and Obligations in Liberal, Traditional, and Social Democratic Regimes* (Cambridge, Mass.: Cambridge University Press, 1998).

5. See Anita Shapira, *Futile Struggle: The Jewish Labor Controversy, 1929–1939* (Tel Aviv, 1977); Michael Shalev, "The Political Economy of Labor Party Dominance and Decline in Israel," in *Uncommon Democracies: The One-Party Dominant Regimes*, ed. T.J. Pempel (Ithaca: Cornell University Press, 1990); David Levi Faur, "Nationalism and the Power of Business: The Manufacturers; Association of Israel," *Environment and Planning C: Government and Policy* 14 (1996): 16.

6. David Levi-Faur, "Nationalism and the Power of Business . . . ," p. 17.

7. See Uri Ben Eliezer "The Meaning of Political Participation in a Nonliberal Democracy: The Israeli Experience," *Comparative Politics* 25, 4 (July 1993): 397–413.

8. See Lev Luis Grinberg, *Split Corporatism in Israel* (New York: State University of New York Press, 1991).

9. Shafir, Gershon, "Business in Politics: Globalization and the Search for Peace in South Africa and Israel/Palestine," *Israel Affairs* 5, nos. 2–3, (winter/spring 1999): 103–120.

10. As reported by Peled and Shafir in "Liberalization and Peace in a Frontier Society," paper presented at the conference on "The Middle East at a Crossroads," organized by the Herzog Center at Ben Gurion University, December 6–8, 1999.

11. See Ron Lubash, "Israeli—The Silicon Wadi," presentation at State Department Conference, May 17, 2000.

12. This of course is the basic message in Shimon Peres' book, *The New Middle East* (New York: Henry Holt, 1993).

13. Most recent data shows that for example, in 1998, out of the total of 310,700 employed immigrants, 38.2 percent had thirteen to fifteen years of schooling, and 25.7 percent had more than 16 years. (1998, CBS, table 5.7).

14. CBS, *Israel Statistical Handbook*, 2001, table 2.1.

15. This particular event received relatively extensive coverage. See *The Jerusalem Post*, January 8, 1991 and *Haaretz*, December 7, 1990. In this same context, rumors spread that the government was offering Arab residents of Nazareth Elite (a suburb of Nazareth adjacent to the above area of expropriated land) large sums of money to leave and move to the predominantly Arab city proper. See Dani Rubenstein, "Nazareth Towards Trilateral-Existence," *Haaretz*, November 29, 1990. This information was confirmed by research conducted by the MK Darawshah. See interview with Darawsheh in *The Jerusalem Post*, February 21, 1992.

16. See *Davar*, March 2, 1992.

17. Arab unemployment is traditionally three times higher then the Jewish unemployment rate. See Majid Al-Haj, "The Employment Situation of Arab Academics in Israel," in *The Employment Distress of the Arab University Graduates in Israel*, ed. Al-Haj (Haifa: The University of Haifa, The Jewish Arab Center, 1991) [Hebrew]; and Lewin-Epstein and Semyonov, "Ethnic Group Mobility in the Israeli Labor Market," *American Sociological Review* 51 (June 1986): 342–51.

18. See Eli Rekhess, "Socio-Economic Implications of the Employment of Arab University Graduates," in M. Al-Haj, *The Employment Distress*, 49–56. Also see Najwa Makhoul, "Changes in the Employment Structure of Arabs in Israel," *Journal of Palestine Studies* 11, no. 3 (spring 1982): 77–102.

19. Such was exactly the case of the largest soft drink factory in Israel—the Tempo factory. This case gained much coverage in the press. A Tempo soft drink factory fired thirty Arab workers, and promptly hired thirty Russians in their stead.

20. See *Davar*, March 2, 1992.

21. Anat Tal-Shir, "Time Bomb," *Yediot Aharanot* (*Seven Days, Supplementary Magazine*) January 11, 1991; Noam Yalin, "Meutei Sikuyim," *Haaretz*, November 14, 1990.

22. See Joel Peters and Becky Kook, "Israel's New Government," Briefing Paper, New Series, No. 5, August, 1999. (London: Royal Institute of International Affairs, 1999), pp. 6.

23. See Ron Lubash, presentation.

24. See *Haaretz*, October 27, 1998, p. 3.

25. See Lustick, Ian, *Arab in the Jewish State: Israel's Control of a National Minority* (Austin: University of Texas Press, 1980).

26. See Jiryis, Sabri (*The Arabs in Israel*, New York: Monthly Review Press, 1976), chapter 7.

27. See Achmed Sa'adi, "Culture as a Dimension of the Political Behavior of the Palestinian Citizens of Israel," *Theory and Criticism* 10 (summer 1997): 193–202.

28. Percentage of Palestinian votes for Arab parties has grown from 31 percent in 1981, to 62.4 percent in 1996. In the 1999 elections no less then five Arab parties competed. See Ilana Kaufman, "From All Comes One: The Vote of the Arabs in Israel during the 1996 Elections," in *The Elections in Israel—1996*, ed. Asher Arian and Michal Shamir (New York: State University of New York Press, 1999); Azmi Bisharah, "The Israeli Arab: Thoughts Concerning a Fragmented Political Discourse," in *Zionism: A Contemporary Discourse*, ed. Pinchas Ginossar and Avi Bareli, (Beer Sheva: Ben Gurion University Press, 1996), pp. 312–39 [Hebrew].

29. See Achmed H. Sa'adi, "Israeli as Ethnic Democracy: What are the Implications for the Palestinian Minority?" *Arab Studies Quareterly* 22, no. 1 (winter 2000): 25–37.

30. Malik, Ibrahim, *The Islamic Movement in Israel* (Givat Haviva: Institute for Arab Studies, 1990).

31. See Azmi Bisharah, "The Israeli Arab: Thoughts Concerning a Fragmented Political Discourse," pp. 332–34; Ramzi Suleiman and Benjamin Beit-Hallahmi, "National and Civic Identities of Palestinians in Israel," *The Journal of Social Psychol-*

ogy 137, no. 2: 219–228; Nadim Rouhana, *Palestinian Citizens in an Ethnic Jewish State: Identities in Conflict* (New Haven, Conn.: Yale University Press, 1997).

32. Assad Ghanem and Sara Osotzki-Lazar, *The Arab Vote to the 15th Parliament* (Givat Haviva: The Institute for Peace Research, October 1999); Azmi Bisharah, ibid.; Suleiman and Beit-Hallahmi, ibid.

33. Assad Ghanem and Sara Osotzki-Lazar, *The Arab Vote to the 15th Parliament*, (Givat Haviva: The Institute for Peace Research, October 1999).

Conclusion

STATE-CENTERED EXPLANATIONS

One of the paradoxes of national identities is that while they all share the basic mold of nationalism—janus faced, powering towards the future while rooted in the past—they are, at the same time, each a unique and singular entity. American national identity is entrenched, both in its more conventional as well as later traditions, in basic political, liberal values: equality, freedom, individualism. If one were to search for a common thread that ran through all accounts, and that served as the guiding light for both ideologists and theorists of American national identity, it is the idea of agency; the belief that membership in the nation is a function of hard work and a determined will. Even the more critical theorists who argue that membership is contingent on political realities, accept and embrace the principle—and ideal—of voluntary and willed membership.

The Israeli identity, on the other hand, is heir to a long established tradition of Jewish religio-national thinking. It is defined by the history, culture, and of course religion of the Jewish people—its values, its prejudices, its sentiments, and its community. Hence discussions of Israeli identity are theological in nature, as is Israeli politics, and the relationship between the Israeli and Jewish identities, while subject to debate and discussion, presents itself as an internal, almost intimate, Jewish affair—a matter for Jews from the Diaspora and from Israel to argue about. If agency pervades American identity, fate and destiny pervade Israeli identity. Israelis and Jews alike are taught that belonging and membership are beyond the question of will, and constitute a force more severe than that of any given individual. In the nationalist, political Israeli version of Jewish identity, not all members are capable of living up to the strict standards and demands of membership in the Israeli nation, and those who fail—"descend," (quite literally) and are, in the words of former prime minister Yizthak Rabin, "nefolet nemushot."[1]

Again, like all national identities, despite their differences, they share certain fundamental similarities. Both set out to incorporate diverse immigrant groups, and while so doing, actively and often violently excluded a significant civic minority from the boundaries and benefits of membership. While in both cases exclusion was/is justified ideologically, it is, as argued above, better understood as part and parcel of the exclusionary nature of all democratic regimes. In other words, *the logic of democratic exclusion derives not from the logic of national ideology, but rather from the logic of democratic political governance.* Democratic governments exclude groups as a mechanism of maintaining stability, and hence of maintaining the efficient provision of public goods, while minimizing the advent of free riding.

Similarly, periodic acts or processes of *inclusion* are best seen as part of the political dynamic of regime stability. In the United States, the growing demands of an integrated, centralized nation-state; the growing importance of the African American vote; the impact of the media; and finally, the constraints of a cold war foreign policy all dictated the logic of inclusion. Legal racial discrimination was no longer as conducive to stability and hence a new political realignment was necessary. The American nation-state, for close to the first two hundred years of its history defined the nation through racial exclusion.[2] The particular political and economic conditions that constrained and guided this definition began to change during the first half of the twentieth century, fully ripening during the 1960s. Hence, the American state—as represented first by the Kennedy and then the Johnson administration, pushed through legislation whose purpose was to end the exclusion of African Americans. In 1964 and 1965, the American state acted, while not autonomously, but in pursuit of a set of clear, identifiable interests. These interests accommodated certain societal forces and contradicted others. Backed by civil rights sympathizers, the passing of the two legislative acts marked a victory for the Johnson administration, and the supremacy of what at the time were defined as interests of the American, federal state.

The status of the Palestinian citizens in Israel represents a different situation entirely. As demonstrated above, the legal, economic and political exclusion of the Palestinian citizens of the state is intimately linked to perceptions of political—both domestic and international—stability. The production of public goods in Israel, indeed, the entire orientation of public and political policy, has been aimed, for much of Israel's history, exclusively towards its Jewish citizens. The test of the efficiency of public goods provision in Israel for a long time was confined to the Jewish sector. The maintenance of such a discriminatory system of provision was possible precisely because of the strict system of control maintained over the Palestinian population, and the benefits accrued to the Jewish citizens from such an exclusionary public system.

Thus, exclusion of the Palestinian citizens in Israel was (and as yet remains) at once more, and less, severe than the exclusion of African Americans in the United States. While granted the franchise, their freedom of association was severely limited; while granted basic civic freedoms, their mobility in the labor market, their ability to purchase land and their share in government funding has been extremely controlled and limited. But most serious of all is the fact that given the nationalist character of Israeli society, the exclusion of the Palestinians from the contours of the national identity has marked their total exclusion and alienation from the mainstay of Israeli society.

Israel at the dawn of the new millenium, was a society fraught in bitter and violent conflict with the Palestinian nation at large. The Oslo Accords were all but declared dead, and negotiations that seemed so promising just a year earlier had led to deadlock and a second, more intense Intifada. For the first time in its history, the Palestinian citizens of the state took an active position alongside the Palestinians and found themselves deeply involved in this national conflict. However, it was difficult to deny that their status, both in terms of legal as well as symbolic indicators, had improved. The Katzir ruling, the debate over the legitimacy of the Law of Return as a membership marker, the legitimacy of the call for a redefinition of Israel as a Jewish state, and the pervasiveness of the debate concerning the compatibility of Israel's definition as a Jewish and democratic society, are all clear indicators of a liberalization in both the reality and the discourse concerning Israeli national membership. Despite the persistence of socio-economic gaps between Israel's Jewish and Palestinian citizens, the legal fortress of discrimination had begun a certain process of decay. Most significantly, the issue of the rights and equality of the Palestinian citizens had captured a legitimate place on the public and political agenda. Discrimination is no longer so easily explained away by theories of modernization, or hushed discussions of security behind closed doors.

How should one best explain and then interpret the meaning of these changes? Society-centered explanations are insufficient. Despite a growing civil society, the Russians' growing demand for secularization, and the emergent high-tech business sector with an inherent interest in political liberalization—neither group have reason to adopt the interests of the Palestinian population. Moreover, while the Palestinians themselves have clearly undergone a process of empowerment and politicization, they alone are incapable of sustaining a successful movement for change. The reason for this is simple, and marks the fundamental difference between the situation of the Palestinians in

Israel and that of African Americans in the United States: the ultimate success of the civil rights movement was in its ability to ignite imaginations—White, liberal, American—imaginations. The African American struggle resonated strongly with the way in which White, liberal Americans imagined themselves. Not so in Israel. Hence, the Israeli media does not represent a sympathetic vehicle for their plight. Violent demonstrations are presented to the Israeli public as perpetrated not by Israeli police forces, but by the Palestinian demonstrators themselves. In Selma and Birmingham the cameras focused on the waterhoses and the billy clubs; in Um el Fahm they are not focused on the snipers and the tear gas, but rather on the stone-throwing, masked Palestinians.

The only viable explanation would lie therefore in the political logic of the Israeli state. As I demonstrated, the interests promoted by the Russians, the emergent business class and the changing nature of the state imply that the maintenance of an exclusionary national identity no longer promises the same kind of stability it did in the past. To accommodate to the growing liberalization of state-society relations and to the gradual decline in ideology, the Israeli state—its ruling government coalitions, its Supreme Court judges—are manifesting a distinct interest in rendering the boundaries of membership less rigid, and more liberal. As of yet, this interest represents a conglomerate of specific interests, all dictated by the logic of democratic governance.

Finally, the Israeli case is, to a large extent, an incomplete one, with the end of the story perhaps not even in sight. What are the comparative lessons that can be learned? What marked the inclusion of African Americans into the American collective national identity, and what constituted both the necessary and the sufficient conditions for democratic inclusion?

Clearly, the removal of the legal barriers to equality constituted the most significant, and hence the most consequential dimension of inclusion. The passing of the 1964 and 1965 legislation marked the end of legal discrimination, and cultural, social, and symbolic inclusion was soon to follow. As the discussion of textbooks, history books, and other commemorative symbols demonstrates, African Americans, from the mid-1960s and onward have constituted an integral—indeed some may say central—component of American identity. Their inclusion forced a reassessment, and re-representation of what it meant to be American. The contours of American national identity were forever changed by the inclusion of African Americans into the ranks.

In Israel on the other hand, since change in the legal contours of the identity is only in its very beginning stages, it is difficult to predict what direction the change will take. Presumably however, as the incipient changes in the symbolic—mainly written—texts illustrate, the reappraisal of Israel's relationship to its Palestinian minority is forcing a reassessment of Israeli national identity as a whole. *Hence, inclusion, as we saw, always forces a reassessment, a new narrative.*

Two factors seem to have provided the necessary and sufficient conditions for the inclusion of African Americans. The first was the evolving commitment of the federal government, which, as shown, resulted from the convergence of a number of interests. This commitment, and the ability to define the converging interests as *significant government interests* is related to the second condition, namely, the evolving legitimacy of the issue of civil rights. For expanding sectors of American society, civil rights, and equality for Blacks was seen as a politically and ethically legitimate issue. And herein lies the most significant difference between both cases: fundamentally, equality for Palestinian citizens is as yet an issue beyond the pale of mainstream political legitimacy. Two factors collude in the constitution of this reality. The first the political conflict between Israel and the Palestinians. The terror and violence which encapsulate and define the Israeli-Palestinian conflict prevent, at this point in time, the transformation of the issue of civil rights for Palestinian citizens into a legitimate issue, around which it would be possible to mobilize both public opinion and the ruling coalition. Hence, it is not *security* per se, but rather the perception of security, and the significance of the value of security to the Israeli ethos that constitutes the first fundamental obstacle towards equality. Were this the sole factor, then presumably the subsidence of the conflict would herald the victory of the liberal paradigm. This factor, however, is enjoined by another which strikes at the core of Israeli-Zionist identity. Slogans of equality do not resonate with the liberal Israeli public because of the deep-seated notions of Zionist ideology, which is entrenched, as yet, in a strict, exclusive conception of community. While the decline of ideology and the other factors listed above have begun to erode this basis, the ongoing security "crisis" feeds into these notions, allowing them to persist, and even flourish despite the fact that they seem to functionally have outgrown their use. Inclusion will become a concrete and realistic possibility only with the convergence of these two trends.

THE AMBIVALENT IMPLICATIONS OF INCLUSION

The main argument of this analysis has been that inclusion in the national identity is a necessary condition for the equal distribution of basic rights and services accorded to citizens by the nation-state. Hence, for those populations, like African Americans in the United States and Palestinians in Israel, who inhabit the margins of national identities, citizenship is not a sufficient condition for the attainment of equality within society. The implications of membership in the national identity, particularly within democracies, transcend the psychological or symbolic, and drive deep into the essence of material and political realities. National membership and with it representation in the national symbolic matrix goes a long way towards fighting the sense of alienation and distancing which results from national exclusion, and facilitates the process of political entitlement. Nonetheless, politics and symbols should serve as a backdrop to the more meaningful and significant dimension of national membership: the equal distribution of social and economic state resources.

The extent to which inclusion in the national membership truly advances not merely the political and legal standing of the excluded group, but their socioeconomic status as well remains to be seen. And here unfortunately the picture remains glum indeed. Thirty-five years following the passing of the 1964 and 1965 legislation, the economic and social standing of African Americans within American society remains dire. The average life expectancy of an African American male is no higher than that of a Sudanese or Bangladeshi male, two of the poorest third world countries.[3] Moreover, the gap between the life expectancy of White and Black men in the United States remains inordinately high. Thus while African Americans have made significant gains since the civil rights decade, much of the promise of the 1960s remains unfulfilled. As leading American scholars contend, the American nation remains a divided one.

Similarly in Israel, the advances made in national membership have not necessarily become reflected in other, more material, dimensions. Recent research has demonstrated that despite rising levels of education amongst Palestinian youth (particularly girls), the positioning of the Palestinians within the Israeli labor market remains unchanged, and unemployment is rising.[4] This data is particularly revealing and relevant to the argument made here. In the context of excluded and marginalized minorities, rising levels of education almost always reflect significant change in government policy. Education is an invaluable resource, and serves, when made more readily available to minorities, as the basis of future cultural and human capital. In Israel, however, the growing human capital amongst Palestinians in Israel is not directly translatable into economic and social resources. Hence, the liberalization of the Israeli polity has resulted in a curious hybrid.

Trying to reveal the *limitations* of national membership would appear to be beyond the purview of this project. However, a few concluding thoughts. The impact of globalization on the ability of the nation-state to supply welfare remedies to its more needy citizens has had a mixed impact. On the one hand, the ability of minorities to appeal to international human rights organizations has provided these groups with significant support and empowerment. The international context was significant for African Americans, as it is for the Palestinians in Israel. Moreover, the growing impact of the international media has made abuses of civil rights much more visible, and has forced states, such as Israel, to be careful in the way in which they present their treatment of minorities.

At the same time, the growing impact of international economic processes has caused a gradual decline in the concept of state-sovereignty and the ability of the state to provide for the needs of its weaker and needier citizens. Hence, one might propose that globalization has brought about a gradual decline in the significance of national membership and its relevance to the equal distribution of state resources. As international forces play an increasingly important role in the stability of national economies, and as the flow of international labor and capital play an important role in the dynamics of domestic economies and labor markets, national membership seems to play a weaker role in the way in which rights and resources are distributed. The future of the state-arena as the ultimate source of entitlement is uncertain. Future research will need to focus on the multiple arenas which will cater to the demands of marginalized minorities, and the different types of political strategies appropriate for each.

NOTES

1. This was attributed to Rabin during his first tenure as prime minister in 1975. "Nefolet Nemushot" roughly translates into "the cowardly of the cowards."

2. Anthony Marx, *Making Race and Nation.*

3. See Amartya Sen, *Development and Freedom* (New York: Random House, 2000), p. 5.

4. Paper given by Dr. Andrei Mazawi, at a conference on "Jewish-Arab Relations in Israel: Past and Future," Ben Gurion University, November 27, 2000.

Bibliography

Ackerman, B. A. *Social Justice in the Liberal State*. New Haven, Conn. Yale University Press, 1980.

Agassi, Joseph. *Between Religion and Nationality*. Tel Aviv: Papyrus, 1984 [Hebrew].

Agassi, Joseph, Judith Buber Agassi, and Moshe Berent. *Who Is an Israeli?* Tel Aviv: Kivunim, 1991 [Hebrew].

Almond, Gabriel, and Bingham Powell. *Comparative Politics: a Developmental Approach*. Boston: Little, Brown and Company, 1966.

Almond, Gabriel, and Sidney Verba. *The Civic Culture: Political Attitudes and Democracy in Five Nations*. 1963. Reprint, Boston: Little, Brown and Company, 1965.

Aloni, Nimrod. *To be a Person*. Tel Aviv: Hakibbutz Hameuchad, 1998 [Hebrew]

Aloni, Shulamit. *The Citizen and his State*. Tel Aviv: Ministry of Defense, 1985 [Hebrew].

Anderson, Benedict. *Imagined Communities*. Rev. and exp. ed. London: Verso, 1991.

Anderson, Lisa. "The State in the Middle East and North Africa." *Comparative Politics* 20, no. 1 (October 1987): 1–19.

Apter, David. *The Politics of Modernization*. Chicago: University of Chicago Press, 1965.

Arian, Asher. *The Choosing People: Voting Behavior in Israel*. Cleveland: Press of Case Western Reserve University, 1973.

Arian, Asher. and Michal Shamir, eds. *The Elections in Israel, 1981*. Albany: State University of New York Press, 1982.

Arian, Asher, and Michal Shamil, eds. *The Elections in Israel—1996*. New York: State University of New York Press, 1999.

Arian, Asher, *Politics in Israel*. New Jersey: Chatham House, 1985.

Arieli, Yehoshua. *Individualism and Nationalism in American Ideology*. Baltimore: Penguin Books, 1964.

Armstrong, John. *Nations Before Nationalism*. Chapel Hill: University of North Carolina Press, 1982.

Arthur, John, and Amy Shapiro. *Campus Wars: Multi-culturalism and the Politics of Difference*. Boulder, Colo.: Westview Press, 1995.

Avineri, Shlomo. *The Making of Modern Zionism*. New York: Basic Books, 1981.

Avineri, Shlomo, and Avner de-Shalit, eds. *Communitarianism and Individualism*, Oxford: Oxford University Press. 1992.

Avishai, Bernard. *The Tragedy of Zionism: Revolution and Democracy in the Land of Israel*. New York: Farrar Straus Giroux, 1985.

Aviv, Aviva. *Israeli Society: Formative Processes*. Tel Aviv: Ministry of Defense, 1990 [Hebrew].

Azaryahu, Maoz. "Street Names in Haifa." *Studies in Zionism*. 10, no. 1, (fall 1991).

Azaryahu, Maoz. "The Power of Commemorative Street Names." *Environment and Planning D: Society and Space* 14 (1996): 311–30.

Barnett, Michael N. *Israel in Comparative Perspective: Challenging the Conventional Wisdom*. Albany, N.Y.: State University of New York Press, 1996.

Barry, Brian, "John Rawls and the Search for Stability." *Ethics* 105 (July 1995): 874–915.

Barry, Brian, "Self Government Revisited." In *The Nature of Political Theory*. David Miller and Larry Siendentop, ed. Oxford: Oxford University Press, 1983.

Barth, Fredrik. *Models of Social Organization*. London: Royal Anthropological Institute, 1966.

Barzun, Jacques. *The House of Intellect*. New York: Harper Brothers, 1959.

Bates, Robert H., Avner Greif, Margaret Levi, Jean-Lauren Rosenthal, and Barry R. Weingast. *Analytic Narratives*. Princeton, N.J.: Princeton University Press, 1998.

Bell, Derrick. "*Brown* and the Interest-Convergence Dilemma," In *Shades of Brown: New Perspectives on School Desegregation*, ed. Derrick Bell, pp. 90–108. New York: The Teachers College Press, 1980.

Bellah, Robert. "Civil Religion in America." *Daedalus* 96, no. 1: 1–21.

Bendix, Reinhard. *Nation-building and Citizenship*. 1964. Reprint, Berkeley: University of California Press, 1977.

Benhabib, Seyla. "Toward a Deliberative Model of Democratic Legitimacy." In *Democracy and Difference: Contesting the Boundaries of the Political*, ed. Seyla Benhabib, 67–95. Princeton, N.J.: Princeton University Press, 1996.

Ben-Rafael, Eliezer. *The Emergence of Ethnicity: Cultural Groups and Social Conflict in Israel*. London: Greenwood Press, 1982.

Ben-Sira, Ze'ev. *Identity, Alienation in Israeli Society: Inter-Ethnic Relations*. Jerusalem: Magnes, 1978 [Hebrew].

Benziman, Uzi, and Atallah Mansour. *Subtenants*. Jerusalem: Keter Publishing House, 1992 [Hebrew].

Bergman, Peter, and Thomas Luckman. *The Social Construction of Reality: A Treatise in the Sociology of Knowledge*. 1980. Reprint, New York: Irvington Publishers, 1996.

Billig, Michael. *Banal Nationalism*. 1995. Reprint, London: Sage Publishers, 1997.

Birch, Anthony H. *Nationalism and National Integration*. London: Unwin Hyman, 1989.

Birnbaum, Pierre. *States and Collective Action: the European Experience*. Cambridge: Cambridge University Press, 1998.

Bisharah, Azmi. "The Arab Israeli: Discussions in a Fragmented Political Discourse." In *Between I and We: The Construction of Identities and Israeli Identity*, ed., Azmi Bisharah, pp. 169–90. Jerusalem: Hakkibutz Hameuchad, 1999.

Bisharah, Azmi. "The Palestinian Minority." In *Israeli Society: Critical Perspectives*, ed. Uri Ram. Tel Aviv: Breirot, 1993.

Black, Hillel. *The American Schoolbooks*. New York: William Morrow, 1967.

Blight, David W. "For Something beyond the Battlefield: Frederick Douglass and the Struggle for the Memory of the Civil War." In *Memory and American History*, ed. David Thelen, pp. 27–50. Bloomington: Indiana University Press, 1990.

Blondel, Jean, and E. Drexel Godfrey. *The Government of France*. New York: Thomas Cromwell Company, 1968.

Bodnar, John. *Remaking America: Public Memory, Commemoration, and Patriotism in the 20th Century*. Princeton, N.J.: Princeton University Press, 1992.

Boorstin, Daniel. *The Americans: The National Experience*. New York: Random House, 1965.

Bourdieu, Pierre. *Distinction: A Social Critique of the Judgement of Taste*. Cambridge, Mass.: Harvard University Press, 1984.

Bracey, J. H., A. Meier, and E. Rudwick, eds. *Black Nationalism in America*. Indianapolis and New York: Bobbs-Merrill, 1970.

Brass, Paul. "Elite Groups, Symbol Manipulation and Ethnic Identity among the Muslims of South Asia." In *Political Identity in South Asia*, ed. Taylor and Yapp. London: SOAS Curzon Press, 1979.

Breuilly, John. *Nationalism and the State*. Manchester: Manchester University Press, 1982.

Brigham, John. *Civil Liberties and American Democracy*. Washington, D.C.: CQ Press, 1984.

Brogan, D. W. *American Themes*. New York: Hamish Hamilton, 1948.

Brubaker, William Rogers, ed. *Immigration and the Politics of Citizenship in Europe and North America*. Lanham, Md.: University Press of America, 1989.

Bryce, Lord James. *Modern Democracies*. New York: Macmillan, 1921.

Buchanan, J. M. *The Demand and Supply of Public Goods*. Chicago: Rand McNally, 1968.

Burnham, Walter Dean. *The Current Crisis in American Politics*. New York: Oxford University Press, 1982.

Burstein, Paul. "Public Opinion, Demonstrations, and the Passage of Anti-Discrimination Legislation." *Public Opinion Quarterly* 43 (1979): 157–73.

Button, James W. *Blacks and Social Change: Impact of the Civil Rights Movement in Southern Communities*. 1989. Reprint, Princeton, N.J.: Princeton University Press, 1993.

Button, James W. *Black Violence*. Princeton, N.J.: Princeton University Press, 1978.

Carmichael, Stokely, and Charles Hamilton. *Black Power: the Politics of Liberation in America*. Middlesex, England: Penguin Books, 1967.

Carmines, Edward G., and James A. Stimpson. *Race and the Transformation of American Politics*. Princeton, N.J.: Princeton University Press, 1989.

Carpenter, Charles. *History of American Schoolbooks*. Philadelphia: University of Pennsylvania Press, 1963.

Carr, E. H. *What is History?* Middlesex, England: Penguin, 1961.

Cartwright, William H., and Richard L. Watson Jr., eds. *Interpreting and Teaching American History*, 31st Yearbook of the National Council for the Social Studies. Washington, D.C.: National Educational Association, 1961.

Cartwright, William H., and Richard L. Watson Jr., eds. *The Reinterpretation of American History and Culture*, Washington, D.C.: National Council for the Social Studies, 1973.

Citrin, Jack, Beth Reingold, and Donald P. Green. "American Identity and the Politics of Ethnic Change." *Journal of Politics* 52, no. 4 (1990): 1124–54.

Clayborne, Carson. *In Struggle: SNCC and the Black Awakening of the 1960s*. Cambridge, Mass.: Harvard University Press, 1981.

Cohen, Abner. "Political Anthropology: The Analysis of the Symbolism of Power Relations." *Man* 4 (June 1969): 427–48.

Cohen, Erik. "Citizenship, Nationality and Religion in Israel and Thailand." In *The Israeli State and Society: Boundaries and Frontiers*, ed. Baruch Kimmerling. Albany: State University of New York Press, 1989.

Cohen, Jean, and Andrew Arato. *Civil Society and Political Theory*. Cambridge, Mass.: MIT Press, 1992.

Cohen, Robin. "Migrants in Europe: Processes of Exclusion and Inclusion." *New Community* 18, no. 2 (January 1992): 332–36.

Combs, Michael W. "The Supreme Court and African Americans: Personnel and Policy Transformations." *Howard Law Journal* 36 (1993): 139–84.

Commager, Henry Steele. *The American Mind: An Interpretation of American Thought and Character Since the 1880's*. New Haven, Conn.: Yale University Press, 1950.

Congressional Digest. "The Controversy over the 'Equal Employment Opportunity' Provisions of the Civil Rights Bill." March 1964: 67–93.

Congressional Digest. "The Controversy over the 'Public Accommodations' Provisions of the Kennedy Civil Rights Proposals," November 1963: 259–83.

Connor, Walker. *Ethnonationalism: The Quest for Understanding*. Princeton, N.J.: Princeton University Press, 1994.

Connor, Walker. "Nation-Building or Nation Destroying?" *World Politics* 24, no. 3 (April 1972): 319–55.

Couper, Kristin. "Immigration, Nationality and Citizenship in the UK." *New Political Science* 35, nos. 16/17 (fall/winter 1989): 91–101.

Couture, Jocelyne, Kai Nielsen, and Michel Seymour, eds. *Rethinking Nationalism*. Calgary: Calgary University Press, 1996.

Curti, Merle. *American Issues: The Social Record*. 4th ed. New York: J. B. Lippincott Company, 1971.

Curti, Merle. *The Growth of American Thought*. 3d ed. New York: Harper and Row, 1964.

Curtis, Michael, and Mordechai Chertoff, eds. *Israel: Social Structure and Change*. New Brunswick: Transaction Books, 1973.

Dahl, Robert. *Democracy, Liberty, and Equality*. Denmark: Norwegian University Press, 1986.

Dahl, Robert. *Polyarchy, Participation and Opposition.* New Haven, Conn.: Yale University Press, 1977.

Dahl, Robert. *A Preface to Democratic Theory.* Chicago: The University of Chicago Press, 1956.

Dale, Richard. "Nation-Building in Namibia: The Search for International Legitimacy." *Canadian Review of Studies in Nationalism* 18, nos. 1/2 (1991): 33–43.

Davidson, Chandler, and Bernard Grofman, eds. *Quiet Revolution in the South: The Impact of the Voting Rights Act 1965–1990.* Princeton, N.J.: Princeton University Press, 1994.

Deutsch, Karl. *Nationalism as Social Communication.* New York: M.I.T. Press, 1966.

Divine, Robert A. ed. The Great Society. Vol. 2 of *The Johnson Years.* Lawrence: University Press of Kansas, 1987.

Doron, Gideon. "Civil Society in Israel." In *Civil Society in the Middle East,* ed. Augustus Richard Norton. Leiden: E. J. Brill, 1995.

Doron, Gideon, and Michael Harris. *Public Policy and Electoral Reform in Israel.* Lanham, Md.: Lexington Books, 2000.

Drotning, Phillip T. *Black Heroes in Our Nation's History.* New York: Washington Square Press, 1969.

Dryzek, John S. "Political inclusion and the Dynamics of Democratization." *American Political Science Review* 90 (1996): 475–87.

Dubnow, Simon. *Nationalism and History: Essays on Old and New Judaism.* New York: Atheneum, 1970.

Dudziak, Mary L. "Desegregation as Cold War Imperative." *Stanford Law Review* 41 (November 1988): 61.

Dudziak, Mary L. "The Little Rock Crisis and Foreign Affairs: Race, Resistance, and the Image of American Democracy." *Southern California Law Review* 70 (September 1997).

Duncan, Graeme and Steven Lukes. "The New Democracy." *Political Studies* 2 (1963): 156–77.

Edelman, Martin. *The Symbolic Uses of Politics.* 1967. Reprint, Chicago: University of Illinois Press, 1985.

Eisenstadt, S. N. *The Development of the Ethnic Problem in Israeli Society.* Jerusalem: Jerusalem Institute for Israeli Studies, 1989.

Eisenstadt, S. N. "Israeli Identity: Problems in the Development of the Collective Identity of an Ideological Society." *The Annals of the American Academy of Political and Social Science* 370 (March 1967): 116–23.

Eisenstadt, S. N. *Israeli Society.* London: Weidenfeld and Nicholson, 1967.

Eisenstadt, S. N. *The Transformation of Israeli Society.* London: Weidenfeld and Nicolson, 1985.

Eisenstadt, S. N. and Stein Rokkan. *Building States and Nations.* Beverly Hills: Sage Publications, 1973.

Eisenstadt, S. N., Rivka Bar-Yoseph, and Chaim Adler, eds. *Integration and Development in Israel.* London: Weidenfeld and Sons, 1970.

Elazar, Daniel., ed. *Constitutionalism: The Israeli and American Experience.* Lanham, Md.: University Press of America, 1990.

Elson, Ruth Miller. *Guardians of Tradition: American Schoolbooks in the Nineteenth Century*. Lincoln: University of Nebraska Press, 1964.

Elster, Jon. *The Cement of Society: A Study of Social Order*. Cambridge: Cambridge University Press, 1989.

Elster, Jon, ed. *Rational Choice*. New York: New York University Press. 1986.

Enloe, Cynthia. *Ethnic Conflict and Political Development*. Boston: Little, Brown and Company, 1973.

Etzioni, Amitai. *The Spirit of Community: The Reinvention of American Society*. New York: Touchstone Books, 1993.

Etzioni-Halevy, Eva, (with Rina Shapira). *Political Culture in Israel*. New York: Praeger Publishers, 1977.

Even-Zohar, Itamar. "The Emergence of a Native Hebrew Culture in Palestine 1882–1948." *Studies in Zionism* 4 (1986): 167–84.

Evron, Boaz. *A National Reckoning*. Tel-Aviv: Dvir, 1988 [Hebrew].

Farley, Reynolds. *Blacks and Whites: Narrowing the Gap*. Cambridge, Mass.: Harvard University Press, 1984.

Fedyck, Micheline. "Conceptions of Citizenship and Nationality in High School American History Textbooks, 1913–1977." Unpublished Ph.D. Dissertation, Columbia University, 1980.

Firth, Raymond. *Symbols: Public and Private*. London: Allen and Unwin, 1973.

Fisherman, Haya, and Joshua A. Fishman. "The 'Official Languages' of Israel: Their Status in Law and Police Attitudes and Knowledge Concerning Them." In *Multilingual Political Systems: Problems and Solutions*, ed. Jean-Guy Savard and Richard Vigneault. Quebec: Les Presses de L'Universite Laval, 1975.

Fitzgerald, Francis. *America Revised*. New York: Vintage Books, 1980.

Foner, Eric. "The Blacks and the Constitution." *New Left Review* no. 183 (Sept/Oct 1990): 63–75.

Frohlich, N., J. Oppenheimer, and O. R. Young. *Political Leadership and Collective Goods*. Princeton: Princeton University Press, 1971.

Fuchs, Lawrence H. *The American Kaleidoscope: Race, Ethnicity, and the Civic Culture*. Hanover: Wesleyan University Press, 1990.

Fukayama, Francis. *The End of History and the Last Man*. New York: The Free Press, 1992.

Gabriel, Ralph H. *The Course of American Democratic Thought: An Intellectual History Since 1815*. 2d ed. New York: The Ronald Press Company, 1956.

Garcia, Jesus, and Julie Goebel. "A Comparative Study of the Portrayal of Black Americans in Selected US History Textbooks." *The Negro Educational Review* 36, nos. 3/4 (1985): 118–27.

Garrow, David J. "Hopelessly Hollow History: Revisionist Devaluing of *Brown v. Board of Education*." *Virginia Law Review* 80 (February 1994): 156.

Geertz, Clifford. *The Interpretation of Cultures*. New York: Basic Books, 1973.

Gellner, Ernest. *Nations and Nationalism*. Oxford: Basil Blackwell, 1983.

Gertz, Nurit, ed. *Perspectives on Culture and Society in Israel*. Tel Aviv: Everyman's University, 1988 [Hebrew].

Ghanem, Assad, and Sara Osotzki-Lazar. *The Arab Vote to the 15th Parliament*. Givat Haviva: The Institute for Peace Research, October 1999.

Giddens, Anthony. *The Nation-State and Violence*. Vol. 2 of *A Contemporary Critique of Historical Materialism*. Cambridge: Polity Press, 1987.

Gillis, John R., ed. *Commemorations: The Politics of National Identity*. Princeton, N.J.: Princeton University Press, 1994.

Glazer, Nathan, and Daniel P. Moynihan. *Beyond the Melting Pot*. Cambridge, Mass.: 1963. Reprint, Harvard University Press, 1970.

Glazer, Nathan, and Reed Ueda. *Ethnic Groups in History Textbooks*. Washington D.C.: Ethics and Public Policy Center, 1976.

Gleason, Philip. "American Identity and Americanization." In *Concepts of Ethnicity*, ed. William Petersen, Michael Novak, Philip Gleason. Cambridge, Mass.: Harvard University Press, 1980.

Goldfarb, Jefferey C. *The Cynical Society: The Culture of Politics and Politics of Culture*. Chicago: The University of Chicago Press, 1990.

Gorni, Yosef. *The Quest for Collective Identity*. Tel Aviv: Am Oved, 1990 [Hebrew].

Graetz, Heinrich. *The Structure of Jewish History and Other Essays*. New York: The Jewish Theological Seminary of America, 1975.

Granott, A. *The Land Issue in Palestine*. Jerusalem, 1936.

Greenberg, Stanley. *Race and State in Capitalist Development*. New Haven, Conn.: Yale University Press, 1980.

Grinberg, Lev Luis. *Split Corporatism in Israel*. New York: State University of New York Press, 1991.

Grob, Gerald N., and Robert N. Beck, eds. *American Ideas; Source Readings in the Intellectual History of the U.S.* London: The Free Press of Glencoe, 1963.

Groman, Rachel. *The Arab Minority in Israel*, Lelach Publishers: Petah Tikva, 1995.

Grossman, David. *Present Absentees*. Tel Aviv: Ha'kibbutz Ha'Meuchad, 1992 [Hebrew].

Gutman, Amy. "Communitarian Critiques of Liberalism." *Philosophy and Public Affairs* 14, no. 3 (summer 1985): 308–22.

Ha'am, Ahad. "The Truth from Eretz Israel." In *Writings of Ahad Ha'am*. Jerusalem, 1946, pp. 25–6 [Hebrew].

Habermas, Jurgen. "Citizenship and National Identity." In *The Condition of Citizenship*, ed. Bart van Steenbergen. London: Sage Publications, 1994.

Haidar, Aziz. *Social Welfare Services for Israel's Arab Population*. Boulder, Colo.: Westview Press, 1990.

Haines, Herbert. *Black Radicals and the Civil Rights Mainstream, 1954–1970*. Knoxville: University of Tennessee Press, 1988.

Al-Haj, Majid. *Education, Empowerment and Control*. Albany: SUNY University Press, 1995.

Al-Haj, Majid. *Education and Social Change Amongst the Arabs in Israel*. Tel Aviv: International Center for Peace in the Middle East, 1991 [Hebrew].

Al-Haj, Majid. "The Employment Situation of Arab Academics in Israel." In *The Employment Distress of the Arab University Graduates in Israel*. ed. Majid Al-Haj. Haifa: The University of Haifa, The Jewish Arab Center, 1991 [Hebrew].

Al-Haj, Majid. "Ethnic Relations in an Arab Town in Israel." In *Studies in Israeli Ethnicity: After the Ingathering*. ed. Alex Weingrod. London: Gordon and Breach, 1985.

Al-Haj, Majid. "The Impact of the Intifada on Arabs in Israel: The Case of a Double Periphery." In *Framing the Intifada: Media and People*, ed. Akiva Cohen and Gadi Wolsfeld. Ablex Publishing Corporation, 1991.

Al-Haj, Majid, and Avner Yaniv. "Uniformity or Diversity: A Reappraisal of the Voting Behavior of the Arab Minority in Israel." In *The Elections in Israel 1981*, ed. Asher Arian and Michal Shamir. Albany: State University of New York Press, 1982: 139–64.

Halpern, Ben. *The Idea of a Jewish State*. Cambridge, Mass, Harvard University Press, 1961.

Hamilton, Alexander, James Madison, and John Jay. *The Federalist*, ed. Benjamin Fletcher Wright. Cambridge, Mass.: Belknap Press of Harvard University Press, 1961.

Hamilton, Charles V. "Political Access, Minority Participation and the New Normalcy." In *Minority Report*, ed. Leslie W. Dunbar. New York: Pantheon Books, 1984.

Hamilton, Charles V. "Social Policy and the Welfare of Black Americans: From Rights to Resources." *Political Science Quarterly* 101, no. 2 (1986): 239–55.

Hammar, Tomas. *Democracy and the Nation State: Aliens, Denizens and Citizens in a World of International Migration*. Aldershot: Avebury, 1990.

Harden, D. *Contemporary Jewish National Thinking*. Jerusalem: World Zionist Organization Publication, no. 5, 1970 [Hebrew].

Hardin, Russel. *Collective Action*. Baltimore: John Hopkins University Press, 1982.

Hardin, Russel. *One for All: The Logic of Group Conflict*. Princeton, N.J.: Princeton University Press, 1995.

Hareven, Aluph, ed. *On the Difficulty of Being an Israeli*. Jerusalem: The Van Leer Foundation, 1983 [Hebrew].

Hartz, Louis. *The Liberal Tradition in America: An Interpretation of American Political Thought Since the Revolution*. New York: Harcourt, Brace and World, 1955.

Head, John G. *Public Goods and Public Welfare*. Durham, N.C.: Duke University Press, 1974.

"Hearing of the Committee on Post Office and Civil Service House of Representatives." June 7, 1983. U.S. Government Printing Office, Washington, D.C.

Hechter, Michael. *Internal Colonialism: The Celtic Fringe in British National Development, 1536–1966*. Berkeley: University of California Press, 1975.

Hechter, Michael. "Nationalism as Group Solidarity." *Ethnic and Racial Studies* 10, no. 4 (October 1987): 415–26.

Hechter, Michael. *Principles of Group Solidarity*. Berkeley: University of California Press, 1987.

Held, David. *Models of Democracy*. Cambridge: Polity Press, 1987.

Hempel, Carl. *Philosophy of Natural Science*. Englewood Cliffs, N.J.: Prentice Hall, 1966.

Hertzberg, Arthur. *The Zionist Idea*. New York: Meridian, 1960.

Higham, John. *Send these to Me*. New York: Atheneum, 1975.

Higham, John. *Strangers in the Land: Patterns of American Nativism, 1860–1925*. New York: Atheneum Press, 1966.

Higham, John, ed. *Civil Rights and Social Wrongs: Black-White Relations Since World War II*. University Park: The Pennsylvania State University Press, 1997.

Hobbes, Thomas. *Leviathan*. London: Dent, 1973.

Hobsbawm, Eric. *The Age of Capital*. 1979. Reprint, New York: New American Library, 1984.

Hobsbawm, Eric. *Nations and Nationalism Since 1780*. Cambridge: Cambridge University Press, 1990.

Hobsbawm, Eric. and Terence Ranger, eds. *Invention of Tradition*. Cambridge: Cambridge University Press, 1983.

Homans, George Casper. "Contemporary Theory in Sociology." In *Sociological Methods*, ed. Norman K. Denzin. Chicago: Aldine, 1970.

Hornsby, Alton, Jr., ed. *Chronology of African-American History*. Detroit: Gale Research, 1991.

Horowitz, Dan, and Moshe Lissak. *Origins of the Israeli Polity*. Chicago: University of Chicago Press, 1978.

Horowitz, Donald L. *Ethnic Groups in Conflict*. Berkeley: University of California Press, 1985.

Huggins, Nathan Irwin. *Harlem Renaissance*. New York: Oxford University Press, 1971.

Huntington, Samuel P. *American Politics: The Promise of Disharmony*. Cambridge: Harvard University Press, 1981.

Huntington, Samuel. *Political Order in Changing Societies*. New Haven, Conn.: Yale University Press, 1968.

Hurewitz, J. C. *The Struggle for Palestine*. 1950. Reprint, New York: Schoken Books, 1976.

Ibrahim, Malik. *The Islamic Movement in Israel*. Givat Haviva, paper no. 4, 1990.

Ignatieff, Michael, 1995. *Blood and Belonging: Journeys into the New Nationalism*. New York: Farrar, Straus, Giroux, 1995.

Inbar, Michael, and Chaim Adler. *Ethnic Integration in Israel*. New Jersey: Transaction Books, 1977.

Inglehart, Ronald. *Culture Shift in Advanced Industrial Society*. Princeton, N.J.: Princeton University Press, 1990.

Issacs, Harold R. *The World of Negro Americans*. 1963.

Jaynes, Gerald David, and Robin M. Williams Jr., eds. *A Common Destiny: Blacks and American Society*. Washington, D.C.: National Academy Press, 1989.

Jiryis, Sabri. *The Arabs in Israel*. New York: Monthly Review Press, 1976.

Kahane, Reuven, and Simcha Kopshtein, eds. *Israeli Society 1967–73*. Jerusalem: Academon, 1974 [Hebrew].

Kalderon, Nissim. *Pluralists Despite Themselves*. Haifa: Haifa University Press, 2000 [Hebrew].

Kammen, Michael. *The Machine that Would Go of Itself: The Constitution in American Culture*. New York: Knopf, 1986.

Kane, Michael B. *Minorities in Textbooks: A Study of Their Treatment in Social Studies Texts*. New York: Quadrangle Books, 1970.

Karl, Popper. *The Poverty of Historicism*. 1957. Reprint, London: ARK Paperbacks, 1961.

Karst, Kenneth L. *Belonging to America: Equal Citizenship and the Constitution.* New Haven, Conn.: Yale University Press, 1989.

Karst, Kenneth L. "Paths to Belonging: The Constitution and Cultural Identity." *North Carolina Law Review* 64 (1986): 303–77.

Katz, Jacob. *Jewish Emancipation and Self-Emancipation.* Philadelphia: Jewish Publication Society, 1986.

Katz, Jacob. *Out of the Ghetto: The Social Background of Jewish Emancipation, 1770–1870.* New York: Schoken Books, 1978.

Katz, William Loren. *Teachers' Guide to American Negro History.* Chicago: Quadrangle Books, 1971 (1968).

Kaufman, Ilana. "From All comes One: In The Vote of the Arabs in Israel during the 1996 Elections." In *The Elections in Israel—1996,* ed. Asher Arian and Michal Shamil. New York: State University of New York Press, 1999.

Keane, John, ed. *Civil Society and the State: New European Perspectives.* London: Verso, 1988.

Kedourie, Elie. *Nationalism.* London: Hutchinson, 1960.

Kedourie, Elie, ed. *Nationalism in Asia and Africa.* London: Weidenfeld and Nicolson, 1971.

Kelley, R. *The Cultural Pattern in American Politics.* New York: Knopf, 1979.

Kelty, Mary G. *Teaching American History in the Middle Grades of the Elementary School.* New York: Ginn and Company, 1928. [Property of Board of Education, Mar 4, 1930, City of New York].

Keohane, R. *After Hegemony: Cooperation and Discord in the World Political Economy.* Princeton, N.J.: Princeton University Press, 1984.

Kettner, James. *The Development of American Citizenship: 1608–1870.* Chapel Hill: University of North Carolina Press, 1978.

Kilson, Martin. "Blacks and Neo-Ethnicity in American Political Life." In *Ethnicity,* ed. Nathan Glazer and D. P. Moynahan. Cambridge, Mass.: Harvard University Press, 1975.

Kimmerling, Baruch. "Between the Primordial and the Civil Definition of the Collective Identity: Eretz Israel or the State of Israel?" In *Comparative Social Dynamics,* ed. E. Cohen, M. Lissak, U. Almagor. Boulder, Colo.: Westview Press, 1985: 262–283.

Kimmerling, Baruch. "The Impact of the Land and Territorial Components of the Jewish-Arab Conflict on the Building of Jewish Society in Palestine." Ph.D. Dissertation, The Hebrew University, Jerusalem, 1975 [Hebrew].

Kimmerling, Baruch. "Sociology, Ideology and Nation-Building: The Palestinians and Their Meaning in Israeli Sociology." *American Sociological Review* 57, no. 4 pp. 446–60.

Klarman, Michael J. "*Brown,* Racial Change, and the Civil Rights Movement." *Virginia Law Review Association* 80, no. 4 (February 1994).

Klarman, Michael J. "How *Brown* Changed Race Relations: the Backlash Thesis." *Journal of American History* 81 (June 1994): 81–118.

Kluger, Richard. *The History of* Brown vs. Board of Education *and Black America's Struggle for Equality.* New York: Vintage Books, 1977.

Kohn, Hans. *American Nationalism: An Interpretive Essay*. New York: Macmillan, 1957.

Kohn, Hans. *The Idea of Nationalism: A Study in its Origins and Background*, 1944. Reprint, New York: Macmillan, 1967.

Kook, Rebecca. "Dilemmas of Ethnic Minorities in Democracies: The Effect of Peace on the Palestinians in Israel." *Politics and Society* 23 (1995): 309–36.

Kook, Rebecca. "Towards the Rehabilitation of 'Nation Building' and the Reconstruction of Nations." Paper presented at the Annual Meeting of the APSA Sept. 1995, p. 5.

Krasner, Stephen, ed. *International Regimes*. 1983. Reprint, Ithaca, N.Y.: Cornell University Press, 1986.

Kretzmer, David. *The Legal Status of The Arabs in Israel*. Boulder, Colo.: Westview Press, 1990.

Kull, Andrew. *The Color Blind Constitution*. Cambridge, Mass.: Harvard University Press, 1992.

Kymlicka, Will. *Multicultural Citizenship*. Oxford: Clarendon Press, 1995.

Kymlicka, Will, and Wayne Norman. "Return of the Citizen: A Survey of Recent Work on Citizenship Theory." *Ethics* 104 (January 1994): 257–89.

Laitin, David D. *Hegemony and Culture*. Chicago: The University of Chicago Press, 1986.

Laitin, David D., Carlota Sole, and Stathis N. Kalyvas. "Language and the Construction of States: The Case of Catalonia in Spain." *Politics and Society* 22 (1994): 5–29.

Lakatos, Imre. *The Methodology of Scientific Research Programmes*. Cambridge: Cambridge University Press, 1978.

Langer, Suzanne K. "On Cassirer's Theory of Language and Myth." In *The Philosophy of Ernst Cassirer*, ed. Paul A. Schlipp. Evanston: Library of Living Philosophers, 1949.

Laqueur, Walter. *A History of Zionism*. London: Weidenfeld and Nicolson, 1972.

Lasswell, Harold. *Power and Society*. New Haven, Conn.: Yale University Press, 1950.

Laver, Michael. *Private Desires, Political Action*. London: Sage Publications, 1997.

Lawson, Steven F. *Black Ballots: Voting Rights in the South 1944–1969*. New York: Columbia University Press, 1976.

Lee, Susan Pendleton. *A School History of the U.S.* Richmond: R. J. Johnson, 1895.

Levi-Faur, David. "Nationalism and the Power of Business: The Manufacturers' Association of Israel," *Environment and Planning C: Government and Policy* 14 (1996): 14–26.

Levine, Lawrence W., and Robert Middlekauff, eds. *The National Temper: Readings in American Culture and Society*. 2d ed. New York: Harcourt, Brace Jovanovich, 1972.

Lewin-Epstein, Noah, and Moshe Semyonov. "Ethnic Group Mobility in the Israeli Labor Market." *American Sociological Review* 51 (June 1986): 342–51.

Liebman, Charles, and Eliezer Don Yehiya. *Civil Religion in Israel*. Berkeley: University of California Press, 1983.

Lijphart, Arend. "Comparative Politics and the Comparative Method." *American Political Science Review* 65 (1971): 682–93.

Lijphart, Arend. *Democracies: Patterns of Majoritarian and Consensual Government in Twenty One Countries.* New Haven, Conn.: Yale University Press, 1984.

Lipset, Seymour Martin. *The First New Nation: The United States in Historical and Comparative Perspective.* 1963. Reprint, New York and London: W. W. Norton and Company, 1979.

Lissak, Mosh, ed. *Sect, Nationality and Class in Israeli Society.* Tel Aviv: Everyman's University, 1989 [Hebrew].

Locke, John. *Two Treatises of Government.* Cambridge: Cambridge University Press, 1988.

Lorwin, Val R. "Segmented Pluralism: Ideological Cleavages and Political Cohesion in the Smaller European Democracies." *Comparative Politics* 3, no. 2 (January 1971): 148.

Lowi, Theodore. *The End of Liberalism: The Second Republic of the United States.* 2d ed. New York: W. W. Norton, 1979.

Lukes, S., ed. *Power.* Oxford: Blackwell, 1986.

Lustick, Ian. *Arabs in the Jewish State.* Austin: University of Texas Press, 1980.

MacIntyre, Alasdair. *After Virtue: A Study in Moral Theory.* Notre Dame, Indiana: University of Notre Dame Press, 1981.

MacIntyre, Alasdair. "Is a Science of Comparative Politics Possible?" In *Philosophy, Politics and Society,* ed. Peter Laslett, W. G. Runciman, and Quentin Skinner, pp. 8–27. Oxford: Basil Blackwell, 1972.

Mackintosh, Barry. *The Historic Sites Survey and National Landmarks Program: A History.* Washington, D.C.: History Division, National Park Service, Department of the Interior, 1985.

Macpherson, C. B. *Democratic Theory: Essays in Retrieval.* Oxford: Clarendon Press, 1973.

Makhoul, Najwa. "Changes in the Employment Structure of Arabs in Israel." *Journal of Palestine Studies* 11, no. 3 (spring 1982): 77–102.

Malik, Ibrahim. *The Islamic Movement in Israel.* Givat Haviva: Institute for Arab Studies, August 1990.

Malinowski, B. *The Coral Gardens and Their Magic.* London: Allen and Unwin. 1935.

Mandel, Neville J. *The Arabs and Zionism Before World War I.* Berkeley: University of California Press, 1976.

Mansour, Atallah. "On Integration, Equality and Co-Existence." In *One out of Every Six Israelis,* ed. Alouph Hareven, pp. 77–96. Jerusalem: The Van Leer Jerusalem Foundation, 1981 [Hebrew].

March, J. G., ed. *Handbook of Organizations.* Chicago: Rand McNally, 1965.

Marshall, T. H. *Class, Citizenship and Social Development.* New York: Anchor Books, 1965.

Martin, Ben L. "From Negro to Black to African American: The Power of Names and Naming." *Political Science Quarterly* 106, no. 1 (1991): 83–107.

Marx, Anthony W. *Making Race and Nation: A Comparison of the United States, South Africa, and Brazil.* New York: Cambridge University Press, 1998.

Mason, Andrew. "Political Community, Liberal-Nationalism, and the Ethics of Assimilation." *Ethics* 109 (January 1999): 261–86.

Mayer, Jacob P. *Prophet of the Mass Age: A Study of Alexis de Tocqueville.* New York: Arno Press, 1979.

Mayer, Thomas S. *The Awakening of the Moslems in Israel.* Givat Haviva: Institute for Arab Studies, 1988.

Mayo, James M. "Remembrance as Political Critique." In *War Memorials as Political Landscape: The American Experience and Beyond.* New York: Praeger, 1988.

Medvedev, Roy. *Let History Judge.* New York: Columbia University Press, 1989.

Mehta, Uday S. "Liberal Strategies of Exclusion." *Politics and Society* 18, no. 4 (1990): 427–54.

Meinecke, Friedrich. *Cosmopolitanism and the National State.* trans. Robert B. Keiber. Princeton N.J.: Princeton University Press, 1970.

Merelman, Richard M., Greg Streich, and Paul Martin. "Unity and Diversity in American Political Culture: An Exploratory Study of the National Conversation on American Pluralism and Identity." *Political Psychology* 34 (1998): 781–807.

Mill, J. S. *Considerations on Representative Government.* 1861. Reprint, Chicago: Regnery, 1962.

Miller, Eugene F. "Positivism, Historicism and Political Inquiry." *American Political Science Review.* 66 (September 1972): 796–874.

Morris, Aldon D. *The Origins of the Civil Rights Movement: Black Communities Organizing for Change.* New York: The Free Press, 1984.

Morris, Benny. *The Birth of the Palestinian Refugee Problem, 1947–1949.* Cambridge: Cambridge University Press, 1987.

Motyl, Alexander. *Sovietology, Rationality, Nationality.* New York: Columbia University Press, 1990.

Motyl, Alexander. *Will the Non-Russians Rebel?* Ithaca, N.Y.: Cornell University Press, 1989.

Moynahan, Daniel, and Nathan Glazer. *Ethnicity.* Cambridge, Mass.: Harvard University Press, 1975.

Musgrave, R. A. *The Theory of Public Finance.* New York: McGraw-Hill, 1959.

Myrdal, Gunnar. *An American Dilemma: The Negro Problem and American Democracy.* New York: Harper and Row, 1944.

Newman, Saul. "Does Modernization Breed Ethnic Political Conflict?" *World Politics* 43 (April 1991): 451–78.

Nora, Pierre. *Constructing the Past.* Cambridge: Cambridge University Press, 1985.

Olson, Mancur, Jr. *The Logic of Collective Action.* Cambridge, Mass.: Harvard University Press, 1965.

Olson, Mancur. *The Rise and Decline of Nations.* New Haven, Conn.: Yale University Press, 1982.

O'Neill, William L., ed. *Insights and Parallels: Problems and Issues of American Social History.* Minneapolis: Burgess Publishing Company, 1973.

Orni, E. *Land in Israel: History, Policy, Administration, Development.* Jerusalem: Jewish National Fund, 1981.

Ozacky-Lazar, Sarah. *Ikrit and Biram: Surveys on the Arabs in Israel*, No. 10. Givat Haviva: The Arab Institute, 1993.

Ozacky-Lazar, Sarah, and Assad Ghanem. *Green Line, Red Line: The Israeli Arabs and the Intifada.* Givat Haviva: The Arab Institute Publishing, 1990 [Hebrew].

Ozacky-Lazar, Sarah and Assad Ghanem. *The Arab Vote for the 14th Knesset, May 29 1996.* Givat Haviva: The Institute for Peace Research, 1996.

Paine, Thomas. "Common Sense." In *Life and Works*, ed. W. M. Van der Wyde. Vol. 2. New Rochelle, 1925: 123–24.

Pappe, Ilan. "An Uneasy Coexistence: Arabs and Jews in the First Decade of Statehood." In *Israel: The First Decade of Independence*, ed. S. Ilan Troen and Noah Lucas, pp. 617–58. Albany: State University of New York Press, 1995.

Parekh, Bikhu. "Defining National Identity in a Multicultural Society." In *People, Nation and State: The Meaning of Ethnicity and Nationalism*, ed. Edward Mortimer. London: I. B. Taurus, 1999.

Parsons, Talcott. *The Structure of Social Action.* New York: McGraw-Hill, 1937.

Peled, Yoav. "Ethnic Democracy and the Legal Structure of Citizenship: Arab Citizens of the Jewish State." *American Political Science Review* 86, no. 2 (1992): 432–42.

Peled, Yoav, and Gershon Shafir. "Liberalization and Peace in a Frontier Society." Paper presented at the conference on "The Middle East at a Crossroads," organized by the Herzog Center at Ben Gurion University, December 6–8, 1999.

Peleg, Ilan, and Ofira Seliktar, eds. *The Emergence of Binational Israel.* Boulder, San Francisco, and London: Westview Press, 1989.

Peres, Shimon. *The New Middle East.* New York: Henry Holt, 1993.

Peres, Yochanan. *Ethnic Relations in Israel.* Tel Aviv: Sifriyat Hapoalim, 1976 [Hebrew].

Peretz, Don. *Israel and the Palestinian Arabs.* Washington, D.C.: The Middle East Institute, 1956.

Peri, Yoram. *Minorities in Israel.* Petah Tikva: Lelach Publishers, 1998.

Plamenatz, John. "Two Types of Nationalism," In *Nationalism*, ed. Eugene Kamenka, pp. 22–38. London: Edward Arnold, 1976.

Platek, Yitzhak, and Muhamad M'Hamid. *The Mark of Coal: The World of Young Arabs in Israel.* Givat Haviva: Institute for Arab Studies, 1989 [Hebrew].

Ploski, Harry A., ed. *The Negro Almanac: A Reference Work on the African American.* 5th ed. Detroit: Gale Research, 1989.

Plummer, Brenda Gayle. *Rising Wind: Black Americans and US Foreign Affairs, 1935–1960.* Chapel Hill: The University of North Carolina Press, 1996.

Poggi, Gianfranco. *The State: Its Nature, Development and Prospects.* Stanford: Stanford University Press, 1990.

Politika. Vol. 2, no. 8 (1988).

Polenberg, Richard. *One Nation Divisible.* New York: Penguin Books, 1980.

Powell, Bingham G., Jr. *Contemporary Democracies.* Cambridge, Mass.: Harvard University Press, 1982.

Rabinowitz, Dan. "Eastern Nostaligia: How Palestinians became 'Israeli Arabs.'" *Theory and Criticism* 4 (autumn 1993): 141–159 [Hebrew].

Rabinowitz, Dan. *Overlooking Nazareth: The Ethnogoraphy of Exclusion in Galilee*, Cambridge: Cambridge University Press, 1997.

Raffert, Max Lewis. *What Are They Doing to Your Children?* New York: New American Library, 1964.

Rahat, Rivka. *Social Patterns in Israel: Unity and Disruption and Ethnic Group Relations*. Ramat Aviv: Everyman's University, 1983 [Hebrew].

Ram, Uri. *The Changing Agenda of Israeli Sociology: Theory, Ideology and Identity*. Albany: State University of New York Press, 1995.

Raulet, Gerard. "Citizenship, Nationality and Internationality." *Contemporary European Affairs* 3, no. 3 (1990): 150–71.

Rawls, John. "Justice as Fairness: Political not Metaphysical." *Philosophy and Public Affairs* 14, no. 3 (summer 1985): 224–51.

Rawls, John. *Political Liberalism*. New York: Columbia University Press, 1993.

Reeve, Andrew. "The Theory of Property: Beyond Private versus Common Property." In *Political Theory Today*, ed. David Held. Stanford: Stanford University Press, 1991.

Reinhold, Robert. "Class Struggle: California's Textbook Debate." *New York Times Magazine*, September 21, 1991: 26–30.

Reiss, Nira. *The Health Care of Arabs in Israel*. Boulder, Colo.: Westview Press, 1990.

Reiter, Yitzhak, and Reuben Aharoni. *The Political Life of Arabs in Israel*. Raananah: The Institute for Israeli Arabs Studies Beit Berl, 1992 [Hebrew].

Rekhess, Eli. *The Arab Village in Israel—A Renewed Political/National Center*. Tel Aviv: The Dayan Center for Africa and the Middle East, Tel Aviv University, May 1985.

Rekhess, Eli. *Israeli Arabs and the Expropriation of Lands in the Galilee*. Tel-Aviv: Shiloah Institute, 1977 [Hebrew].

Rekhess, Eli. "Socio-Economic Implications of the Employment of Arab University Graduates." In *The Employment Distress*, ed. Majid Al-Haj, pp. 49–56. Haifa: The University of Haifa, The Jewish Arab Center, 1991.

Riker, William H. "Public Safety as a Public Good." In *Is Law Dead?* ed. Eugene V. Rostow, pp. 370–85. New York: Simon and Schuster, 1971.

Robertson, R. "The Sociological Significance of Culture: Some General Considerations." *Theory Culture and Society* 5 (1988): 3–24.

Rosenberg, Gerald N. *The Hollow Hope: Can Courts Bring About Social Change?* Chicago: University of Chicago Press, 1991.

Rothschild, Joseph. *Ethno-Politics*. New York: Columbia University Press, 1981.

Rouhana, Nadim. "Collective Identity and Arab Voting Patterns," In *The Elections in Israel, 1984*, ed. Asher Arian and Michal Shamir, pp. 121–49. New Brunswick and Oxford: Transaction Books, 1986.

Rouhana, Nadim. *Palestinian Citizens in an Ethnic Jewish State*. New Haven, Conn.: Yale University Press. 1997.

Rouhana, Nadim. "The Palestinian Dimension in the National Identity of the Arabs in Israel." Paper presented at the Conference on "The Arab Minority in Israel: Dilemmas of Political Orientation and Social Change," organized by the Moshe Dayan Center for Middle Eastern and African Studies at Tel Aviv University, June 3–4, 1991.

Rouhana, Nadim. "The Political Transformation of the Palestinians in Israel: From Acquiescence to Challenge." *Journal of Palestine Studies* 17, no. 3 (spring 1989): 50.

Rousseau, Jean-Jacques. *On the Social Contract*, ed. and trans. Donald A. Cress. Indianapolis: Hackett, 1987.

Rosenhek, Zeev. "New Developments in the Sociology of Palestinian Citizens of Israel: an analytical review." *Ethnic and Racial Studies* 21, no. 3 (May 1998): 558–78.

Rubenstein, Amnon. *The Constitutional Law of Israel*. 3d. ed. Tel Aviv: Schocken, 1980 [Hebrew].

Rubenstein, Amnon. *From Herzl to Rabin and On*. Jerusalem: Schoken, 1997 [Hebrew].

Rubenstein, E. "Zionist Attitudes in the Arab-Jewish Dispute to 1936." *The Jerusalem Quarterly*, no. 22 (winter 1982).

Ruggie, J. G. "Collective Goods and Future International Cooperation." *American Political Science Review* 66 (September 1972): 874–92;

Russet, Bruce, and John Sullivan. "Collective Goods and International Organization." *International Organization* 25 (autumn 1971): 845–65.

Sa'adi, Achmed. "Culture as a Dimension of the Political Behavior of the Palestinian Citizens of Israel." *Theory and Criticism* 10 (summer 1997): 193–202.

Sa'adi, Achmed. "Israeli as Ethnic Democracy: What are the Implications for the Palestinian Minority?" *Arab Studies Quareterly* 22, no. 1 (winter 2000): 25–37.

Sabari. "The Legal Status of Israel's Arabs." *Iyunei Mishpat* 2, no. 568 (1972) [Hebrew].

Sachar, Howard M. *A History of Israel*. New York: Knopf, 1976.

Sandel, Michael J. *Liberalism and the Limits of Justice*. Cambridge: Cambridge University Press, 1982.

Sandel, Michael J., ed. *Liberalism and Its Critics*. New York: New York University Press, 1984.

Sanders, Elizabeth M. "New Voters and New Policy Priorities in the Deep South: A Decade of Political Change in Alabama." Paper presented at the Annual Meeting of the American Political Science Association, Washington, D.C., 1979.

Sartori, Giovanni, ed. *Social Science Concepts: A Systematic Analysis*. California: Sage Publications, 1984.

Sartori, Giovanni. *Democratic Theory Revisited*. New Jersey: Chatham House, 1987.

Schlesinger, Philip. "On National Identity: Some Misconceptions and Misconceptions Criticized." *Social Science Information* 26, no. 2 (1987): 219–64.

Schoenbrun, David, Robert Szekely, and Lucy Szekely. *The New Israelis*. New York: 1973.

Schweid, Eliezer. "The Attitude Toward the State in Modern Jewish Thought Before Zionism." In *Kinship and Consent*, ed. Daniel J. Elazar, pp. 127–51. New York: University Press of America, 1983.

Segal, Ze'ev. *Israeli Democracy; Constitutional Law*. Tel Aviv: Ministry of Defense, 1988 [Hebrew].

Segev, Tom. *1949: The First Israelis*. Jerusalem: Domino Press, 1984 [Hebrew].

Segre, Dan. *A Crisis of Identity*. Oxford: Oxford University Press, 1980.

Seton-Watson, Hugh. *Nations and States: An Inquiry into the Origins of Nations and the Politics of Nationalism*. Boulder, Colo.: Westview Press, 1977.

Shafir, Gershon. "Business in Politics: Globalization and the Search for Peace in South Africa and Israel/Palestine." *Israel Affairs* 5, nos. 2/3, (winter/spring 1999): 103–20.

Shalev, Michael. "Jewish Organized Labor and the Palestinians: A Study of State/Society Relations in Israel." In *The Israeli State and Society: Boundaries and Frontiers*, ed. Baruch Kimmerling. Albany: SUNY Press, 1989.

Shalev, Michael, *Labor and the Political Economy in Israel*. Oxford: Oxford University Press, 1992.

Shalev, Michael. "The Political Economy of Labor Party Dominance and Decline in Israel." In *Uncommon Democracies: The One-Party Dominant Regimes*, ed. T. J. Pempel. Ithaca: Cornell University Press, 1990.

Shapira, Anita. *Futile Struggle: The Jewish Labor Controversy, 1929–1939*. Tel Aviv. 1977.

Sharkansky, Ira. *Wither the State? Politics and Public Enterprise in Three Countries*. Chatham, N.J.: Chatham House Publishers, 1979.

Shavit, Yaacov. *The Season of the Hunt: The "Season"—The Confrontation between "Organized Settlement" and the Underground, 1937–1947*. Tel Aviv: Hadar, 1976 [Hebrew].

Schnapper, Dominique. "Beyond the Opposition: Civil Nation versus Ethnic Nation." In *Rethinking Nationalism*, ed. Jocelyne Couture, Kai Nielsen, and Michel Seymour, pp. 219–37. Calgary: Calgary University Press, 1996.

Shklar, Judith N. *American Citizenship: The Quest for Inclusion*. Cambridge, Mass.: Harvard University Press, 1991.

Shohamy, Elana. "Issues of Language Planning in Israel: Language and Ideology." In *Language Planning Around the World: Contexts and Systemic Change*, ed. Richard D. Lambert. Washington D.C.: National Foreign Language Center Monograph Series, Johns Hopkins University, 1994.

Silberman, Charles E. *Crisis in the Classroom: The Remaking of American Education*. New York: Random House, 1970.

Sitkoff, Harvard. *A New Deal for Blacks: The Emergence of Civil Rights as a National Issue. Vol. 1: The Depression Decade*, New York: Oxford University Press, 1978.

Sivan, Emmanuel. *Islam and Politics*. Tel-Aviv: Am-Oved, 1988.

Skocpol, Theda. "Bringing the State Back In." In *Bringing the State Back In*, ed. Peter B. Evans, Dietrich Rueschemeyer, and Theda Skocpol. New York: Cambridge University Press, 1985.

Sleeter, Christine E., and Carl A. Grant. "Race, Class, Gender and Disability in Current Textbooks," In *The Politics of the Textbooks*, ed. Michael W. Apple and Lina K. Christian-Smith, pp. 97–120. London and New York: Routledge, 1991.

Smith, Anthony D. *The Ethnic Origin of Nations*. Oxford: Basil Blackwell, 1986.

Smith, Anthony D. *The Ethnic Revival*. Cambridge: Cambridge University Press, 1981.

Smith, Anthony D. *National Identity*. London: Penguin, 1992.

Smith, Anthony D. *Theories of Nationalism*. 1971. Reprint, London: Duckworth, 1983.

Smith, Robert C. "Black Power and the Transformation from Protest to Politics." *Political Science Quarterly* 96 (fall 1981): 439.

Smith, Rogers M. "The 'American Creed' and American Identity: The Limits of Liberal Citizenship in the United States." *The Western Political Quarterly* 41, no. 2 (June 1988): 225–51.

Smith, Rogers M. "Beyond Tocqueville, Myrdal and Hartz: the Multiple Traditions in America." *American Political Science Review* 87 (1993): 549–66.

Smith, Rogers M. *Civic Ideals: Conflicting Visions of Citizenship in U.S. History*. New Haven, Conn.: Yale University Press. 1997.

Smooha, Sami. *Arabs and Jews in Israel: Conflicting and Shared Attitudes in a Divided Society*. Vol 1. Boulder, Colo.: Westview Press, 1989.

Smooha, Sami. "Existing and Alternative Policy Towards the Arabs in Israel." *Ethnic and Racial Studies* 26, no. 1 (January 1982): 71–99.

Smooha, Sami. *Israel: Pluralism and Conflict*. Berkeley: University of California Press, 1978.

Smooha, Sami. "Minority Status in an Ethnic Democracy: The Status of the Arab Minority in Israel." *Ethnic and Racial Studies* 13, no. 2 (1990).

Smythe, Mabel M. *The Black American Reference Book*. Englewood Cliffs, N.J.: Prentice Hall, 1976.

Snidal, Duncan. "Public Goods." *International Studies Quarterly* 23, no. 4 (December 1979): 539.

Soffer, Arnon. "Twenty Years to the Six-Day War: Demographic and Geographic Changes in Eretz-Israel." In *Twenty Years for the Six-Day War*, ed. Arnon Soffer, pp. 7–15. Haifa: University of Haifa, Jewish Arab Center, 1988 [Hebrew].

Spillman, Lyn. 1997. *Nation and Commemoration: Creating National Identities in the United States and Australia*, Cambridge: Cambridge University Press.

Statistical Abstract of Israel. Jerusalem: Government of Israel, Central Bureau of Statistics, 1995.

Steele, Joel Dorman, and Esther Baker Steele. *A Brief History of the U.S. for Schools*. New York: A. S. Banest Company, 1871.

Steinberg, Stephen. *The Ethnic Myth*. Boston: Beacon Press, 1989.

Steiner, Peter O. "The Public Sector and the Public Interest." In *Public Policy and Public Expenditure*, ed. Robert H. Haveman and Julius Margolis. Chicago: Markham, 1970.

Steinmetz, Georg. *State/Culture: State-Formation after the Cultural Turn*. Ithaca, N.Y.: Cornell University Press. 1999.

Stern, Mark. *Calculating Visions: Kennedy, Johnson and Civil Rights*. New Brunswick, N.J.: Rutgers University Press, 1992.

Stewart, Jeffery C., and Fath Davis Ruffins. "A Faithful Witness: Afro-American Public History in Historical perspective, 1828–1984." In *Presenting the Past: Essays on History and the Public*, ed. Susan Porter Benson, Stephen Brier, and Roy Rosenzweig. Philadelphia: Temple University Press, 1986.

Suleiman, Ramzi and Benjamin Beit-Hallahmi. "National and Civic Identities of Palestinians in Israel." *The Journal of Social Psychology* 137, no. 2 (1997): 219–28.

Sullivan, John, and Michal Shamir, eds. *Political Tolerance in Context: Support for Unpopular Minorities in Israel, New Zealand and the United States.* Boulder, Colo.: Westview Press, 1985.

Suny, Ronald Grigor. *The Making of the Georgian Nation.* Bloomington: Indiana University Press, 1988.

Suny, Ronald Grigor. "The Revenge of the Past: Socialism and Ethnic Conflict in Transcaucasia." *New Left Review* 184 (Nov/Dec 1990): 5–37.

Swirski, Amos. *Not Failing, but Failed.* Haifa: Research Notebooks, 1981 [Hebrew].

Tamir, Yael. *Liberal Nationalism.* Princeton, N.J.: Princeton University Press. 1995.

Talmon. J. L. *The Origins of Totalitarian Democracy.* 1952. Reprint, London: Mercury Books, 1961.

Taylor, Charles. "The Politics of Recognition." In *Campus Wars: Multi-culturalism and the Politics of Difference,* ed. John Arthur and Amy Shapiro, pp. 249–64. Boulder, Colo.: Westview Press, 1995.

Taylor, Charles. *Sources of the Self: The Making of the Modern Identity.* Cambridge, Mass.: Harvard University Press, 1989.

Taylor, Michael. "Intentional Action." *Politics and Society* 17, no. 2 (June 1989): 115–163.

Thernstorm, Stephan, and Abigail Thernstorm. *America in Black and White: One Nation, Indivisible.* New York: Simon and Schuster, 1997.

Thornbrough, E. L., ed. *Black Reconstructionists; Great Lives Observed.* New Jersey: Prentice Hall, 1972.

Tilly, Charles, ed. *The Formation of National States in Western Europe.* Princeton, N.J.: Princeton University Press, 1975.

Tiryakian, Edward A., and Ronald Rogowski, eds. *New Nationalisms of the Developed West toward Explanation.* Boston: Allen and Unwin, 1985.

Tocqueville, Alexis de. *Democracy in America.* New York: Knopf, 1951.

Todd, Lewis Paul, and Merle Curti. *America's History.* New York: Harcourt Brace, 1950.

Vital, David. *Zionism, the Formative Years.* Oxford: Clarendon Press, 1982.

Vogel, Jerome. "Culture, Politics and National Identity in Cote d'Ivoire." *Social Research* 57, no. 2 (summer 1991): 439–56.

Walzer, Michael. "Pluralism in Political Perspective." In *The Politics of Ethnicity,* ed. Michael Walzer, Edward T. Kantowicz, John Hijham and Mona Harrington, pp. 1–29. Cambridge: Harvard University Press, 1982.

Walzer, Michael. *Spheres of Justice: A Defense of Pluralism and Equality.* New York: Basic Books, 1983.

Walzer, Michael. "What Does It Mean to Be an 'American'?" *Social Research* 57, no. 3 (fall 1990): 591–614.

Warwick, Paul V. *Culture, Structure or Choice?: Essays in the Interpretation of the British Experience.* New York: Agathon Press. 1990.

Weber, Eugene. *Peasants into Frenchmen: The Modernization of Rural France, 1870–1914.* London: Chatto and Windus, 1979.

Weinberg, Meyer. "The Civil Rights Movement and Educational Change." In *The Education of African Americans*, ed. Charles V. Willie, Antoine M. Garibaldi and Wornie L. Reed. Westport, Conn.: Greenwood, 1991.

Weller, Leonard. *Sociology in Israel*. Westport, Conn.: Greenwood Press, 1974.

West, Willis Mason, and Ruth West. *The American People: A New History for High Schools*. 1928. Reprint, Boston: Ginn, 1934.

West, Willis Mason, and Ruth West. *The Story of Our Country*. Boston: Allyn and Bacon, 1948.

Whalen, Charles, and Barbara Whalen. *The Longest Debate: A Legislative History of the 1964 Civil Rights Act*. New York: New American Library, 1985.

Wilkinson, Harvie J., III. *From Brown to Bakke: The Supreme Court and School Integration, 1954–1978*. New York: Oxford University Press, 1979.

Wolin, Sheldon. *The Presence of the Past: Essays on the State and the Constitution*. Baltimore: The Johns Hopkins University Press, 1989.

Woodward, C. Vann. *The Strange Career of Jim Crow*. New York: Oxford University Press, 1966.

Wynn, *The Afro American and the Second World War*, 1976.

Yiftachel, Oren. "Debate: The Concept of 'Ethnic Democracy' and its Applicability to the Case of Israel." *Ethnic and Racial Studies* 15, no. 1 (January 1992): 124–34.

Yiftachel, Oren. "Ethnocracy: The Politics of Judaizing Israel/Palestine." *Constellations* 6, no. 3: 364–91.

Young, Iris Marion. *Justice and the Politics of Difference*. Princeton, N.J.: Princeton University Press, 1990.

Young, Iris Marion. "Polity and Group Difference: a Critique of the Ideal of Universal Citizenship." *Ethics* 99 (1989): 250–74.

Zangwill, Israel. *The Melting Pot*. 1909. Reprint, New York: Macmillan, 1942.

Zelinsky, Wilbur. *Nation Into State*. Chapel Hill and London: The University of North Carolina Press, 1988.

Zureik, Elia. *Palestinians in Israel: A Study in Internal Colonialism*. London: Routledge and Kegan Paul, 1979.

Index